ORGANIZATIONAL PSYCHOLOGY

Dr. UMA WARRIER
Chief Counselor,
Jain University
and
Associate Professor CMS - JU
Bangalore.

Himalaya Publishing House
ISO 9001:2015 CERTIFIED

First Edition : 2013
Reprint : 2017
Reprint : 2022

Published by : Mrs. Meena Pandey for **Himalaya Publishing House Pvt. Ltd.,**
"Ramdoot", Dr. Bhalerao Marg, Girgaon, Mumbai - 400 004.
Phone: 022-23860170, 23863863; **Fax:** 022-23877178
E-mail: himpub@bharatmail.co.in; **Website:** www.himpub.com

Branch Offices :

New Delhi : "Pooja Apartments", 4-B, Murari Lal Street, Ansari Road, Darya Ganj, New Delhi - 110 002. Phone: 011-23270392, 23278631; Fax: 011-23256286

Nagpur : Kundanlal Chandak Industrial Estate, Ghat Road, Nagpur - 440 018. Phone: 0712-2738731, 2721216

Bengaluru : Plot No. 91-33, 2nd Main Road, Seshadripuram, Behind Nataraja Theatre, Bengaluru - 560 020. Phone: 080-41138821; Mobile: 09379847017, 09379847005

Hyderabad : No. 3-4-184, Lingampally, Besides Raghavendra Swamy Matham, Kachiguda, Hyderabad - 500 027. Phone: 040-27560041, 27550139

Chennai : No. 34/44, Motilal Street, T. Nagar, Chennai - 600 017. Mobile: 09380460419

Pune : First Floor, "Laksha" Apartment, No. 527, Mehunpura, Shaniwarpeth (Near Prabhat Theatre), Pune - 411 030. Phone: 020-24496323, 24496333; Mobile: 09370579333

Lucknow : House No. 731, Shekhupura Colony, Near B.D. Convent School, Aliganj, Lucknow - 226 022. Phone: 0522-4012353; Mobile: 09307501549

Ahmedabad : 114, "SHAIL", 1st Floor, Opp. Madhu Sudan House, C.G. Road, Navrang Pura, Ahmedabad - 380 009. Phone: 079-26560126; Mobile: 09377088847

Cuttack : Plot No 5F-755/4, Sector-9, CDA Market Nagar, Cuttack - 753 014, Odisha. Mobile: 09338746007

Kolkata : 108/4, Beliaghata Main Road, Near ID Hospital, Opp. SBI Bank, Kolkata - 700 010. Phone: 033-32449649; Mobile: 07439040301

DTP by : Sri Siddhi Softtek
Bengaluru.

Printed by : Trinity Academy, Mumbai. On behalf of HPH.

Dedication to
my children

Sidharth and Aparna

Foreword

In the last decade, there has been a rapid growth of interest in organizational psychology and its applications. This is a unique book containing numerous topics in the discipline with dual concern for theory and practice providing original insights at various levels of work related causes and consequences.

While reading this book, one can easily learn the behavioral patterns of human being in an organization in terms of shared social identities and the difference between interpersonal and group behavior of an individual. Also, one can observe the effect of organizational characteristics on an individual and group.

This book is intended for organizational psychologists, management institutions and students. This book is also useful for practicing HR managers.

I wish the reader an enjoyable experience of thought provoking study.

Dr. Chenraj Roychand
President - Jain University Trust

Preface

Employees form the core of any organization. The roadmap to organization success is paved by the painstaking efforts of its employees and employers. Thus organization behavior is the bedrock for organizations to succeed and prosper in today's tough business environment. Sound knowledge in organizational psychology will help management and employees alike, in bringing harmony in the work place. Several books on organizational psychology have been written in the past and each and every one of them has their themes and merit. This book on organizational psychology was written keeping in mind the fundamental aspects of organizational psychology interwoven with the contemporary concepts, practices and issues related to this field. The flow in this book helps in distilling the basic concepts and incentivizes students to get actively involved in the subject thus enabling them to develop competencies for becoming successful managers and entrepreneurs.

The book is a lucid presentation of logical sequences of concepts relevant in the field of organizational psychology. The first chapter introduces the reader to the concept of organizational psychology, followed by perception in the next chapter that deals with different concepts in perception and its application in business management. Subsequent chapters cover personality, learning, work related attitudes, motivation, group dynamics, power and politics in organizations. Case studies, subject related activities, self assessment questions and model questions are provided in each chapter to enhance the learning experience.

This book is a humble dedication to my children, Sidharth and Aparna who have given their unflinching support during the writing of this book and have taught me during the course of my work that everything is possible if a firm resolve is in place. I have seen a whole new world through their eyes. This book is a true reflection of my love to them.

I would like to acknowledge my better half Surendranath Warrier for being a pillar of strength all through this journey. I thank my colleagues Roopa Traisa and Sneha Vatsa, my students Aiswarya Rao and Swati Prasad and all my well wishers for giving me the moral support while writing this book.

Special thanks to **Dr. Chenraj Roychand,** President, Jain Group of Institutions and Professor **Dinesh Nilkant**, Principal, Centre for Management Studies (CMS) for being the true inspiration in the creation of book.

Happy learning students. Your learning is my inspiration!

Dr Uma Warrier
Chief counselor,
Jain University
Bangalore.

Contents

CHAPTER 1

INTRODUCTION TO ORGANIZATIONAL PSYCHOLOGY

Learning Objectives of the Chapter

- Meaning
- Structure
- Theoretical framework of OB
- Contributing disciplines to OB field.

Introduction to organizational behaviour

Organisational behavior is the discipline that deals with the way people in the organization- (as individuals and groups) - behave and its impact on the organization's performance. Organisational behaviour can be termed as an art, as it deals with management of human behavior. It is also a science since it provides information on effective practices that can be adapted in the organization for improved organizational performance. Most of the concepts discussed in organizational behavior like perception, personality, learning, memory, attitude, motivation are all derived from psychology. Organisational psychology as a discipline seeks to bring in better understanding of social processes in an organization.

OPENING CASE

Shankar Surana is the CEO of Magnum construction group. The company is a well reputed construction company with CRISIL rating .Mr Surana manages a staff of 169 across 3 major cities: Chennai, Mumbai & Bangalore. Mr Surana is a tough task master. He keenly follows a principle of productivity and profits. Sometimes he gets aggressive and pushy if targets are not met. Rightly so, he has streamlined the business operations by his alertness, shrewd business acumen and his flair for efficiency. He had a good rapport with his general manager (operations) Mr. Kausubh Chaterjee. Mr Chaterjee had 30 years of experience in the construction industry and had a deep understanding of organizational issues. His civil engineering background helped him while dealing with product-related issues. Though Mr Chaterjee was not as high-handed as Mr Surana, he definitely believed in managing a cordial relationship with his boss by endorsing both his leadership style and manner of working. He closely followed the instructions of Mr Surana and always made sure that the targets are always achieved. When Mr.Chaterjee reached his superannuation, Mr Surana was in a fix. To get a replacement for Mr Chaterjee was next to impossible. His loyalty, knowledge and complete trust in his boss were not easily traced qualities. Mr Chander Kapoor was selected to fill in the position, after a lot of deliberation. Mr Kapoor was a well-qualified and senior manager with a pleasant disposition. He was a people-centric person. His work related attitude was very different from Mr Chaterjee. He thought that people had to be treated with dignity and concern to help them perform their jobs efficiently. Mr Kapoor believed in a win-win strategy. He opposed the punishment system and favored positive reinforcement for motivating people. In his previous organization, Polaris group Pvt. Ltd, he had used this approach effectively as a deputy general manager. He was confident that people were responsive if the superior was considerate and cared for their interests.

Mr Kapoor wanted to check the pulse of the organization before getting deeply involved with the company. Upon studying the systems of the company carefully, he noticed that there were quite a few rules, which were stringent. Mr Kapoor concluded that the rules of the company were not employee friendly. He wanted to make some changes in the HR and administration rules of the company. He decided to abolish some of the unfriendly rules completely. One particular rule specified that if a person was late to work for 3 consecutive days, his ½ day's leave was to be deducted. In case the employee exhausted all the causal leaves allotted to him/her, the employee had to sustain the loss of a pay leave. Mr Kapoor abolished this policy, expecting that this would improve the morale of employees and they would work with more zeal and enthusiasm. He also adopted an open-door policy for his employees, so that they could walk in and express their concerns, grievances and problems to him. Mr Surana, who was a highly task oriented leader did not react to this developments, but was definitely not pleased with them. He kept a sharp eye on the situation to prevent any deterioration. To his dismay, he saw that the staff indulged in greater unpunctuality in the first month itself. He pointed this out to Mr Kapoor. Mr Kapoor's reaction was very stoic. He felt that there was no cause to be alarmed, but he immediately spoke to department heads whose department registered greater unpunctuality. He told them to counsel the concerned employees to be more careful with their work behaviour. Despite this, in the second month also the level of punctuality improved only marginally. Mr Surana was at his wits end. He asked Mr Kapoor to reintroduce the previous rule. Mr Kapoor knew that this would send wrong signals to the employees and so requested Mr Surana to allow him to continue this at least for 3 months. But Mr Surana was determined to revert back to the previous rule of deducting leave or pay. At the same time, he advised Mr Kapoor to set aside time for meeting employees so that it did not affect his productive work time. Mr Kapoor was not very happy with these developments. However he did accept the suggested changes. He thought to himself that the road ahead definitely looked difficult and recalled his previous boss Mr. Singh with whom he shared perfect rapport and understanding. Even while he contemplated revising his previous stand he was convinced about his approach being the right one.

Discussion questions:

1. What is the underlying issue in this case?
2. What would be the next move of Mr Kapoor?
3. How can Mr Surana improve the situation?

Organization: The term organization can be understood as two or more individuals who interact with one another within a deliberately structured set up and work interdependently to achieve some common objective/s. Organizations play a major role in our lives. An organization draws inputs from the environment and converts them into specified outputs desired by society.

Organizations are economic and social entities in which a number of persons perform many functions to achieve common goals.

Organization may be studied from two perspectives namely-Micro Level: where the focus of study is on individual human beings. Macro Level: Organization is considered as a unit of analysis.

Organizational Behaviour: OB refers to the actions and characteristics of the people in an organization who work towards common goals. An organization consists of people who differ completely in attitudes, cultures, beliefs, norms and values.

Definitions:

Chester Barnard: Organization is a system of consciously coordinated activities of two or more persons.

Parsons: Organizations are social units deliberately constructed and reconstructed to seek specific goals.

Koontz and O'Donnel: "Organization is the establishing of effective authority relationship among selected work, person and work places in order for the group to work efficiently."

Mooney and Reiley: "Organization is defined as the form of human association for attaining objectives."

OB is the study and application of knowledge of how people act/ behave within an organisation.

Stephen P Robbins: "OB is a field of study that investigates the impact that individuals, groups and structure have on behaviour within organisations for the purpose of applying such knowledge towards improving an organisation's effectiveness."

Characteristics of OB:

1. Rational Thinking: Predicting human behavior results in creating situations yielding to success and goals.
2. OB is a body of theory, research and applications.
3. OB encompasses 3 levels of study: individual, groups, and the organizational level.
4. OB is basically a social science.
5. It tries to identify the cause and effect relationship.

6. OB is behavioral branch of Management.
7. OB is oriented towards organizational objectives.

Application of OB in an organisation

OB is applied in all areas of human management, with focus on understanding and managing human behavior.

a) ***Individual behaviour:*** OB studies the response shown by an individual in a particular situation.

b) ***OB helps in effectively handling the managerial roles in an organisation***. The central action figures in OB are managers, those who get things going in organizations. They plan, control, organize and lead people and get work done through others. Managers use technical skills, human skills and conceptual skills. Henry Mintzberg who is an internationally acclaimed author of business management categorized the roles managers play into 10 different types

    1. Figurehead- The oldest assumption of a manager who is merely a symbolic head
    2. Leader- Enhances moral and alleviates stress of employees.
    3. Liaison- Link between contacts who provide favors and information
    4. Monitor- Receives information from various sources in the organization and serves as nerve center in the organization
    5. Disseminator- Transmits information from outsiders and colleagues to the superiors and subordinates of the organization
    6. Spokesperson- Broadcasts information to the public and partners about the company's plans, policies and results
    7. Entrepreneur- Looks for opportunities within the organization and take up projects to bring about development.
    8. Disturbance handler- They uphold the organization with corrective action when faced with unexpected decisions.
    9. Resource Allocator- They approve significant decisions in the organization
    10. Negotiator- Are responsible for representing the organization at various negotiations

c) ***Interpersonal behavior:*** Behavioral science can help managers understand themselves and others better, it improves inter-personal relations.

d) ***Group-Behavior:*** Group formation, behavior and interaction are studied as group behavior has a synergic effect on performance.

e) ***Inter-group behavior***: OB helps managers in achieving cooperative group relationship, through interaction, avoidance of a win-lose situation.

f) ***Leadership:*** A competent leader is one who uses all the human and physical resources at the maximum level for achieving organizational goals.

g) ***Motivation:*** The levels of motivation vary among individuals. The study of this will enhance inter-personal skills.

h) ***Communication:*** It is a building block of the organization. The communication process and its working in inter-personal dynamics are evaluated by behavioral sciences.

i) ***Organization change and development:*** change is introduced through group dynamics and appropriate education of employees through effective communication.

j) ***Organizational climate:*** climate is the sum total of the entire organizational situation effecting human behavior. It is the conception of an atmosphere of effective supervision, the opportunity for the realization of personal goals, good relations and a sense of accomplishment.

Organizational Psychology (OP)

Psychology is an academic and applied discipline that involves the scientific study of human or animal mental functions and behaviour.

The word psychology literally means, "Study of the soul". It derives from Ancient Greek: "ψυχη" (psychç, meaning "breath", "spirit", or "soul"); and "λογα" (-logia, translated as "study of").

Organizational Psychology is a specialized area that applies psychological knowledge and skills to work, with the aim of improving organizational effectiveness and the quality of work life Here, unlike in OB, the emphasis is on aspects of perception, personality, learning, motivational stimuli, job satisfaction, decisions making process etc, which are exclusive topics with respect to an individual employee and the employee's psychology. Hence the concept of Organisational psychology, where the concepts from sociology and social psychology like group formation, power and organisational politics are covered in this syllabus.

OP- Definition

"Organisational psychology is the scientific study of individual and group behaviour in formal organisational settings" (Jex, 2002)

"OB/OP is a field of study that examines the effect that the individuals, groups and organizational structure have on behavior within the organization. The information procured from the study is used to improve the effectiveness of an organization."

"OB/OP is a systematic study of the actions and attitudes that people exhibit within organizations."- Stephen Robbins

Difference between Organisational behavior and Organisational psychology

The two disciplines often overlap in terms of the content and there are not many obvious differences between both. However, both are not the same. OP deals with individual and group behavior where as OB deals with organizational structure and strategy which are macro level processes , apart from individual and group behavior. OB is more eclectic or diverse in nature, drawing inputs from varied disciplines like sociology, anthropology, economics, management, political science etc where as OP is a little more convergent study, drawing inputs basically from its sub disciplines .

Contributing Fields to Organizational Behaviour

Psychology:

It is a practiced science, which strives to account for human behavior in a circumstantial situation and anticipates actions of individuals. It studies why people think and act in a certain manner

Psychology is the study of human behavior that analyses the attributes of individuals and gives a reason as to why an individual carries oneself in a particular manner.

Psychology has tended towards explicit theories on learning, motivation, personality, training and development, leadership, individual decision making, job satisfaction, performance appraisal, self appraisal, ego state, attitude, work stress, job design and conflict management. After deliberation of these theories, personal skills can be improved which will bring about a change in the attitude and develop positive approach to organizational systems.

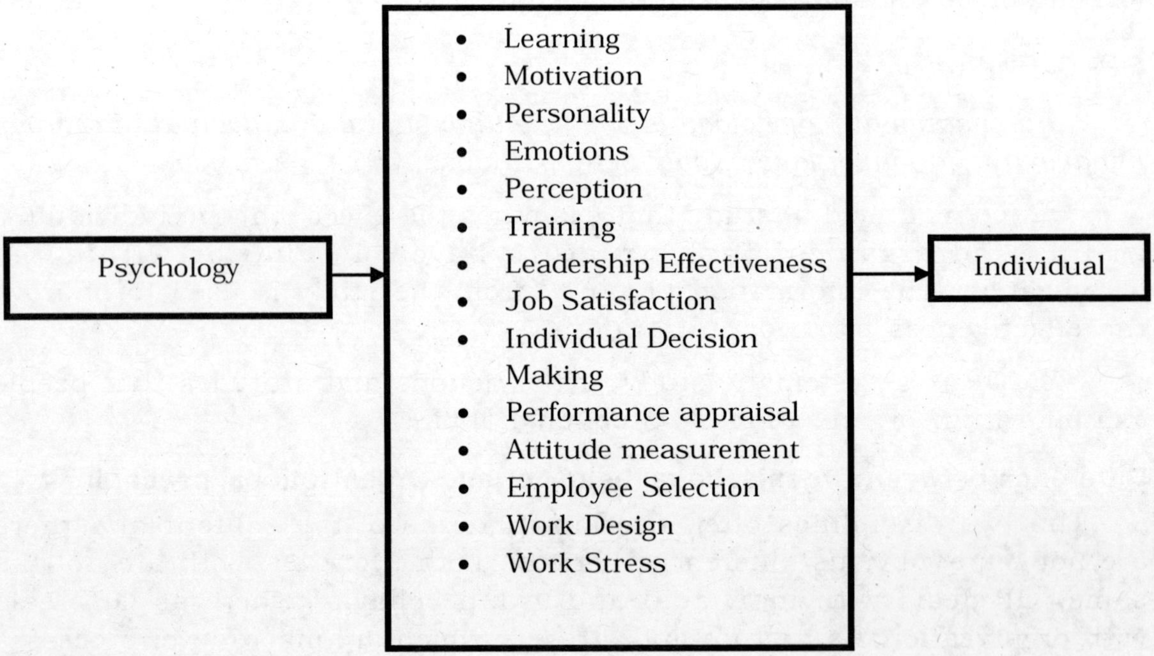

Sociology:

It is the study of group behavior, dependence among social groups and societies, and the continuation of social order. It is the study of people in association to their contemporaries.

Sociology studies group behavior and has endowed a large amount of information to the area of group-dynamics, roles that an individual plays in the communication, organization, conflict management , status, power, norms , group processes, formal organization theory and group decision-making. The field has conferred to administer change, group decision-making, Group dynamics, design of work teams, organizational culture, formal organization theory and structure, organizational technology, conflict, inter group behavior, inter group behavior etc , which are useful contributions of sociology.

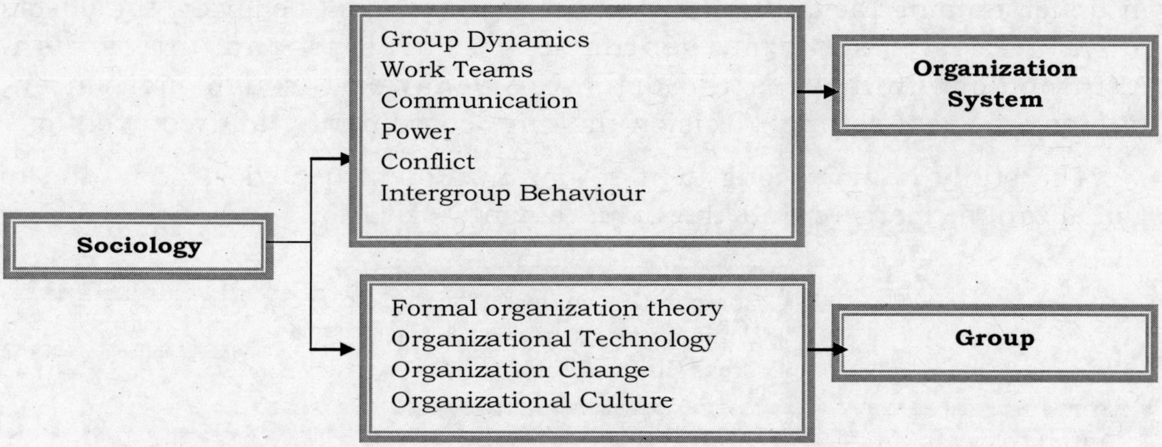

1. Social Psychology:

This is a field that blends psychology and sociology and seeks to explain why people behave in a certain way in groups in a particular situation. It is an area within psychology that blends concepts from psychology and sociology and throws light on the effect of people on one another.

Social psychology is the analysis of human behavior with reference to social situations. A few major concepts that contribute to OP are group decision making, inter-group behaviour and team work. This discipline also helps in measuring, understanding and changing attitudes of an individual ways in which groups efforts and activities can satisfy individual needs, and the group decision making process.

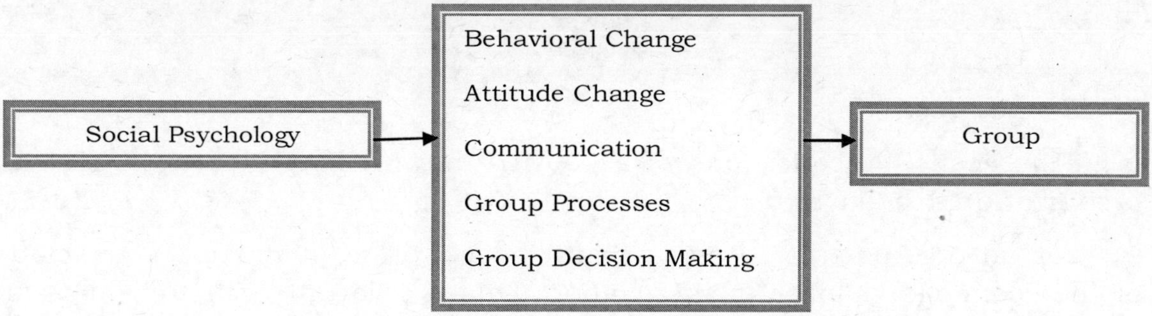

2. Anthropology

It is the research carried out on societies to understand humans and their activities. The main focus of inspection is on the cultural system, beliefs, customs, ideas and values (within a group or society) and the comparison of the behavior of individuals among different cultures. It helps in understanding the cultural effects on organizational behavior, the effects of value systems, norm, sentiments, cohesions and interaction. Anthropology influences the employee behavior through motivation, interaction, goal-setting, decision-making, coordinating and controlling.

The study is more congruent to organizational behavior today due to globalization, mergers and the achievements of various industries.

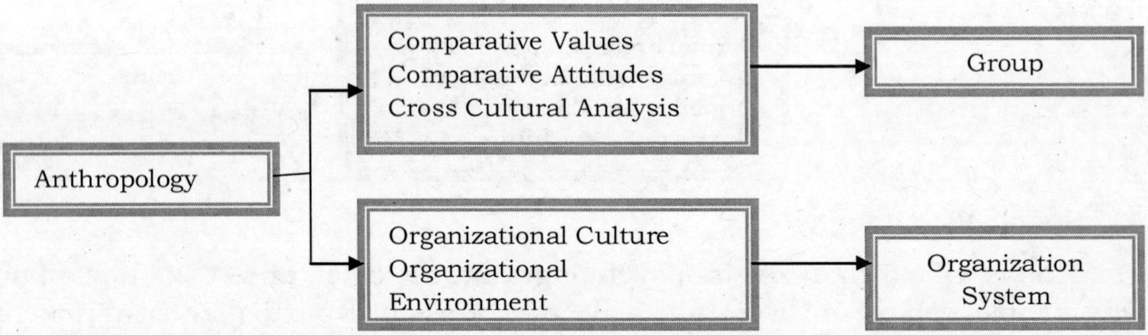

3. Political Science:

It is the analyses of the conduct of individuals and associations in a political environment. It compares individuals and groups in specific conditions regarding power dynamics.

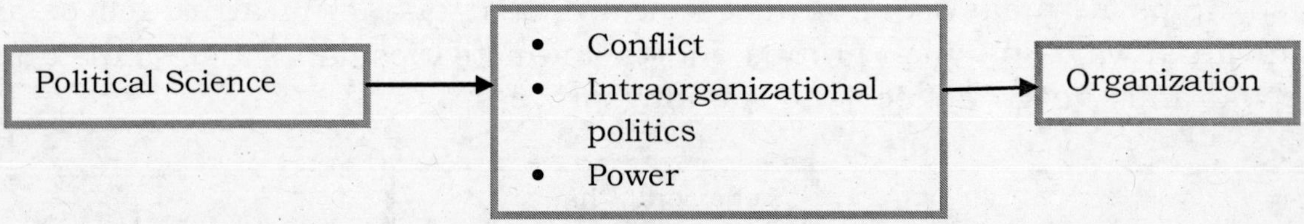

4. Economics:

The economic conditions of a country have a long lasting impact on organizational behavior.

For an organization to stay afloat and continue, it must be conscious of the economic viability of their labor. This is relevant even to non-profit and free-willed organizations.

Theoretical Frameworks of OP

Cognitive Framework

Cognition can be simply denoted as the act of knowing an element of information. In the cognitive framework, cognition antecedes behavior and creates inputs to the person's thinking, perception, problem solving, and information processing.

The work of Edward Tolman corresponds to the cognitive theoretical approach. According to Tolman, learning consists of the anticipation of the fact that a particular event will lead to a particular outcome. This cognitive conception of expectancy shows that the organism thinks about, or is attentive to or aware of the goal and result of a behavior demonstrated by it. It simply means that a person craves for a goal and also knows the behavior that will be responsible for the accomplishment of the goals.

Example: With goals, certain behavior is exhibited to achieve them.

Behavioristic Framework

Pioneer behaviorists Ivan Pavlov and Jon B. Watson asserted the seriousness of studying visible behaviors instead of the elusive mind. They argued that behavior could be better comprehended in terms of stimulus and response (S-R). They cross-examined the impact of stimulus and felt that learning manifested when the S-R connection was made. Modern behaviorism, that marks its birth with B.F. Skinner, supports the fact that behavior in reverberation to a stimulus is controlled by certain environmental consequences. Thus, it is important to note that the behavioristic approach is based on visible behavior and environmental irregularities (which are also observable).

Example: Classical conditioning theory- Dog and the Bell experiment.

Social Cognitive Framework

The social part ratifies the social origins of human thought and activity (what the individual absorbs from society), whereas the cognitive portion pinpoints the prominent addition of thought processes to human motivation, attitudes, and action of individuals.

In social cognitive theoretical framework, organizational members are at the same time both the products and producers of their personality, respective environments, and behaviors.

The participants as a group produce the environment; every individual is a product of the environment and through his actions, the environment changes for others as well as for himself.

Every individual is a invention of his personality, but also affects his personality as a reflection of the results of his behavior.

Historical Evolution of OB

Study of OB has evolved from the late 1800s. Prior to the 1900s, organizational theory focused mainly on the division of labour and importance of machinery to facilitate labour. The following are different landmark phases of OB evolution with its distinct features:

Industrial revolution

- Materialism
- Discipline
- Monotony
- Boredom
- Work-interdependence

Scientific Management (1910s)

This era described management as a science. The focus of **scientific management** was the application of scientific methods to increase an individual worker's productivity. It vested employers with specific but different responsibilities, encouraged scientific selection training and development of employees. According to the principles of scientific management, there is a division of work between managers and workers. F. W Taylor is considered as father of scientific management

The Human Relations movement (1920s)

The Human Relations movement was based on the belief that an important link existed among managerial practices, morale, and productivity. It focused on attitudes and the emotions of employees

The key point of the movement was that satisfied workers are more productive. It was believed that given the proper working environment, virtually all workers would be highly productive.

Hawthorne studies (1930s) by Elton Mayo.

The "Hawthorne Experiments" were a sequence of analyses of worker yield undertaken at the Cicero plant beginning in 1924 and ending in 1932, initially conducted by the National Research Council and later by Western Electric and Harvard University

Illumination Studies, 1924 -1927: Does the Use of Electric Lights Increase Productivity?

Relay Assembly Test Room Experiments, 1927-1929

The Harvard research team set up a study with 5 females from the Relay Assembly area to analyze the effect of incentives and work conditions on worker fatigue.

Productivity and worker satisfaction increased when conditions were improved or made worse.

3rd Hawthorne Experiment

It was performed on the Mica Splitting Test group, from 1928-1930. The relation between work conditions and yield was focused on, and the situation was altered by providing a piece-rate incentive and by changing certain work conditions. The yield was elevated by about 15% and researchers concluded that yield was affected by non-pay considerations

Hawthorne studies concluded that social dynamics was the footing of worker performance. There was a lot of stress on work done in groups. It was understood by the study that human factors are more important than physical conditions for motivating employees to achieve greater productivity.

The Hawthorne effect

The Hawthorne effect is named after what was one of the most famous experiments (or, more accurately, series of experiments) in industrial history. It marked a sea change in thinking about work and productivity. Previous studies, in particular Frederick Taylor's influential ideas, had focused on the individual and on ways in which an individual's performance could be improved. Hawthorne set the individual in a social context, establishing that the performance of employees is influenced by their surroundings and by the people that they are working with as much as by their own innate abilities.

The experiments took place at Western Electric's factory at Hawthorne, a suburb of Chicago, in the late 1920s and early 1930s. They were conducted for the most part under the supervision of Elton Mayo, an Australian-born sociologist who eventually became a professor of industrial research at Harvard.

The original purpose of the experiments was to study the effects of physical conditions on productivity. Two groups of workers in the Hawthorne factory were used as guinea pigs. One day the lighting in the work area for one group was improved dramatically while the other group's lighting remained unchanged. The researchers were surprised to find that the productivity of the more highly illuminated workers increased much more than that of the control group.

The employees' working conditions were changed in other ways too (their working hours, rest breaks and so on), and in all cases their productivity improved when a change was made. Indeed, their productivity even improved when the lights were dimmed again. By the time everything had been returned to the way it was before the changes had begun, productivity at the factory was at its highest level. Absenteeism had plummeted.

The experimenters concluded that it was not the changes in physical conditions that were affecting the workers' productivity. Rather, it was the fact that someone was actually concerned about their workplace, and the opportunities this gave them to discuss changes before they took place.

A crucial element in Mayo's findings was the effect that working in groups had on the individual. At one time he wrote:

The desire to stand well with one's fellows, the so-called human instinct of association, easily outweighs the merely individual interest and the logic of reasoning upon which so many spurious principles of management are based.

Later in life he added:

The working group as a whole actually determined the output of individual workers by reference to a standard that represented the group conception (rather than management's) of a fair day's work. This standard was rarely, if ever, in accord with the standards of the efficiency engineers.

Fritz Roethlisberger, a leading member of the research team, wrote:

The Hawthorne researchers became more and more interested in the informal employee groups, which tend to form within the formal organisation of the company, and which are not likely to be represented in the organisation chart. They became interested in the beliefs and creeds which have the effect of making each individual feel an integral part of the group

Source: The Economist, November 3rd 2008

1. Organization Development era (1946)

Kurt Lewin conducted research in the field of organizational change and group dynamics. He postulated the change theory. Kurt Lewin is known as father of organization development

2. Hierarchy of Needs (1954)

Abraham Maslow published a book called Motivation and Personality in which he introduced the concept of the hierarchy of needs, which will be discussed in detail under the topic of motivation in coming chapters. This theory gives a frame work for employers to gain employee commitment.

3. Leadership/Management (1954)

Peter Drucker wrote a book The Practice of management, where he enlisted five roles of managers. A lot of emphasis was given to organisation structure too. Peter Drucker is known as father of modern management.

4. Hygiene and Motivational Factors (1959)

Frederick Herzberg made modifications in the concepts of Maslow's need hierarchy to make it more suitable for work situations. According to him, hygiene factors should be already provided in the job before motivating factors can be deployed by the management to elicit better performance.

5. Theory X and Theory Y (1960)

Douglas McGregor came up with 2 theories, which basically divides employees into a group that was inherently lazy and the management needed to use coercion to get work out of them (Theory X) and another, where employees are self-motivated and who did not need close supervision to complete the task(Theory Y)

6. Management Grid (1964)

Robert Blake and Jane Mouton made a model which describes managerial behavior by two aspects. They formed a grid with two axes, "Concern for task" on the Y axis and "Concern for people" on the X axis.

7. Learning Organization (1990)

According to Peter Senge, a learning organization is any organization (e.g. school, business, government agency) that understands itself as a complex, organic system that has a vision and purpose.

Approaches to the study of OB

1. The Systems Perspective

A system is an interrelated set of elements that work as a whole. The Systems Approach yields a framework for interpreting how the elements of an organization cooperate among themselves and with their environment.

The Systems Approach to Organizations

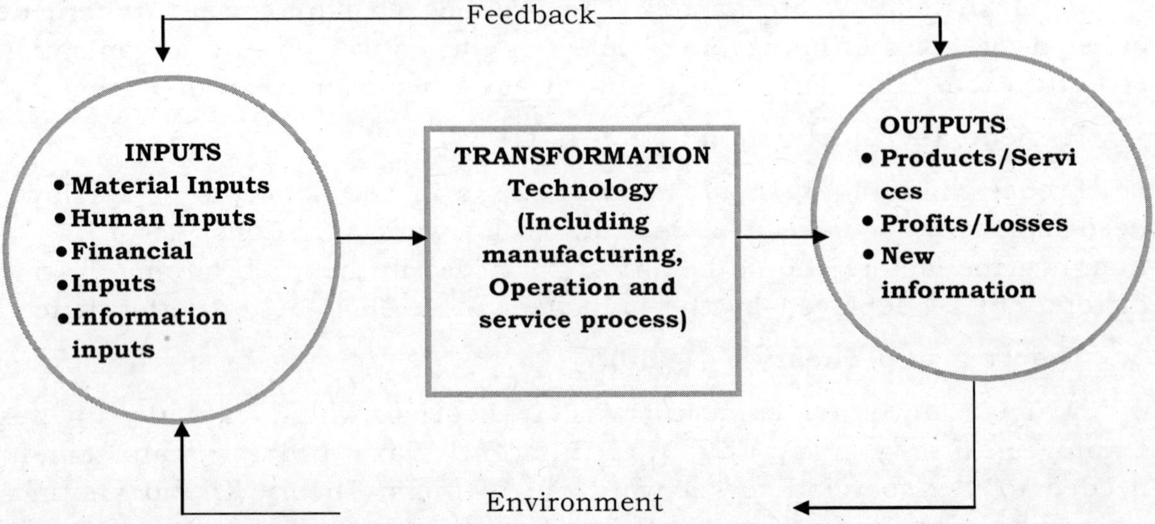

2. The Universal Perspective

Proposes that whenever a manager comes across a problem, a universal approach exists that will lead to the necessary outcome.

3. The Contingency Perspective

This proposes that whenever a manager comes across a problem, the means to use is contingent on other variables. Dependent variables: a feedback that is influenced by an independent variable. The variables in OB are productivity, efficiency and effectiveness, absenteeism, turnover, organizational citizenship behavior, job satisfaction etc

Contingent variables- are variables that moderate the relationships between dependent and independent variables

Universal Approach

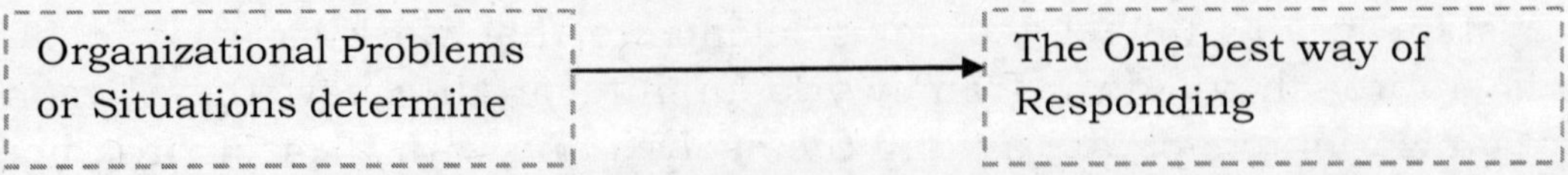

Contingency Approach

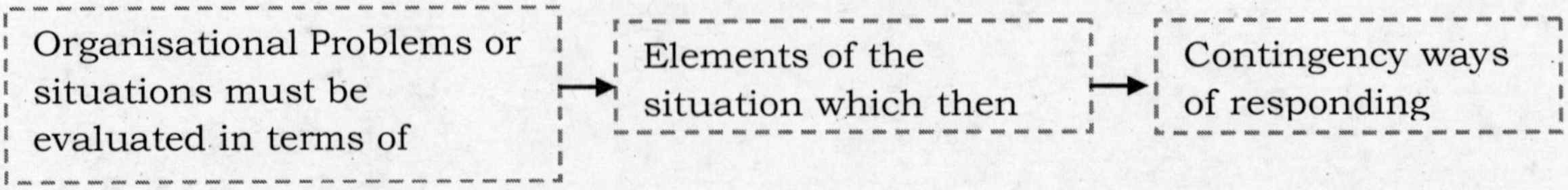

4. Interactionalism Approach: People and Situations

In terms of interactional psychology, this view expects that individual behavior results from the stable and multidirectional communication between the attributes of the person and the attributes of the situation. Interactionalism tries to account for how people select, interpret, and change various situations

5. The Human relations approach/Supportive approach:

This approach recognizes the fact that people are the central resource in any organization and they should be developed towards higher levels of competency, creativity and fulfillment. People thus developed will contribute to the success of the organization.

6. The Productivity Approach

Productivity is the ratio of output to input, a measure of organization effectiveness. It also reveals a manager's efficiency in optimizing resource utilization. The higher the numerical value the greater is the efficiency.

Productivity is also measured in terms of human and social inputs and outputs. **Example:** Better OB can improve Job satisfaction (a human input or benefit).

Organizational Structure:

Organization is a formal configuration between individual and the groups with respect to the allocation of tasks, responsibility and authority within an organization.

Structure is the framework of an organization where the jobs of each and every person is defined, described and coordinated to achieve organizational goals. It includes control, command, division of work, placement of jobs, centralization, differentiation and related factors.

Need for organisation structure

a) Ensure efficiency and effectiveness of activities.

b) Divide and allocate work authority

c) Establish working relationship and operating mechanism.

d) Establish means by which work is controlled.

e) Retain experience, knowledge and expertise.

f) Provides the basis of fair and equitable reward system.

g) Gives a concrete shapes to the organization.

Features of good organization structure:

1. Clear lines of authority.
2. Adequate delegation of authority.
3. Less managerial levels.
4. Appropriate span of control.
5. Simple and flexible structure.

Factor influencing organization structure:

1. Internal contingency factor:
   a) Goals
   b) Size of the organization.
   c) Employee's characteristics.
2. External contingency factors:
   a) Dependence on external factors.
   b) Volatility of environment.
   c) Technology.

Elements of good structure:

1. Work specialization.
2. Departmentaation.
3. Chain of command.
4. Span of command
5. Centralisation/decentralization.
6. Formalisation.

It is the degree of complexity, formalization and centralization in the organization.

- **Complexity** is the degree of vertical, horizontal and spatial differentiation in an organization
- **Formalization** is the degree to which jobs within the organization are standardized
- **Centralization** is the degree to which decision making in concentrated at a single point in the organization.

Entrepreneurial structure:

Owner-manager makes decisions. Little specialization of tasks. Few rules, little formalization.

Gives high flexibility. Accelerated product introduction. Few coordination problems

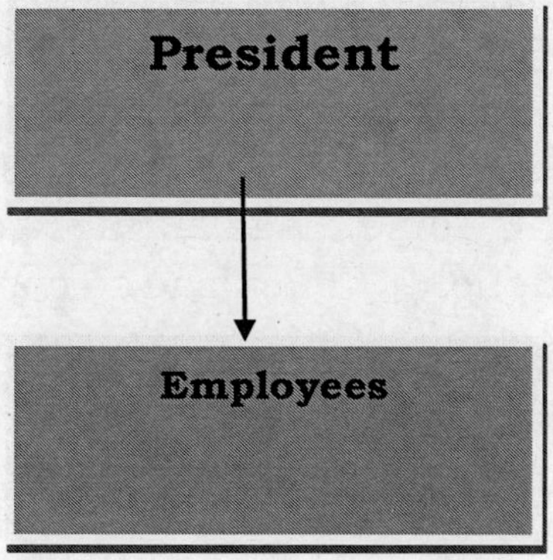

Functional Structure

- Consolidated control of operations. Boosts complete functional expertise. Intensifies operating efficiency where tasks are routine. Some of the disadvantages of this structure are Functional coordination problems, Inter-functional rivalry, Overspecialization and narrow viewpoints,

  Hinders development of cross-functional experience, Slower to respond in turbulent environments etc.

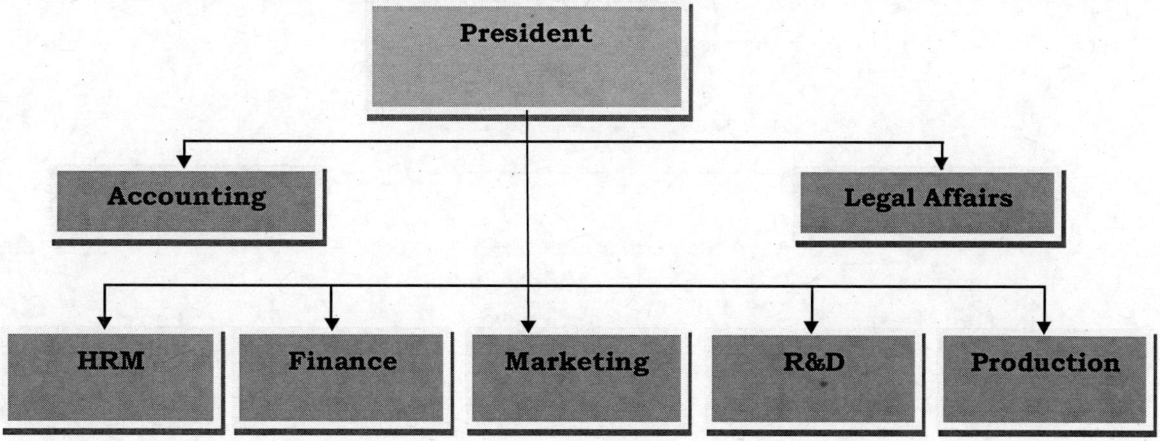

Product Structure

Organization based on products versus functions. Divisions are discrete, in which day-to-day decisions are entrusted to divisional managers. Divisions are maintained using strategic controls: detailed knowledge of firm operations allows managers to remain keenly involved. Over diversification leads to inefficiency in processing detailed information and a reliance on financial controls to evaluate managers. Decentralized decision making is a characteristic feature of product structure. Each business is classified around products. This kind of structure facilitates quick response to environmental changes. It allows efficient management of a large number of units. Some disadvantages of this structure are related to increased cost of production. It may lead to costly duplication of functions, Inter-divisional clashes etc. Corporate managers may lose detailed understanding

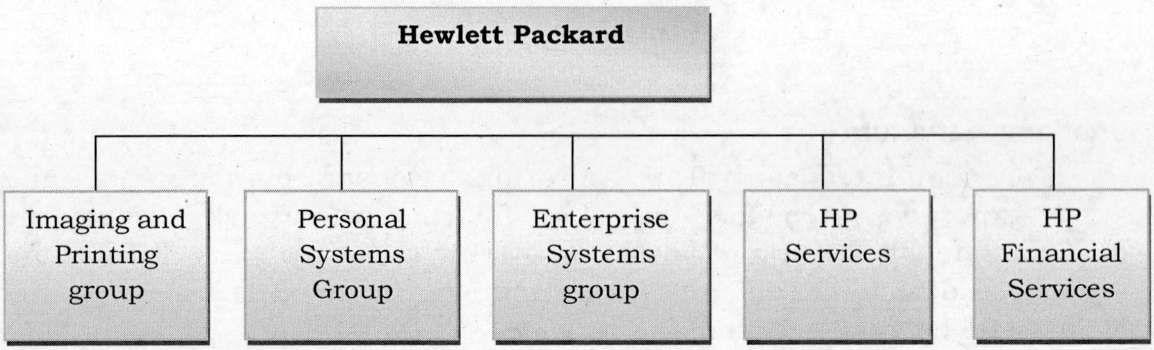

Place/Area Structure:

Similar to product structure, covering wide geographic area

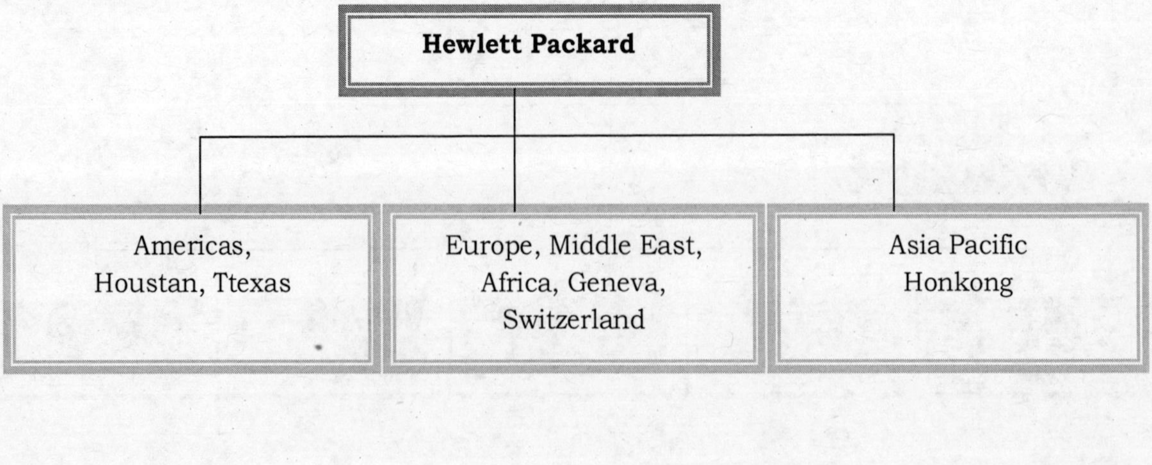

Matrix structure:

Violates Fayol's principle of unity of command. Combines the advantages of the pure functional structure and the product organizational structure. Creates checks and balances between clashing viewpoints. Provides an entire view of the firm. Encourages collaboration and consensus building. Some of the disadvantages of this structure are it can be highly expensive and complex, Shared authority maximizes communication time, Quick response nearly impossible, May promote bureaucracy and hinders innovation (in large firms)

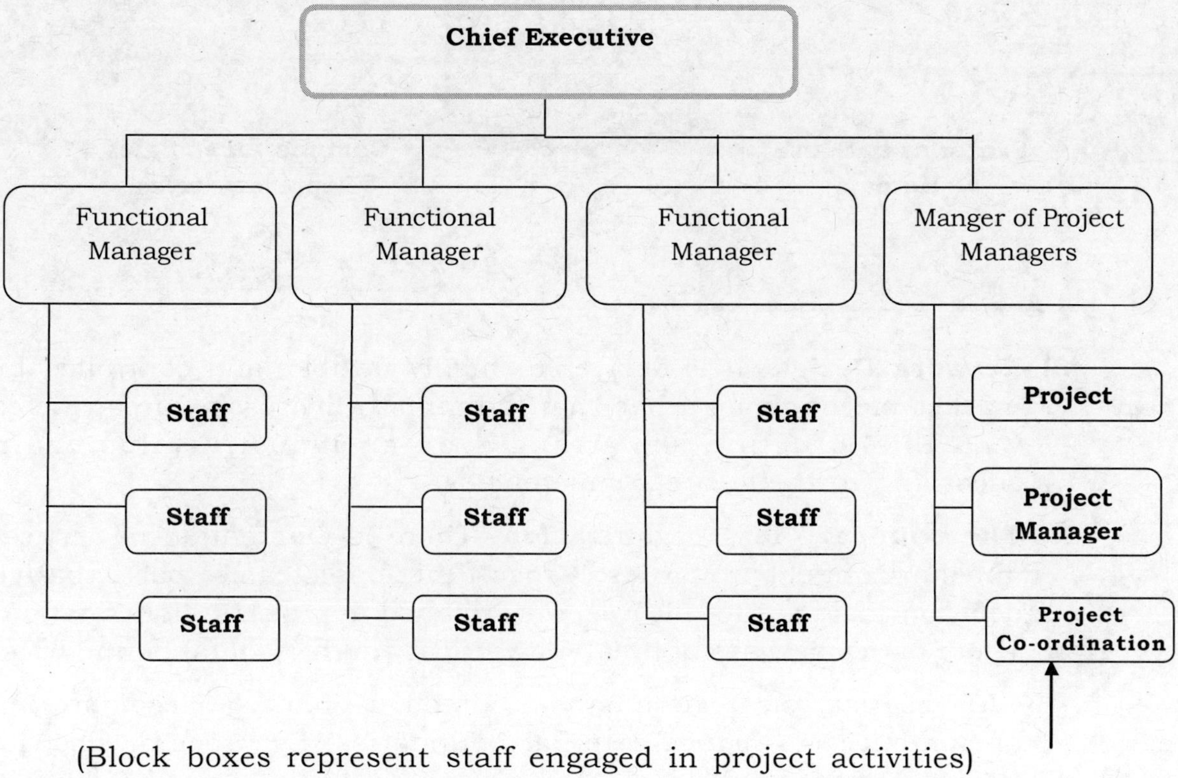

(Block boxes represent staff engaged in project activities)

Ex: Asea Brown Bovery (ABB)

Contemporary organization structures

1. **Team structure:** Organization uses teams as its central co-ordination devices. It breaks down departmental barriers and decentralizing decisions making to the level of the work team. Features: a) Organization revolves around process. b) Hierarchy is flattened. c) Customer driven performance. d) Team performance is rewarded. f) Suppliers and customer contact is maximized.

2. **Virtual organization**: It is a temporary network of companies that come together quickly to exploit fast changing opportunities. Eg. Nike, Cisco system, Exxon mobile corp.

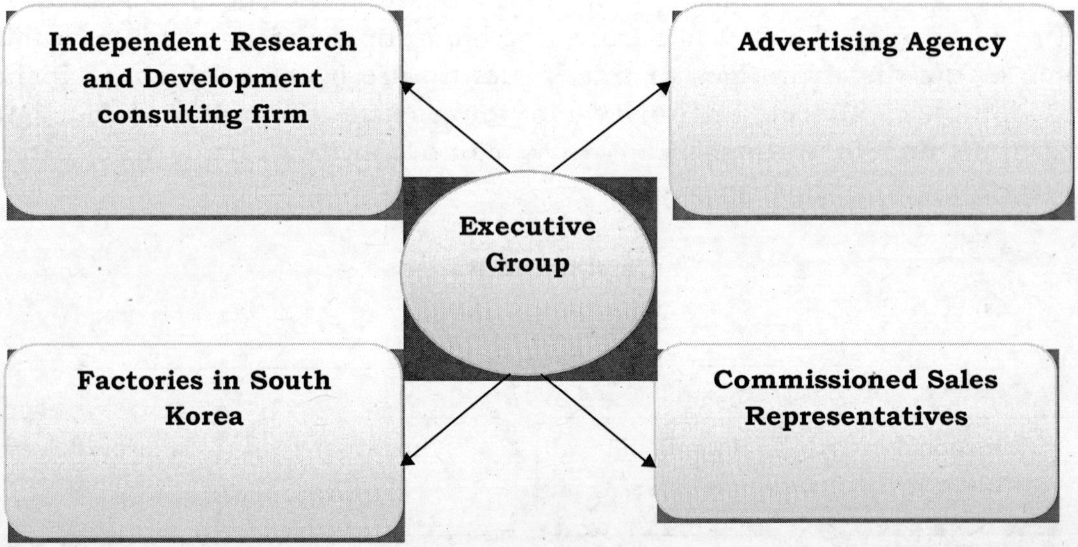

3) **Network Design:** It is delayered, highly flexible, and controlled by market mechanism rather than administrative procedures. Firms with this structure are arranged on an industry value chain according to their core competencies.

4) **The boundary less organization:** There is elimination of vertical and horizontal boundaries. Cross-functional teams, participative decision making, 360 degree performance appraisals, Job rotation. These are some ways of breaking vertical and horizontal boundaries.

   Globalization, strategic alliance, customer-linkage, telecommuting are practices to reduce external boundaries. Eg, General electric, Boeing, Apple computers.

Implication of Organizational structure on OB

- Work specialization contributes to higher employee productivity, but it reduces job satisfaction.
- The benefits of specialization have decreased rapidly as employees seek more intrinsically rewarding jobs.
- The effect of span of control on employee performance is contingent upon individual differences and abilities, task structures, and other organizational factors.

- Participative decision making in decentralized organizations is positively related to job satisfaction.

Strengths of OP

- Acts as a roadmap to life in an organization
- Helps predict organizational life
- Helps influence organizational events
- Helps individuals understand themselves & others better
- Helps the manager grasp the basis of motivation
- OB is advantageous for maintaining cordial Industrial Relations
- It helps individuals shape his/her career

Shortcomings

- OB has almost become a fad with managers
- It has not helped improve interpersonal relations in organizations settings.
- OB is selfish and exploitative.
- OB might not endure the same rate of success under different conditions
- It does not offer "one best" answer to a problem

Challenges and Opportunities for OB

Responding to Globalization:

Management is required to cope with problems of unfamiliar laws, languages, practices, competition, attitude management styles, work ethics etc. The major issues of globalization are increased foreign assignments, working with people from different cultures, Overlook movement of jobs to countries with low-cost labor etc.

Managing Workforce Diversity

Highly diverse work force in terms of Race, National origin, Age, Disability etc. makes a difference in the organisational psyche. Varied cultures and languages can be found at the best workplaces. Longer working hours have become a trend.

Changing demographics of workforce

Dual income career couples, growing number of young employees and presence of baby boomers, generation X, and Y in the same organisation, increasing number of working mothers, steady decline in blue-collar jobs making place for white-collar jobs are some of the issues to be handled.

Changed employee expectations

Employee expectations in terms of empowerment, flexi-time, challenging jobs, career-advancement, better treatment etc pose challenges to the field of OB.

Technology transformation

- Linear organizations
- Wired organizations
- Virtual offices
- Changing nature of management work

Corporate Re-organization: diversification, mergers, acquisitions, take-overs and massive re-organization has impact on organization and employees.

Improving Quality and productivity: TQM, QC, Re-engineering, Kaizen, are implemented with extensive employees participation.

Improving Ethical Behavior: Manager has to create a ethically healthy climate where employees wholeheartedly contribute to the organization

CLOSING CASE

Mrs Rita was a hardworking and intelligent employee of a well run embroidery unit in South India. Job: She had put good number of years in the organization and she was liked by the management and colleagues alike for her commitment towards the job. Three months ago, Mrs Rita looked forward to her promotion to supervisor position, which would have been well deserved career move for her. After four years in the department, she was confident of her abilities, and knew her staff was capable and experienced.

Today, Rita isn't so sure she was cut out to be a supervisor. There seems to be no end to her workday. During office hours her day is filled assigning work and reviewing results. Also, there is a steady flow of visitors, and the phone rings constantly. In the evening, when she would like to relax, she has to take care of administrative matters such as reading mail, answering letters, preparing budgets and completing performance appraisals.

In frustration, Mrs Rita asked her friend, Agnus, to join her for lunch. Mrs Rita said she had something important to talk to her about. At lunch, she told Agnus that she was thinking about giving up her supervisor's job. She said she just couldn't face a career of working 60 hours a week. Agnus listened and then said there might be another way. If the only issue was the time required to do the job, perhaps a review of how Mrs Rita was using her time might help. After listening to Mrs Rita describe a typical week, Agnus asked the following questions:

Consider Mrs Rita's situation and answer the following questions:

1. Does she appear to be making effective use of delegation?

 ____

 ____

2. If her visitors are employees, how might she avoid interruptions?

 ____

 ____

3. Should Mrs Rita consider establishing a "quiet time" when she would receive no calls or visitors? If so, when might be the best time of day?

 ____

 ____

4. Mrs Rita feels she should assign all departmental work and review all results. Is there a more efficient way?

 ____

 ____

5. What other ways could Mrs Rita gain more control over her use of time?

 ____

 ____

Reference

a. Slocum/Hillriegel, Fundamentals of organizational behavior, Cengene Learning

b. Fred Luthans, Organizational Behavior, 11th edition, Mc-Graw Hill International

c. Stephen P Robbins, Timothy A. Judge, Seema Sanghi, Organizational Behavior, Pearson Education, 12th Edition

Test your knowledge

Multiple Choice Questions

A) Organizational behavior

a. Is the study of large organizations and their structure
b. Seeks to understand, explain, predict and change human behaviour
c. Is the process of organizing the company
d. Is the process of corporate governance

B) Interpersonal, decisional and informational managerial roles were identified by whom:

a. Hawthorn
b. Hertzberg
c. Mintzberg
d. Wheatley

C) The roots of organizational behaviour come from research results from:

a. Sociology and Psychology
b. Political science
c. Anthropology
d. All of the above
e. a) and c)

D) Which statement is true?

a. Organizational behaviour explores managerial roles and challenges
b. Organizational behaviour is the study of financial capital applications
c. Organizational behaviour is the study of technological capital applications
d. Organizational behaviour is the dividing up of tasks and work roles

E) The benefit(s) of studying Organizational Behaviour are/is:

a. Improved managerial effectiveness
b. Effective managers
c. Become better at influencing others
d. Manage your life outside work better
e. All of the above

F) The formal organization includes:

a. Beliefs, assumptions, values and unspoken norms of behaviour
b. Technology, structure and other visible parts of the organization
c. Both the overt and covert aspects of the organization
d. The open systems interactions

G) A system of control and performance monitoring of top management is:

a. Behaviour science
b. Formal organization structure
c. Informal organization structure
d. Corporate governance

H) All the following statements are true regarding Organizational Behavior except

a. OB focuses on observable behaviors
b. OB deals with internal states such as thinking and perceiving
c. OB focuses on theoretical management issues rather than practical ones
d. OB analyzes the behavior of groups and organizations
e. OB focuses only on the external factors.

MODEL QUESTIONS

Section–A

(Each question carries 2 marks)

1. Define OB.
2. Define Organization and State the difference between OB and OP
3. State the different stages of evolution of OB
4. State the various approaches to the study of OB
5. Explain the impact of globalization on employees in organization
6. State the organizations of the future
7. What do you understand by Organization structure?
8. What are the three theoretical frameworks of OP?

Section–B

(Each question carries 5 marks)

1. Explain the process of evolution of OP.
2. Briefly explain the assumptions to the field of OP/OB.
3. Explain the importance of OB in today's scenario.
4. State the advantages and disadvantages of Functional structure.
5. State the advantages and disadvantages of Virtual structure.
6. Explain the 3 theoretical frameworks to the field of OB/OP.

Section–C

(Each question carries 15 marks)

1. State the Challenges and Opportunities to the field of OP.
2. Explain the contributing disciplines to the field of OP.
3. Explain in detail the strengths and weakness to the field of OB.

◈◈◈◈

Read More on the Web

We all know what organizational psychology is. However, this collective psyche is the amalgamation of numerous factors, the smallest of which is an individual human, or here, an employee. It is very interesting to try to understand why a certain person behaves the way he/she does, or what constitutes to his psyche exclusively. A persons mind is governed by two factors, namely the conscious and the subconscious.

Most of the time, we portray what we want others to see and perceive, with the alert help of our conscious. However, our subconscious pushes its way through anyway (a classic example being Freudian slips). Turning inwards, the conscious is capable of processing very little information and has a memory of about twenty seconds, when the subconscious is capable of processing exponentially more (to the tune of 11 million bits per second) and hence forms a substantially more comprehensive picture of a situation.

But, this vast area is mainly uncharted. Psychiatrists are yet to establish the seemingly mind boggling possibilities of exploring and exploiting this region. Psychiatrists now capitalize on this in the form of psychoanalysis .Coming back, and after realizing the potential of this region (the proof of this theory funnily was observed in an American theatre in the mid-1950's) major companies started to utilize subliminal messaging, a tactic that was sure to ensure that their message would be received loud and clear by the target, whether he was aware of it or not. This quickly caught on; and today, we see subliminal messaging almost everywhere.

The theory behind this tactic was this. The conscious mind would take what it saw, process it and quickly move on. The subconscious would simultaneously see much more, process it, give certain instructions to the conscious, which would then follow the same, without knowing what happened in the background. This is what happened in the theatre: An American market/motivational researcher James Vicary demonstrated the tachistoscope, a device used to flash consciously invisible messages on a screen which could be seen only by the subconscious mind. During one six-week test in a Fort Lee, A New Jersey movie theater, involving 45,699 patrons, messages were flashed on alternate days over Kim Novak's calming face: "Hungry? Eat Popcorn," and "Drink Coca-Cola" During the six weeks, popcorn sales rose 57.7 percent and Coca-Cola sales rose 18.1 percent.

Even so the subconscious isn't a quietly repressed commander. The time where it truly shines is during our sleep, particularly when we are dreaming. The mind is essentially awake, operating at the alpha stage, even though our body is paralyzed to protect itself (more on that later) and our subconscious takes over, telling and teaching us what we may have happened to miss while we were awake, albeit in a strange, encoded manner. Our mind, having received this information (or some of it) wakes up and applies it.

The trick, of course, is harnessing this information and using it - for whatever reason.

Have you ever walked down a road with a clear and unoccupied mind and suddenly a solution comes to mind, for a problem you've been obsessing over for a while? That's your subconscious at play. A few tips to get your subconscious to speak to you are:

- Meditate. It calms your mind, allowing the subconscious to express itself.
- Be creative. This bolsters your subconscious, allowing it to express itself in terms of feelings, colours, music and emotion. This also facilitates the removal of accumulated negativity in a healthy way.

- Learn about the subconscious. The more you know, the more you allow the mind, now armed with knowledge, to explore itself.
- Practice self talk and visualization. This allows you to have a one on one with your mind, for problem solving and even affirmation- if you say you can do something, you will accomplish it.
- Study briefly before bed. Sleep and more particularly dreaming helps in the learning process.
- Pay attention to our dreams. Very often, they tell us things that we don't know things that we aren't ready to acknowledge, or things we want.
- Listen to your intuition. Your intuition is a way your mind has of warning you to dangers or opportunities before your conscious mind has all the information. Quite often, this is a key to avoid potential dangers.
- Be perceptive to your surroundings. Allow as much absorption of information you can and allow your mind to process it in an unbiased manner, as far as possible. Psychologists call this "relaxed awareness"

Sources and References

http://www.sveiby.com/articles/TacitTest.htm (information processing, conscious and subconscious)

https://en.wikipedia.org/wiki/Freudian_slip

http://marcelleliemant.com/your-big-and-beautiful-brain-harnessing-your-subconscious-for-creativity/

http://www.sleeplearning.com/html/subliminal_message.htm (origin of subliminal messaging and preliminary public testing)

http://science.howstuffworks.com/life/inside-the-mind/human-brain/dream2.htm (brain waves)

http://subliminalmanipulation.blogspot.in/ (extra reading)

http://www.wikihow.com/Control-Your-Subconscious-Mind

http://www.calmdownmind.com/programming-your-subconscious-mind/ (extra reading).

CHAPTER 2

PERCEPTION

Learning Objectives of the Chapter

- Meaning of Perception
- Difference between Sensation & Perception
- Perception Process and its elements
- Factors influencing Perception
- Perceptual Organization
- Social Perception
- Attribution and Kelly's Attribution theory
- Impression Management

OPENING CASE

How perception can make or mar a company!

Godrej Appliances, started in 1958, dominated the consumer durables market for decades, especially in refrigerators. But gradually it grew complacent and lost touch with its customers. Liberalisation and the entry of foreign players saw its market share in the segment drop by half. This case study describes how the company reacted to the situation, re-branded its products, and fought its way back.

The findings of a series of market surveys stunned the top management of Godrej Appliances, one of the leading companies of the Godrej group. They said the company and its products were not connecting with young people. The average age of its customers was 35 to 45 years - a serious impediment in a country with 45 per cent of its population below 25. Worse, they claimed, that it was not even perceived as a technology brand - the market did not think its products incorporated the latest advances in technology.

The year was 2005. The surveys had been commissioned to figure out why Godrej Appliances was losing market share. No doubt competition had stiffened following liberalisation and the entry of aggressive foreign players, especially Korean brands like LG and Samsung, and the Japanese like Akai and Aiwa. But Godrej executives had never imagined that such a yawning gap had grown between perception and reality. "There was little or no difference in terms of technology between us and the foreign players," says Ramesh Chembath, Assistant Vice President, Marketing, Godrej Appliances. "Yet the youth considered us a momand-pop brand."

Introduction

The opening vignette clearly states the importance of perception in the business world. The way a consumer perceives a company's product or service will affect buying decision which ultimately affects the company's market share. A job aspirant's perception about a company's image will affect the recruitment process of the company. An employee's perception about the value system of the company as well as his perception about the extent of support provided by his immediate boss decides his tenure in the company, which ultimately affects attrition percentage in the company. These are some of the many organizational significance of perception.

Human beings have the ability to attach meanings and interpretations to our actions. The way each individual understands a particular situation will vary based on many aspects like value system of the individual, cultural background, education level etc. The story of *"Six blind men who went to see an elephant" is* a good example of how people will perceive things differently, based on their understanding, even though the perceived item remains the same.

Figure 2.1 Six blind men and elephant

Meaning of Perception

The sensory stimuli received by our sense organs and transferred to our brain are not completely captured by our mental focus. These stimuli are captured by our individual preferences. Perception is the way that sensory information is chosen and transformed so that it has meaning. The process of perception helps us to select, organize and interpret the sensory stimuli received from the environment. Soon after the sensory input is received, an individual uses perceptual processes to select among sensory input stimuli and to organize them to lead to relevant action. A person's perception is a culmination of past experiences, including one's culture, background etc. The word "Perception" is originated from the Latin word "Percipio" which means receiving. The dictionary meaning of perception is to "take in mentally".

Sensation and perception:

Psychologists distinctly differentiate sensation from perception. Sensation is the process by which external stimuli are received by us through sensory organs and transmitted to the brain. Perception refers to the interpretation of these sensory stimuli received by the brain. It is important to understand the concepts of perception from organisational point of view. Human behavior is the outcome of the way we perceive things around us. Often we fail to understand the other person's behavior in a given situation. To understand each other's behavior, it is essential to understand each other's perception. A conducive organizational environment should be created for favourable perception, which in turn will lead to increased organizational productivity.

Sensation: The process through which the senses pick up visual, auditory, and other sensory stimuli and transmit them to the brain. In the case of sensation, sensory information are registered in the brain but are not been interpreted. Sensation deals with the basic behaviour of a person which is caused by his physiological functions.

Perception: Perception on the other hand is a broader concept. It is the process by which sensory information is actively organized and interpreted by the brain in order to give meaning to the environment. Perception is the course of action by which an individual selects, organizes and interprets stimuli into an indicative picture of the environment. It is less physiological and more cognitive in nature.

Definition of Perception:-

Robbins: "Perception may be defined as a process by which individuals organize and interpret their sensory impressions in order to give meaning to their environment"

It is a process of receiving, selecting, organizing, and interpreting, checking and reacting to sensory stimuli/data"

Nord: "Perception is the manner in which a person organizes, interprets and processes various stimuli that are transmitted in to psychological experience.

Figure 2.2 What does it look like to you ?

Some of you may see a rabbit in the picture and some may see a duck in the same picture. Why? The picture has not changed, but the perception is different.

Figure 2.3 ***Anand Milk, from India, wanted to increase milk consumption among children, McCann Erikson Agency came up with this amazingly creative ad placed on one of Mumbai's buildings, where you can see a child strong enough —a benefit of the milk, of course— to move part of the building***

Perception is your interpretation of reality after filtering out the stimuli or information, which is then organized based on one's existing knowledge, needs, beliefs, values, assumptions and attitude. The meanings of things change when the same thing is perceived from a different angle. Perceiving things in the way it is expected to perceive is very important for an organization. People behave in a particular way based on the perception of reality, not on reality itself. Incorrect perceptions are called illusions.

Perception process

Now let us look at perception process. It is an "Input- Throughput – Output" process. Environmental stimuli in the form of objects, people, events, information etc. are the inputs for perception process. These inputs are filtered and screened before it generates observable behavior. The process of selection has 5 basic stages.

1. The sensory input stage
2. Selective attention
3. Perceptual organization
4. Interpretation
5. Behavioural response

Stages of perception process are depicted in the following diagram:

The sensory input stage:

Stimuli is received through five sensory organs –Tasting, Smelling, Seeing, Hearing, Touching.

↓

Selective attention stage:

External factors	***internal factors***
Habit	Size
Motivation	Contrast
Learning	Repetition
Personality	Movement
Interest	Familiarity
Experience	Novelty
Social background	

↓

Perceptual organization:

Figure ground

Grouping

Constancy

↓

Interpretation

Perceptual set

Attribution

Stereotyping

Halo effect

Defense

Projection

↓

Behavioural response.

Covert	***Overt***
Attitudes	Behaviour
Motivation	
Feeling	

Let us discuss each of these stages in detail.

***1. The sensory input stage*:** The sensory organs capture the stimuli from the environment. The stimuli may include people, events, objects etc. These stimuli are transferred to brain in the form of raw data. Examples of a few stimuli affecting the senses are the noise of TV, others talking, fragrance of flowers, taste of ice cream, smoothness of silk etc.

***2. Selective attention /Perceptual Selectivity*:** From the multitudes of sensory stimuli, we select the ones which are relevant for us, as we cannot pay attention to every stimulus we receive. The selective screening could be by controlled processes or without perceivers' conscious awareness. Perceptual selectivity is the tendency to select certain objects from the environment for attention. A related term for selective perception is subliminal perception. Subliminal perception are the situations in which weak stimuli were perceived without any awareness yet a person is influenced by it. It is often "below the radar of perception" wherein the stimuli presented below the threshold for awareness are found to influence thoughts, feelings, actions, etc. Subliminal perception does not produce long lasting changes in behavior. The concept of subliminal perception is used in advertising to covertly influence buyer behavior. Selection of stimuli could depend on internal and external factors. Internal factors include perceivers' age, learning, interest, IQ etc. External factors include intensity of stimuli, its size, movement, repetition etc

Internal Factors Influencing the Perceptual selection:

People select those stimuli from the environment that call out to them and suit them based on varied aspects like perceiver's learning, interest, motivation, personality, etc. These are intrinsic factors that affect perception. The following are some of the internal factors of perception:

a) Habit: Old habits die hard. Individuals observe objects, locations and conditions differently according to their habits. Example: A person who is habituated to smoking cigarettes whenever he is upset will feel the urge to smoke when encountered with stressful situations.

b) Motivation: Motivation has vital importance in perceptual selectivity. Motivational factors accentuates the individual's sensitivity to those stimuli which he considers as necessary for satisfying his needs in relation to his past experience with them. Primary motives such as hunger and thirst affect the perception of a mankind. A person who is hungry will be more sensitive to the smell of food. Perception is also affected by secondary motives, like attainment of power, affiliation or achievement. Motivation gives the energy to take interest in a particular thing and to attend to things. A person who is motivated by power will perceive a special chair kept along with other regular chairs to be reserved for him.

c) Learning: The state of learning plays an important role in perceptual selection. Even though it is interrelated with motivation and personality, learning itself play's a major role in developing perceptual set/ cognitive awareness. A perceptual set is what a person expects from the stimuli on the basis of his learning and experience relative to same or similar stimuli. People perceive as per their levels of education or knowledge.

Using a perceptual set, the mind organizes information and forms images and compares them with previous exposures to similar stimuli. Learning creates an expectancy, which makes an individual see what he wants to see. Try the activity given below to comprehend this better.

Activity:Can You Read This?

AoccdrnigtorscheearchatanElingshuinervtisy, it deosn'tmttaerin what oredrtheltteersin a word are, only that thefristandlsatltteresare at the rghitpcleas. The rsetcan be a total msesand you can still raeditwouthitaporbelm. This isbcuseaewe do not raederveylteterbyilstef, but the word as a wlohe.

Even though none of the words are correct, we comprehend what is written because of our previous exposure to similar words and sentences.

Learned values can also affect perception. For example, the very thought of eating beef is not accepted by Hindus as cow is considered sacred by Hindu religion.

Another famous illustration of cognitive awareness is given below.

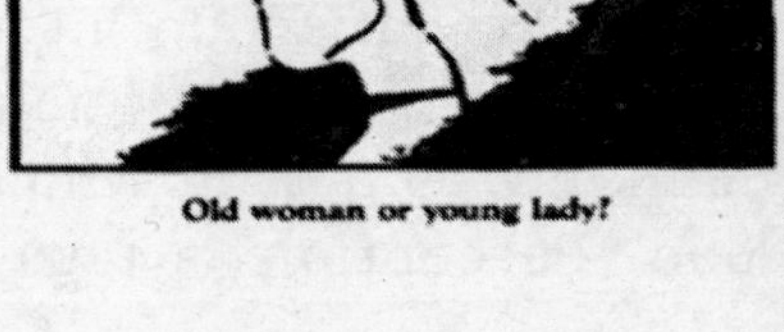

Old woman or young lady?

If a person is shown the clear picture of young women in the picture, right at the beginning, the individual will perceive only the young woman and not the old lady in the picture because of previous experience.

d) Personality: The personality of the perceiver has great impact on the perception process. Our personality trait predisposes us to perceive the world in a particular way. Individual distinctive behavior affects what you perceive about that individual. Optimistic people grasp things in favourable terms and pessimistic looks at anything with skepticism. Another example could be that of an extrovert personality, who responds to others conversation eagerly in comparison to an introvert, who is generally disinterested in striking a conversation with others.

e) Interest: Perception is influenced unconsciously by the interests of the perceiver. For example, an individual who is fascinated by cars will observe different car makes, features etc., which may not be otherwise observed by other people who commute on the same road. Another example could be that of an individual who is interested in losing weight will observe the advertisements for slimming in newspapers, which will be otherwise ignored by people who are not interested in it.

f) Experience: Experience influences perception to a great extent. Successful experiences enhance perceptive ability and lead to accuracy in perception whereas continuous failure erodes self-confidence. For example, a person who has experience of driving sports car will observe sports cars on the road, which may not be noticed by people who have no experience of the pleasure of driving a sports car.

g) Social background: The kind of upbringing also affects perception. Socially and economically backward people may look at things differently compared to socially and economically forward people. For example, a person who was brought up with a lot of superstitious beliefs will look at certain incidents in a particular way, which will be unlike a person who was not brought up with superstitious beliefs.

External Factors Influencing the Perceptual selection

External factors are the building blocks for perception. Once they are received by our sensory organs, the signals are sent to the brain for taking action. The following are some of the external factors that affect perception.

a) Intensity: The intensity of stimulus indicates that the more forceful the stimulus audio or visual, the more is the possibility that it will be perceived. For example, we pay attention to a person who is yelling than the normal voice of people in a crowd. Similarly, brighter colours, intense smell etc. will catch ones attention.

b) Size: The size of the object or stimulus has a powerful effect on the perception process because the size affects attention and absorption in a very effective manner. A tall and well-built individual catches more attention than an individual of regular size. A bigger sized file will catch attention in an admin office compared to a regular sized file. The bigger the size of the perceived stimuli, the higher is the probability that it is perceived. Size attracts the attention of the individual.

c) Contrast: Contrasting objects catch the attention of people and has an effect on their behavior. The contrast principle states that exterior stimuli, which stand out against the background or which are not anticipated by the people, will receive better attention than stimuli which is common. For example, an employee who wears casual clothes on a regular working day when other employees wear formal clothing will get noticed faster. Plant safety signs, which have black lettering on a yellow background or white lettering on a red background, are attention catching as they strike out of the ordinary.

d) Repetition: Repeated stimuli sent more number of times have more impact on performances than single stimuli. This principle is used in marketing extensively. Repetition has the benefit of being attention catching and we will often find marketers displaying their products in front of consumers as often as possible. Few more examples of repetition as a factor of perception could be NIRMA advertisement wherein the jingle, the word NIRMA is repeated many times to catch attention. Breaking news bulletin flashed repeatedly is perceived better. An organizational example could be that of repeated requests of a subordinate, who requests for additional budget support for completing the project, which attract attention than a single request.

e) Movement: A moving object catches attention more in comparison to a static object. For example, wooden template of a motor cycle is perceived in poor light in comparison to a moving miniature model of motor cycle. Another example could be that of a car which is pulling out from a car park where the rest of the cars are stationary, catches attention.

f) Novelty and familiarity: A novel object in the common situation or an everyday object in a novel situation tends to attract attention. For example a fair skinned or black skinned employee in an organization in India will catch better attention, as people of Indian origin are generally of medium complexion. Books with unusual covers, people wearing unusual clothes etc will attract attention.

3. Perceptual organization: The selected stimuli are put in order and pattern to make some meaning out of the stimuli.

Forms of Perceptual Organization/Laws of perceptual organization.

a) Figure-ground differentiation: The tendency to differentiate and concentrate on a stimulus that is classified as figure as opposed to back ground. A form or shape is naturally perceived as **figure** or **object**, while the encircling area is perceived as **ground** or **background**. The eye distinguishes an object from its circumferential area. After balancing both the figure as well as the ground the perceived image will become clear.

b) Perceptual Grouping: Human beings tendency to group several individual stimuli into a meaningful and recognizable pattern is known as perceptual grouping. A person is likely to group several stimuli together into a identifiable pattern based on theory of:

i) Closure: *Closure* takes place when an object is *unfinished* or not *completely enclosed*. If a person is not able to acquire enough information to come to a decision, he tries to fill the gaps by combining the present information with the information from previous experiences. This is called the principle of closure. If enough of the shape is determined or pointed out, people perceive the whole by filling in the missing information.

Ex: The Panda in the above figure is not complete; but just enough is present for the eye to complete the shape. When the *person's perception completes a shape,* **closure**occurs.

ii) Continuity: The principle of Continuation occurs when the eye is compelled to move through one objectand continue to another object. Sometimes people tend to think only in a particular direction. This is called principle of continuity

Ex: Continuation occurs in the above example; the individual's eye will naturally follow a line or curve of the "H" which leads the eye directly to the maple leaf.

Proximity: Proximity occurs when elements are placed together. They tend to be perceived as a group.The nine squares below are placed without proximity. They are perceived as separate shapes.

When the above squares are given close proximity, unity occurs. i.e.

Similarity: The principle of similarity occurs when the object look similar to one another. People often perceive them as a group or as a pattern. The below example depicts the same

The example above contains 11 distinct objects which appear as single unit because all of the shapes have similarity.

Here unity occurs because the triangular shapes at the bottom of the eagle symbol look similar to the shape of the sun.

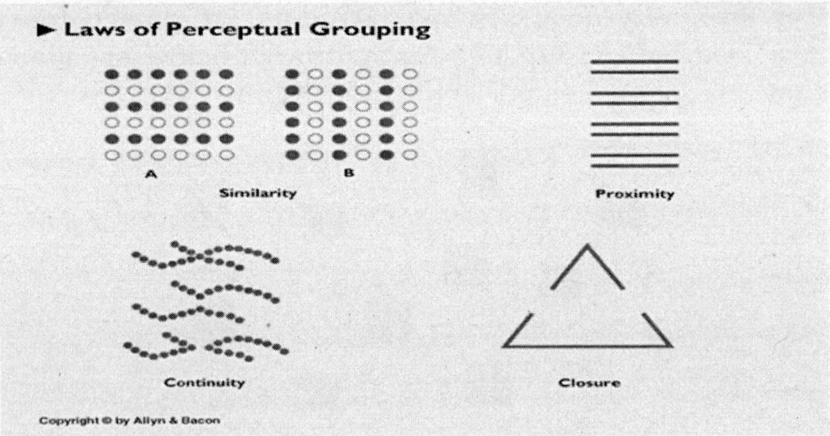

Perceptual Constancy: The perception of elements like size, shape, color, brightness and location of an object remains constant and does not change from individual to individual. The tendency to perceive objects as maintaining stable properties (e.g., size, shape, brightness, and color) despite differences in distance, viewing angle, and lighting

Size constancy: Perceiving objects as being about the same size when they move farther away

Shape constancy: Perceiving objects as having a stable or unchanging shape regardless of changes in the retinal image resulting from differences in viewing angle. According to principle of perceptual constancy, there are some things which are perceived alike by all people, irrespective of the factors influencing perception. It provides a person a sense of stability in this changing world.

4. Interpretation: Trying to make some meaning. The perceptual output includes one's attitude, opinion, feelings and values. Accurate interpretation of perceived, selected and organized stimuli will lead to productive outcome, whereas perceptual distortion may lead to adverse conditions.

a) Perceptual Context: It provides meaning and value to objects, events, situation and other people in the environment. Perceptual context provides meaning and value to stimuli with respect to a particular context

Perceptual Defense: It refers to building of a defense against stimuli or situational events in a particular context that are personally or culturally unacceptable or threatening. According to the principle of perceptual defense, people tend to resist information that is emotionally disturbing or clashes with their personal convictions or cultural values

Activity: Take specific examples in advertising and analyse how creatively the stimulus factors are used to attract the viewers' attention.

5. Behavioural response: Based on the accuracy of perception, there can be varied behavior response.

Activity: Explore your own stereotype thinking by attaching 4 terms that describe most or all of the category of people

a) Teacher ....

b) Politicians ....

c) Accountant ....

d) Artist ....

e) Autoriksha drivers ....

Factors Influencing Perception

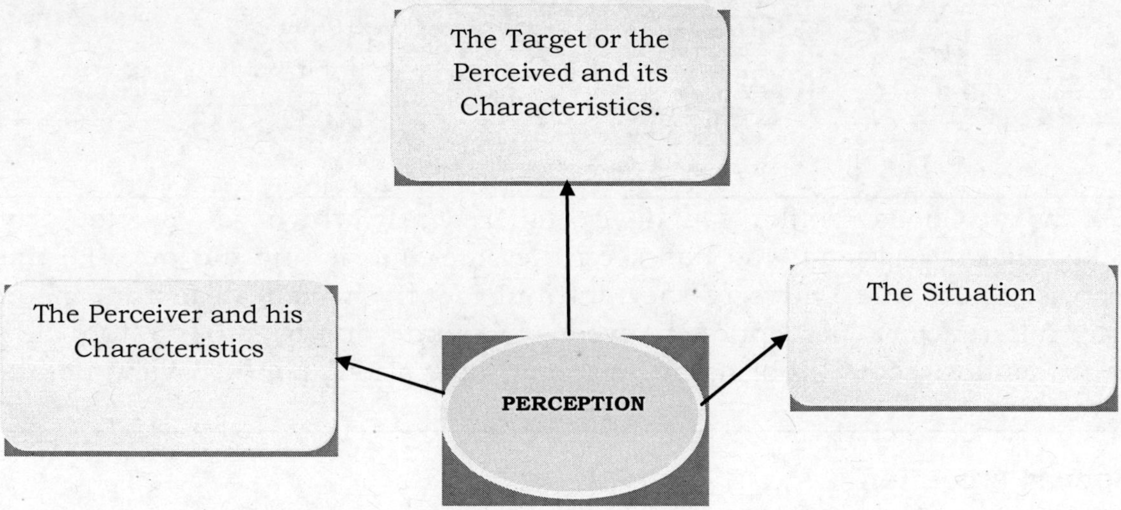

1. The Perceiver and his characteristics

- Needs & Motives
- Self-concept
- Past experience
- Current psychological state
- Beliefs and Expectations
- Situation (surrounding)
- Cultural upbringing

2. The Target or the Perceived and its characteristics

- Physical appearance
- Similarity
- Behavior
- Manner of communication
- Status

3. The Situation

- Physical setting
- Social setting
- Organizational setting

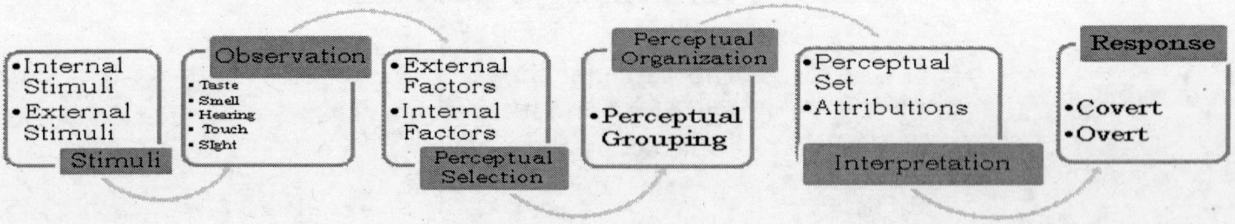

Activity: Choose a film you have seen recently which you particularly like. Identify a friend who has seen the same movie and did not like the movie. Share your views of the film and identify which all factors made the difference in perception between you and your friend (factors like age, gender, social upbringing, interest, education, political view points etc.

Social Perception

Social perception is the process of interpreting information about another person i.e. the opinions you form about another person depends on the amount of information available to you and the extent to which you are able to correctly interpret the information that you have acquired.

It is directly concerned with how one individual perceives other individuals; how we get to know others.

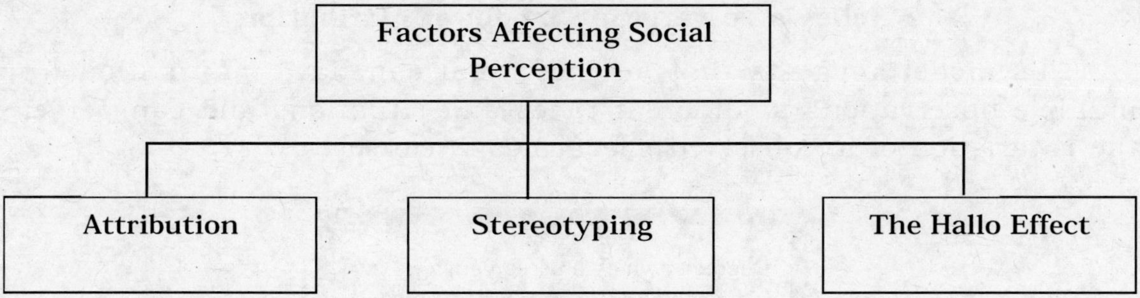

Attribution

It is the process by which we make sense of our environments. Attribution refers to how people attach or attribute causes or reasons of another's or their own behavior. Fritz Heider and Harold Kelley developed attribution theory. Ex: We may attribute high marks secured by a student to his diligence and focus. Some may also attribute the students' success to luck or his contact with people at the evaluating system

Definition: The ways in which people come to understand the causes of their own and others' behaviors

Most often a subconscious process (i.e. people are not normally aware of making attributions)

ATTRIBUTION THEORY

Attribution theory is a social psychology theory developed by Fritz Heider, Harold Kelley, Edward E. Jones, and Lee Ross. According to them, attribution theory deals with how social perceiver uses information to arrive at casual explanation of events. It examines what information is gathered and how it is combined to form a casual judgment.The theory explores how individuals "attribute" causes to events and behavior.

Types of attribution

1. **Internal attribution :**

When individual tends to explain the behavior of others, it is known as internal or personal attribution. Example: Personality traits. We may attribute a person's particular behavior to his honesty. Internal attribution provides us information for predicting a person's future behavior.

2. **External attribution:**

When individuals tend to explain their own behavior, it becomes external or situational attribution.

Kelley's co variation model of Attribution

This model suggests that an individual can have information from multiple observations at different times and situations and can perceive the covariation of an observed effect and its causes.

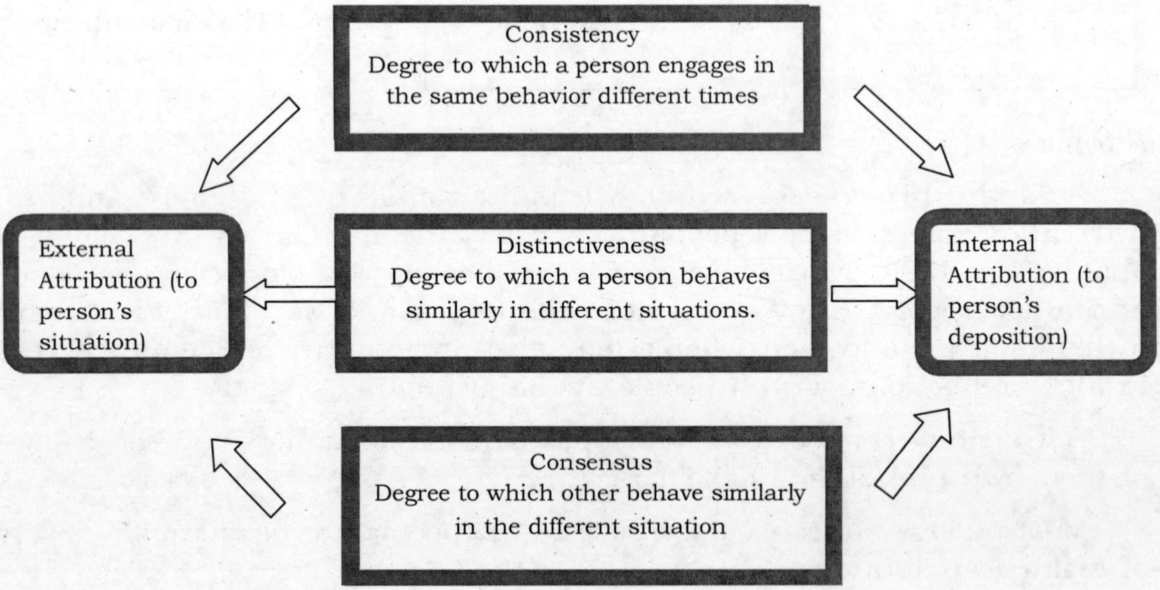

According to Kelley, there are 3 types of casual information which influenced our judgement. They are as follows :

1. **Consistency:** It is the extent to which a person behaves in a particular way every time the situation occurs. It explains how a person acts with same stimulus over time.

   Example: A person X smokes every time when he goes out for lunch with his friends. If he smokes very rarely when he is out with friends, consistency is low.

2. **Consensus**: This is the extent to which other people behave in the same way in similar situations. It is about how *other people act with same* stimulus.

   Example: Continuing with the previous example, X smokes when he goes out with his friends for lunch. If his friends also smoke, his behavior is high in consensus.

3. **Distinctiveness :** It is the extent to which the person behaves in the same way in similar situations

Example: If X smokes *only* when he goes out with friends for lunch, his behavior is high in distinctiveness. But if he smokes at any time or any place, distinctiveness is low.

Activity: Look at the following diagram from different angles. What do you see?

Biases affecting Perception and Attribution in the workplace

Several factors contributing toward interpretation of data are:-

1. **Perceptual set:** Previously held beliefs about objects influence an individual's perceptions of similar objects

2. **Attribution:** It refers to the process by which the individual assigns causes to the behavior he or she conceives.

3. **Stereotyping:** It is the tendency to assign attributes to someone solely on the basis of a category of people to which that person belongs to stereotyping — judging someone on the basis of our perception of the group to which he or she belongs

   The problem, of course, is when we inaccurately stereotype.

   Example: In organizations, we frequently hear comments that represent stereotypes based on gender, age, race, ethnicity, and even weight.

4. **Halo effect:** It refers to the tendency of perceiving people in terms of good or bad and assigning all good qualities to one who is good and bad qualities to one who is bad. The halo effect occurs when we draw a general impression on the basis of a single characteristic. The opposite is known as **Horns effect**

   Example: This phenomenon frequently occurs when students appraise their classroom instructor. Students may give prominence to a single trait such as enthusiasm and allow their entire evaluation to be tainted by how they judge the instructor on that one trait.

5. **Projection:** People project their own feelings, tendencies, or motives into their judgment of others. People tend to see in other person traits that they themselves possess. This tendency to attribute one's own characteristics to other people is called projection.

   Example: When managers engage in projection, they compromise their ability to respond to individual differences. They tend to see people as more homogeneous than they really are.

6. **Similarity Error:** This can happen when a manager rates a subordinate based on the qualities and characteristics possessed or not possessed by himself

   Example: A punctual manager perceives and rates a subordinate high on performance because of his similarity in nature, though being punctual is not the only criteria of performance.

7. **Contrast error:** In this perceptual distortion, the manager rates an employee based on comparison with other employees and not with a previously set benchmark performance.

   Example: A sales manager may rate a sales person a "lower performance" employee though he has completed the assigned target only because his peers have exceeded the targets and way too ahead of him.

8. **Initial impression:** This again is a faulty perception when an individual's first impression on others forms an opinion about him irrespective of his later behavior or performance.

   Example: A teacher gets initial high rating during the start of academic year and the superior considers him as good performer irrespective of the poor sessions taken in the later part of the academic period.

9. **Recency effect:** Here, the supervisor rates the subordinates based on the recent performance (good or bad) rather than considering the whole performance period.

   Example: Some employees resort to a tactic where they perform at their best to get good rating just before the performance appraisal.

10. **Central tendency:** Here the rater evaluates all the employees in the middle of the rating scale, giving them an average score, to avoid taking responsibility of very high or very low score

    Example: A teacher gives average marks to all students in the class irrespective of the difference in academic performance, to avoid the responsibility of extremely high or extremely low scores

11. **Selective exposure/Selective perception:** Employees tend to perceive things which they would want to perceive, though there are varied stimuli in the environment.

12. **Pygmalion effect/Self-fulfilling prophecy:** is the tendency to deny personal responsibility for performance problems but to accept personal responsibility for performance success.

This has application at university and business level. According this theory, when a teacher expects a student to learn well and show his intellectual ability, the student actually performs well academically and if there no such expectation set on students, they do not show any improved academic performance. This applies also in the organizational context where the manager expects the subordinate to very well in job and expresses the same positively to the subordinate, he improves his performance.

Pygmalion effect represented diagramatically

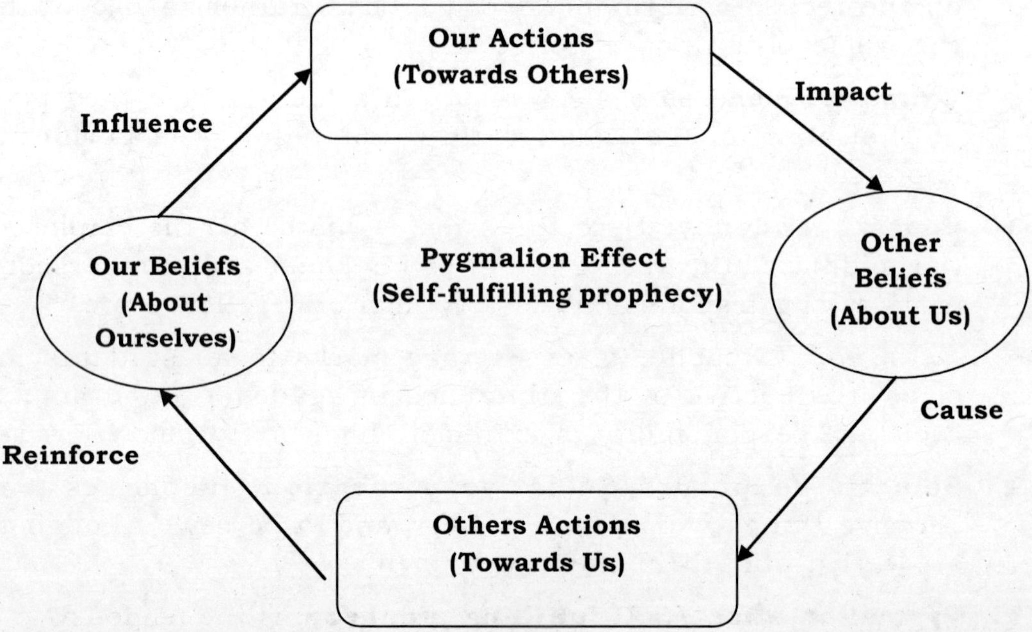

Importance of Perception for an organization

1. Employees behave based on the perception of reality, not by reality itself
2. Helps us to adapt to complex and dynamic work situations by perceptual constancy. (Size, shape and brightness constancy)
3. Perception is used in advertising to draw attention of prospective customers. Hoardings of advertisements are made keeping in mind the principles of shape, size and brightness constancies so that they catch the attention of prospective buyers.
4. Perception is used in ensuring safety. Perception principles are used while making messages of warning.
5. Managing performance. It is understood that people start behaving the way you expect them to behave. Expectation becomes reality. Pygmalion effect can be very effectively used to groom subordinates to star performers.
6. Building relationships. Positive perception forges good relationship among team members
7. Impression management. If a positive impression is created during an interview, candidate is perceived to be a suitable candidate.

Impression Management

It is referred to as "*self- presentation*"

Everyone attempts to make favourable impression of self in the mind of others. This business of impression management becomes more important when you face employment interview. While facing an interview if you happen to create positive impression in the beginning, most likely you happen to establish an early lead. In the beginning, if you do not help experts to create a positive perception or impression for yourself, it becomes difficult to turn the table in later part of the interview. Hence during employment interview it is in your favour to create positive first impression. On the other hand, evidence indicates that interviewers make perceptual judgements that are often inaccurate. However, more matured evaluators do not give undue importance to first impression.

Impression management is done in various other organisational activities. Whereas efforts at impression management may improve the quality of social functioning, overdoing of such actions may occur at the cost of information accuracy and high quality decision making.

Impression Management (sometimes referred to as self-presentation) is the process by which people attempt to manage or control the perceptions others form of them. It has considerable implications for areas such as the validity of performance appraisals and a pragmatic, political tool for one to climb the ladder of success in organizations.

Impression Management Strategies Used By Employees

Demotion - Preventive Strategy	Promotion - enhancing Strategy
▪ Accounts ▪ Apologies ▪ Disassociation	▪ Entitlements ▪ Enhancements ▪ Obstacle disclosure ▪ Association

I) Demotion-Preventive Strategy

It is used when employees want to minimize their responsibilities for negative outcome

- **Accounts**: These are employee's attempts to excuse or justify their actions.

  Example: Excuse for not getting something done on time because of other high-priority assignment.

- **Apologies**: When there is no logical way out, the employee may apologize to the boss for some negative event. Such an apology not only gives the impression that the individual is sorry but also indicates that it will not happen again. The employee is big enough to face up to a problem and solve it.

- **Disassociation**: When employees are indirectly associated with something that went wrong (for example they are a member of a committee or work team that made a bad decision), they may secretly tell their bosses that they fought for the right thing but were overruled. Employees using this approach tend to be removed both from the group and from responsibility for the problem.

II) Promotion-Enhancing Strategy

It is used when employees want to maximize their responsibility for a positive outcome or improve their image.

- **Entitlements:** Employees feeling they have not been given credit for a positive outcome may make sure that it is known through formal channels. Or they may informally note to key people that they are pleased their suggestions or efforts worked out so well.

- **Enhancements**: Here, employees may have received credit but they point out that they really did more and had a bigger impact than originally thought. For example, their effort or idea not only served a customer well or met a difficult deadline, but can be used in the future to greatly increase profits.

- **Obstacle Disclosures**: In this strategy employees identify either personal (either family or health) or organizational (lack of resources or cooperation) obstacles they had to overcome to accomplish an outcome. They try to create the perception that because they obtained the positive outcome despite the big obstacles, they really deserve a lot of credit.

- **Association**: Here, the employees make sure to be seen with the right people at the right time. This creates the perception that the employee is well connected and is associated with successful projects.

How do you improve perception?

1. Use of Johari window for improved perception
2. Improved empathy improves perception
3. Creating positive attitude creates right perspective to perceive things correctly.
4. Consciously try and get rid of common biases
5. Creating an atmosphere of open communication will help perception to be more accurate
6. Enhanced self-esteem and self-concept helps in perceiving and treating others with respect.

CLOSING CASE

Sudhakar, the technical head at Mont. Electronics Ltd., was happy that he was able to fill up the two vacancies in the systems department by selecting Ajay and Ganesh. Ajay was a M.Sc. (Electronics) degree holder along with 6 months of industrial experience. Ganesh was a fresher, with first class degree (in electronics) engineering. Both Ajay and Ganesh were intelligent, hardworking and usually were able to complete the projects assigned to them.

After a few months at Mont.,Sudhakarrealized that Ganesh always perceived himself to be more qualified than Ajay, because of his engineering background coupled with his better communication skills. Once he had overheard Ganesh taking the full credit for overseeing an overseas project completed in an efficient manner. Sudhakar spoke to their (Ajay's and Ganesh's) immediate superior Naveen, who confirmed that completion of the said project was a combined effort, with rather more inputs from Ajay's side. He also told Naveen to have a talk with Ganesh and rectify communication gaps, if any.

The talk seemed to help Ganesh who realised that if he had to come up, he had to transform his image for the good and try to mould himself into a strategic thinker. Ganesh honed his skills and started attending marketing and strategic planning classes to upgrade his knowledge. The classes opened his eyes on how to make assumptions on project sales, revenues, costs and profits. Very often he was seen voluntarily helping his superior to study the company data and analyze it. Seeing the change in Ganesh, Sudhakar was happy. Observing Ganesh's motivation, at the end of the probation period, he was offered a confirmed job as an assistant manager. Meanwhile Ajay was offered the position of a database analyst, after his probation period was completed successfully.

Sudhakar had presumed that both Ajay and Ganesh would be happy on being confirmed and promoted. One day le happened to meet the Human Resources head during an informal meeting of the various heads of departments to discuss about the managerial problems they each grapple with. The HR head was speaking to Sudhakar, "l was satisfied and feeling quite competent as a HR person, when something like this has to occur." "Why? What happened?" Sudhakar enquired. "It is concerning your boy Ganesh. Based on his superior's feedback and your observation of his area of competence, he was offered a confirmed job of an assistant manager. But yesterday he came to meet me and said' l feel I am my own enemy. May be it would be better if I go back to fixing things because I was quite comfortable with that. Now I realise that I have to learn on how to manage the impressions that others have of my role'. ' On further questioning the HR head he realised that quite often Ganesh became, by default, the technological fix-it person on projects because of his "engineering experience background. Also he had to learn to communicate with non-technical people. Now the HR head asked Sudhakar whether he could suggest a remedy or solution to the problem.

Questions:

1. Do you think Sudhakar was wrong in his initial perception about Ganesh being more suitable for carrying out managerial functions?
2. Which facet of socialization is relevant in the above case? Justify your answer
3. Can you suggest ways to solve the problems mentioned in the case?

Check your knowledge:

Multiple choice questions:

1. Which of the following is not true about attribution theory?
   a. In this theory, we attempt to determine whether an individual's behavior was internally or externally caused.
   b. Consistency in a person's behavior refers to whether the person acts the same way over time.
   c. If everyone who is in a similar situation responds in the same way, we can say the behavior shows consensus.
   d. In this theory, distinctiveness refers to whether an individual is memorable.
   e. None of the above.
2. Basic form of Perceptual Organization confirming that perceived objects stand out from their general background is
   a. Figure Ground
   b. Principle of Contrast

c. Principle of Intensity
d. Closure
e. Halo effect

3. Which of the following is true with regard to perceptual constancy?
   a. It gives a person a sense of stability in a changing world
   b. It gives meaning and value to stimuli
   c. It blocks unacceptable and threatening stimuli from registering
   d. It gives a tendency to perceive events as continuous flow
   e. It makes individual to ignore details.

MODEL QUESTIONS

Section–A

(Each question carries 2 marks)

1. Define Perception and State the nature of Perception
2. State the difference between Perception and Sensation
3. What is Social perception?
4. What is Impression management?
5. Define Attribution
6. Explain Stereotyping with examples
7. Explain Halo-effect with examples
8. Explain Projection with examples
9. What do you understand by Subliminal Perception with examples
10. What is Perceptual Set? Give examples
11. Explain Perceptual selectivity and Perceptual organization.
12. Explain the Figure-ground principle

Section–B

(Each question carries 5 marks)

1. What is Social perception? Explain the factors influencing Social Perception.
2. Briefly explain the Attribution theory with examples
3. Discuss the importance of perception in organizations
4. Explain the factors influencing Perceptual interpretation

Section–C

(Each question carries 15 marks)

1. Explain Perception Process in detail
2. Define Impression management and Strategies of Impression management implemented in organizations
3. Explain in detail the factors influencing Perception

REFERENCES

1. Jerald Greenberg & Robert A Baron, Behaviour in organization, Pearson Education (Singapore), ISBN 81-297-0414-5, 2004
2. Luthans, Fred, OrganizationBehaviour, Mac Graw Hill Inc, New York, 2000.1.
3. Morgan, C.T. King, R.A. Weisy, J.R, & Scooper, J. Introduction to Psychology. New Delhi: Tata Mc Grew - Hill, VII, 1993.

FIGURE SOURCES

http://gowingassociates.com/its-a-matter-of-perspective-and-perception/perception_vase/

http://lh4.googleusercontent.com/_hVfE2qcyzXU/TWwhmhjZ9MI/AAAAAAAACEA/bMw_0Um0G_s/s800/building-advertising-anando.jpg

https://encrypted-tbn2.gstatic.com/images?q=tbn:ANd9GcSuw3cQb FDEfZ_srY55zIUzgaDrWoSOJH Ge8dIXGvKTaCxvx-KhKQ

https://encrypted-tbn1.gstatic.com/images?q=tbn:ANd9 GcQWOLXqlJi8_4aT7c1k7KdmH-Oo0j_jMgEj6KSi9NKJWye2rLV18w

https://encrypted-tbn3.gstatic.com/images?q=tbn:ANd9GcSB dkZ_HftBvm0bzlV3kSna5zyXp1Yk2NGuGpT5w 2X_tBPcAkB8ZQ

http://graphicdesign.spokanefalls.edu/tutorials/process/gestaltprinciples/closure/closure_a.gif

https://encrypted-tbn3.gstatic.com/images?q=tbn:ANd9 GcSCOIY5mk834aMt-lDiphlXCmLmYMY739RB6q_OFo6N5mXlY0Bz

http://graphicdesign.spokanefalls.edu/tutorials/process/gestalt principles/proximity/proxa.gif

http://graphicdesign.spokanefalls.edu/tutorials/process/gestalt principles/proximity/proxb.gif

https://encrypted-tbn0.gstatic.com/images?q=tbn:ANd9GcR FwPV9EPUlTuVIDpA9XkrggLeDsG6lyq3rYAZ6GaP-89CVwMSI

◈◈◈◈

Read More on the Web

Perception is again, one of the most important functions that our mind performs for us. Although we see, feel, and hear only what we want to (which is basically the minds version of a coping mechanism when there is an overload we cannot take) our subconscious is open to all external stimuli and processes it, and sometimes even allows us to see what it saw. People often work on this because they know the importance and the perseverance of a first impression. These little inputs we get from our surroundings are often deep rooted and difficult to edit. This is why one 'hates' or 'loves' something, even though one isn't really sure exactly why.

People work hard on the image they want to portray. Also, how we perceive this is a culmination of many things including circumstances, mental climate, and most importantly how we perceive a group of the same. For example, when we think of a lawyer, a cut-throat, devious person comes to mind; one that is completely focused on the task at hand, albeit in a sometimes unethical way. Therefore, when we see a lawyer, this perception is hardwired into our minds, hence making it quite difficult for one to change that preset image, even if the lawyer in question is far removed from that image.

Another thing a lot of manipulators (like certain lawyers) do is to create a story with a lot of gaps which they then spring on someone. This person, now unsure of his/her place, and apprehensive, gets defensive, during the course of which something undesirable usually slips out, to fill that gap. The manipulator now seizes that and goes, "aha! I didn't say that, you did!" This again is because the person under duress perceives that something bad is going to happen and hence takes evasive action (following the saying, 'the best defense is a good offence)

One other thing our mind does is to condition itself to something that is constantly repeated. So if a lie is constantly repeated in some form or the other, we eventually perceives it to be the truth. On a tangent, this is how marketers condition their targets mind. By constantly reinforcing the image of their campaign, they hardwire the mind to connect and associate itself to the same. However, when the mind cannot take something, it turns to defense mechanisms. Basically, here, it cannot deal with certain perceptions it forms. When we lock on to a particular truth, we lock out anything that contradicts it. We create a scotoma, or a blind spot.

Delving a bit further, the RAS (or Reticular Activating System- a network of cells in the cerebral cortex that allows you to concentrate) screens out things that are non essential. Hence, it builds scotomas to information that isn't important to you at that point. This is the reason why, when you're early to college, you don't really notice red lights and traffic jams; but if you're late, you notice them all and your mind even stretches it to longer than it seems. Here, the mind removes a scotoma - the one that filters non essential info, i.e. "I am not late and therefore I needn't pay attention to the red lights and traffic".

Scotomas are useful. They let us concentrate to what we think is important to us at that point. However, when the mind encounters certain situations wherein it cannot cope, it resorts to defense mechanisms, or coping mechanisms. Defense mechanisms are ways by which people distance themselves from full awareness of unpleasant thoughts, feelings and behaviors.

Some common defense mechanisms are:

- Denial
- Regression: where an individual regresses to an earlier stage of behaviour (for example, he could become clingy or whiny in the face of undesirable circumstances)
- Physically acting out
- Dissociation and/or Compartmentalization: This is disconnecting with a situation. It can lead to Multiple Personality Disorder in extreme cases.
- Projection: The misattribution of a person's undesired thoughts, feelings or impulses onto another person who does not have those thoughts, feelings or impulses. Eg. You're angry with a friend and so take it out on a sibling.
- Repression, which is mostly unconsciously done.
- Rationalization: Where an individual tries to reason why a situation or a person behaved so.
- Undoing: Which is basically trying to take back what was done; to erase or nullify something.
- Sublimation: Channeling negativity into more constructive and acceptable impulses, thoughts or emotions. For example, when a person is angry, he/she could channel that impulse into exercise.
- Compensation: Where a person tries to compensate for a shortcoming by being good at something else.

Knowing these tendencies of an employee in an organization is important to be able to predict what they will do when they perceive a situation to be over their head. Predicting this is again based on what the company perceives from the individual: how he/ she is, his/ her behavior, etc. Based on that, the organization decides if a person is childish (he who chooses defenses like regression and denial) or if a person is mature (he who chooses mature defenses like compensation and sublimation). After that, it sent appropriate tasks and to the segregated employees. This again, is based wholly on perceptions received via observation.

Sources and References

http://www.sourcetext.com/sourcebook/essays/scotoma.html (blind spots)

http://psychcentral.com/lib/15-common-defense-mechanisms/0001251 (defense mechanisms)

CHAPTER 3

PERSONALITY

Learning Objectives of the Chapter

- Definition & Meaning of Personality
- Theories of Personality- Type theory, Trait theory, Dynamic theory, Psycho-analytical theory, Social learning theory.
- Personality assessment
- Work related aspects of personality

OPENING CASE

Condoleezza Rice A historic, transformational Personality

"Very rarely in the life of a nation or a culture, a person appears who represents a true healer—from a psychological perspective—of divisions and fault lines, whether of race or gender or ethnicity or socioeconomic status, that occur naturally as the story of that nation or culture takes form.

Such a healer must acknowledge the past shortcomings and injuries and challenges and victories inherent in the collective story, put it in context, and, by his or her own understanding of them and embodiment of them, make them part of a cohesive and good whole, so that the story is seen always to have had an internal axis around which it turned, a sense of ultimate integrity and a quality of manifest destiny.

In Swedish, the word for such a person or event or influential book is,kulturbärer—translated as culture-bearer. Author Robert Pirsig described the kulturbärer as something or someone who "bears the culture on its back" and carries it to a different place."

Condoleezza Rice, with her speech at the Republican National Convention, qualified herself as such a person. Her intelligence is so obvious, and her grasp of the core truths of the American narrative so apparent, that those things alone could be mistaken for the reasons she galvanized the nation last night.

But, from a psychological perspective, there are other reasons. Ms. Rice literally transcends all boundaries of race, gender and socioeconomic status. She is feminine, but strong. She is approachable and warm, yet possessed of an iron will.

She comes from humble beginnings, which she honors, yet has attained success no one would deny her. She is a black American who seems to bear no ill-will toward white Americans. She is a former Democrat turned Republican. She is not old and not young.

Very few people who listened to her would posit that she harbors hatred toward anyone or any group. All of these characteristics in one individual do not merely constitute a candidate, but an event. A psychological, healing kulturbärer.

To be clearer: Whatever vestiges of racial, gender and religious prejudice or self-doubt reside in the American people or our national character, Condoleezza Rice could literally help remove them, by her presence on the national stage, perhaps as part of the Romney administration or, perhaps, eight years from now, by her presence in her own administration. And she can do so without abandoning our national character (as President Obama has done), but, rather, by stating it more clearly than ever, while being evidence of the best of it herself.

Dr. Keith Ablow, August 30, 2012, FoxNews.com

http://www.foxnews.com/opinion/2012/08/30/why-condoleezza-rice-is-historic-transformational-figure/

PERSONALITY

Personality is derived from Latin word "Persona" which means "Mask: to speak through". This means the characteristic pattern and or behavior style revealed by the person from his external appearance. But personality in organizational psychology is beyond this meaning. It is an all inclusive concept which is the sum total of an individual's characteristic as a distinct human being. It is the totality of specific qualities, attributes, traits, factors, and mannerisms that distinguish one individual from other individuals.

While the external attributes are directly observed by all of us, internal aspects are inferred using some cues.

Definition-1: "Personality is the dynamic organization within the individual of those psychological systems that determines his unique adjustment to his environment" [Gordon Allport]

Definition-2: "Personality includes external appearance and behaviour, inner awareness of self as a permanent organizing force & the pattern of inner & outer measurable traits. [Floyd. L. Ruch]"

Equation of Personality

Personality = Individual's reaction to other people + environmental adjustments/interactions

What does Personality mean?

Personality is a stable set of characteristics and tendencies that determine those commonalities and differences in the psychological behavior (thoughts, feeling & actions) of people that have continuity in time and that may not be easily understood as the sole result of the social and biological pressures of the moment.

Nature of Personality:

- Personality is the characteristic set of traits & behaviors of an individual, which is relatively stable and which can predict an individual's behavioral tendencies.
- Personality has both internal (thoughts, values & genetic characteristics that is inferred from observable behaviors) & external (observable behaviors) elements.
- Personality may originate from genes as well as it can be shaped by the environment.
- Individuals vary in their personality. No two individuals will have same personality, not even twins.

Major contributing factors to Personality:

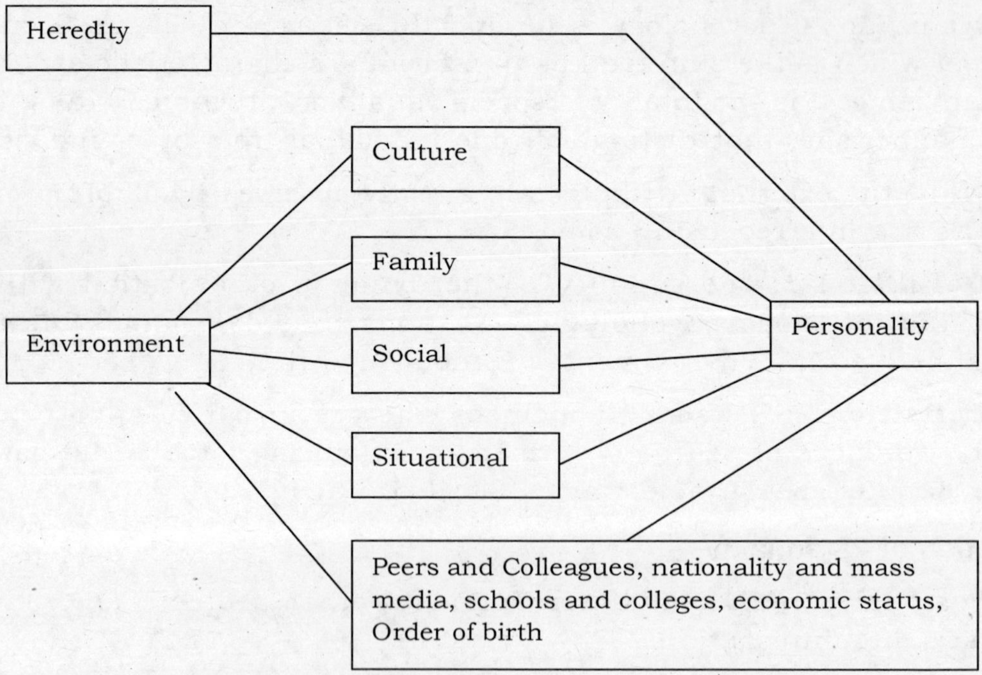

Contributing factors of personalities:

Personality of an individual is moulded by varied factors. Some of these factors can be controlled and manipulated while others are relatively constant. Basic classification of factors affecting personality is Heredity and Environment. The following are the major factors that affect personality formation of an individual.

1. HEREDITY

One major factor which influences personality is heredity. These are the factors that are determined at conception and are transferred through chromosomes. Many physiological & psychological factors like facial attractiveness, skin colour, temperament, energy levels, intelligence, eye & hair colour, height etc. are generally transferred by genes. Researches prove that >50% of personality differences are contributed by heredity. These are more or less permanent traits of personality which are difficult to change. The role of heredity on personality development is still an unsettled area of understanding. Some of the researches do not converge to accept heredity as a major contributor of personality

2. ENVIRONMENT

Environment plays a major role in personality formation. There are various environmental factors which affect personality. They are:

a) CULTURE: The broad spectrum of culture includes factors such as societal culture which influences norms, attitudes and values that create consistencies over time. Even though culture has significant impact on personality, it is not possible to associate a linear relationship between personality and culture. Impacts of culture on all individuals are not uniform because the value systems transferred to individuals are by different people like parents, neighbours, relatives, peers etc. Moreover, an individual's response a particular social condition will be different, which will also affect the formation of personality.

Ex: - Indian culture teaches you to be industrious, frugal, logical, with strong family values; Western culture has more thrust on being Independent, Competitive, Ambitious and Aggressive

b) FAMILY: Influence of family in moulding personality of an individual is high during early stages. The family factors are important in determining personality of an individual. Three major factors: viz., the socialization process, identification process and birth order influence the personality of an individual.

i) **Socialization Process**: It is the process of acquiring a wide range of behavior by an infant from the wide range of behavioural patterns that are available to him at birth. These are the behavioural patterns that are customary and acceptable according to the standards of his family and social groups. Family members ensure that the infant conforms to certain behavior acceptable to the family. Ex: In North Indian families, it is customary to touch the feet of elders when you visit them. Family members insist on this behavioural pattern among all members of the family.

ii) Identification Process: Personality is shaped with more vigour from the time the identification process commences. Identification Process occurs when a person tries to identify himself with some person who is ideal in the family. Ex: A child tries to emulate his father or mother based on whom he considers ideal in his mind.

iii) Birth Order: Birth order is found to have some influence in the personality of an individual. It is widely accepted that first born children are likely to be more dependent, more rational, understanding, ambitious, hardworking, cooperative, and more prone to guilt, anxiety and are less aggressive in comparison to the younger siblings of the same family. Younger ones are more street smart and playful in general. This could be due to the different kinds of exposure the children get who are born at different time in the life cycle of parents.

c) SOCIAL FACTORS: These are distinctly different factors from the previous two factors because the social group at this stage in personality development includes a wider range of coverage like family, schoolmates, friends, friends or colleagues at work place, group to which the individual belongs etc. Behaviour pattern will be customary and acceptable according to standards of his family and social groups. The organization and work groups have a major impact on personality. Ex: An individual interned under a much disciplined manager in the work place will imbibe that quality into his personality.

d) SITUATIONAL FACTORS:

There is increased importance given of late, to the influence of situational factors on personality. Though an individual's personality is stable and consistent, it changes with different situations. A study conducted by Milgram suggested that actions of an individual are determined by the situation. According to him, situation exerts an important influence on the individual. It exercises constraints and may force individual to behave in a particular way.

Ex: Situations like temple, class room, working place, employment interview, Boss's chamber etc. regulate the behavior of the individual to a greater extent, based on the situational requirements. Behaviour exhibited by an individual will not be the same when he is in the playground with his friends.

THEORIES OF PERSONALITY

There are many traditional and contemporary theories of personality. There are more and more new theories emerging in this field. For ease of learning, five different theories of personality are discussed in this chapter.

Theories of personality

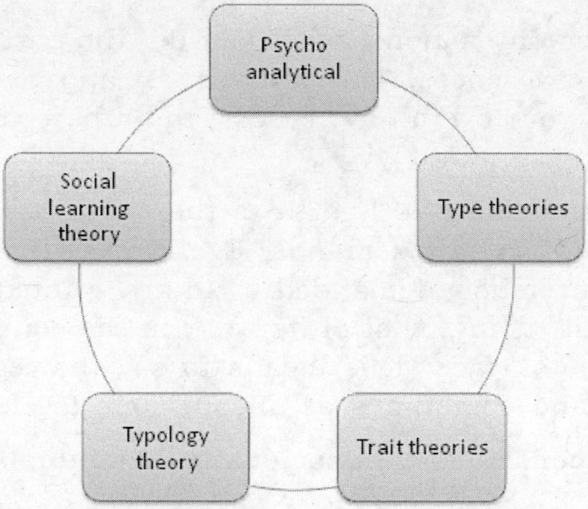

1. **Psycho analytical theory:*(also called the dynamic theory, Freudian theory)***

Sigmund Freud developed this theory. According to him human mind consists of three elements that are responsible for shaping the personality. They are Id, Ego and Super ego. Freud identified 3 levels of consciousness: Preconscious,(Memories that can be recalled) , Conscious (What we're aware of) and Unconscious levels (Wishes, feelings, impulses that we are not aware of). Unconscious mental activity determines behaviour. Conscious element is guided by reasoned reality principle.

1. **Id = unconscious = pleasure principle**

It is the storehouse of instincts and primitive needs of an individual (Anamatistic). Id is the totality of instincts oriented towards increasing pleasure, avoiding pains and striving for immediate satisfaction of desires.

The personality characteristics of an individual are built on the foundation of the Id. The Id is present at birth and represents our instinctual drives such as hunger, sex and aggression, which motivate most of our behaviour.

The Id is completely unconscious and operates on the "pleasure principle". These "unconscious drives" operate without conscious awareness. This is because our unconscious desires are too difficult or too painful to face directly

2. Ego = conscious = reality principle

The ego begins to develop during the first year of life and balances the Id's urges with reality. Hence, the ego is guided by the "Reality Principle". It balances the demands of Id and Super ego.

This is your everyday actions, what you do, the part of your mind that holds your current awareness. This is the most apparent layer, and while only a small part of your overall awareness, this where your focus generally lies.

10% of one's personality is Ego. It is the conscious mediator between realities of world and the id's demands. Ego keeps the Id in check so that the pleasures unconsciously demanded by Id are granted at an appropriate time and place. While doing most of its work in the conscious, a portion is working beneath the surface. This means to say that ego primarily works at conscious level and sometimes at unconscious level.

3. Superego = preconscious & conscious level = morality principle

The superego is the embodiment of societal rules, ethics and morals. It is the ethical and moral arm of personality. It is the individual's internal expression of societies moral and ethical code of conduct. Super ego is a moralistic segment of human personality consisting of noblest thoughts, ideals, feelings developed through absorption of cultural values and attitudes.

The super-ego strives to act in a socially appropriate manner, whereas the Id just wants instant self-gratification. Super ego acts like a "brake" which prevents the impulsive responses stemming from Id. The super-ego controls our sense of right and wrong and guilt. It helps us fit into society by getting us to act in socially acceptable ways. The superego sets high standards for behavior and monitors the decisions of the ego. Perfection, rather than pleasure is its goal. The superego causes feelings of guilt and shame when its standards aren't met. The super-ego works in contradiction to the Id. All humans have Id, Ego and the Superego, but in varying amounts.

Sigmund Freud's View of human mind: The mental ice berg

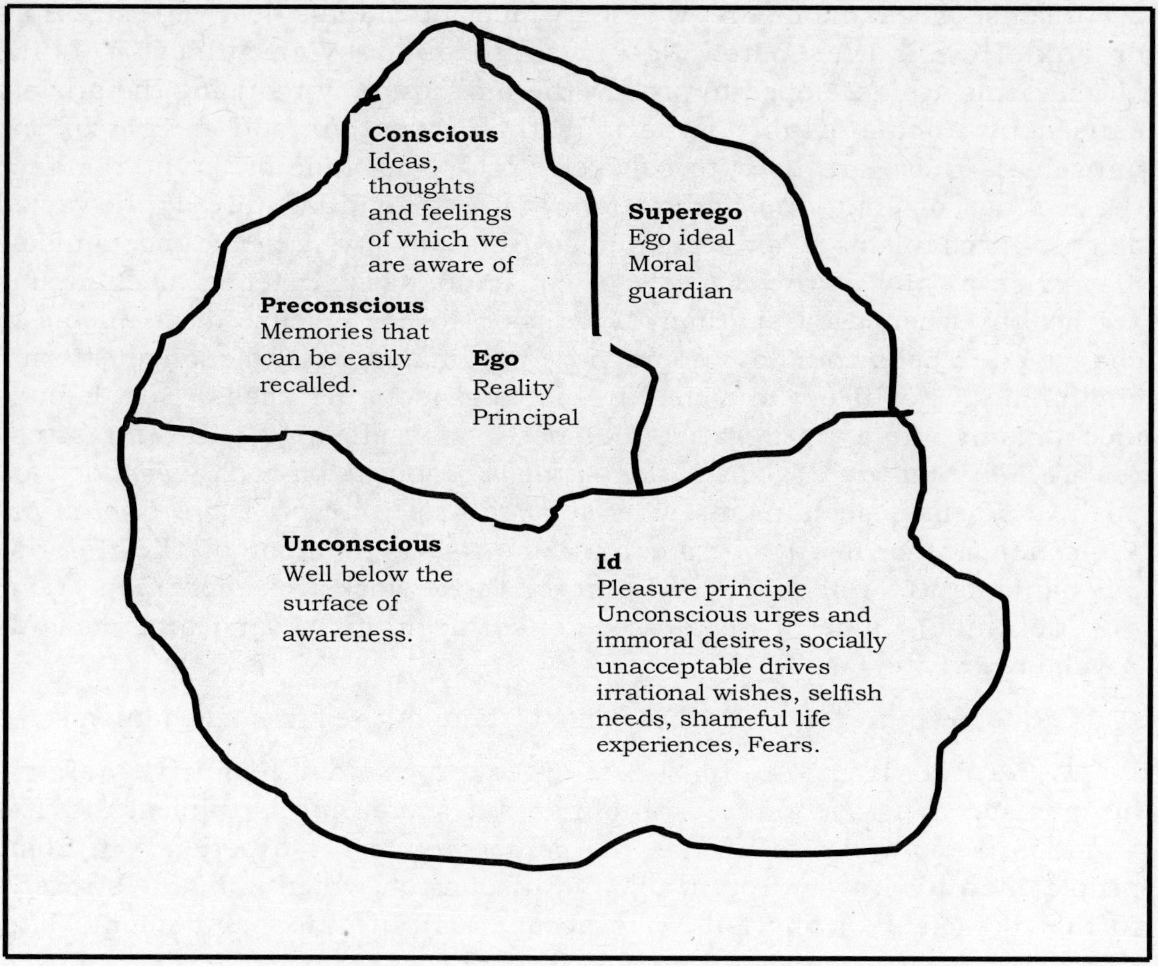

Assessing the Unconscious:

As it is evident, it is difficult to assess the unconscious. Rorschach ink blot tests and TAT tests are two projective tests used to assess the unconscious part of an individual's personality. Details of these tests are given under assessment of personality later in this chapter.

The extent to which Ego does the balancing act between the demands of Id and Super ego determines the personality makeup of the individual. A balanced personality is possessed by individuals who have a powerful Ego. A maladjusted personality is displayed by a person with weak Ego. When Super ego overtakes Ego, it does not permit the fulfillment of desired wishes thereby producing Neurotic personality. But if the Id takes over the Ego, individual may get into immoral and unlawful activities, leading to Delinquent personality.

Defense mechanisms:

Defense mechanisms are ways by which individuals deal with stressors or anxieties in life. When Ego is threatened by impulses, defense mechanisms are developed to protect the individual by reducing the anxiety caused by uncomfortable situations that threatens self-esteem of the individual. These are used to solve the problems, hide or counterbalance the feelings of emotions and actions. One individual may apply varied defense mechanisms to protect the ego from anxiety. Defense mechanisms may arise at any of the 3 levels of consciousness. Defense mechanisms are healthy when used sparingly. It is good to use defense mechanisms to change one's behaviour to become more productive, able to change external environment positively and modify his unreasonable needs. But defense mechanisms often are negative and not a very effective outlet for stress release. *Rationalisation, Substitution Altruism, Anticipation and Sublimation* are positive defense mechanisms whereas *Regression, Repression, Denial and Projection* are undesirable mechanisms. Though most of the defense mechanisms are unconscious, some of them work from conscious level too. Continuous use of negative defense mechanism can cause serious psychological illness.

The following are some of the most common defense mechanisms.

1. Denial: It is one of the simplest and most primitive defense mechanism. A person refuses to admit that something is unpleasant. If a situation is too much to handle, the person refuses to experience it. Some people often turn away from a topic of discussion which is highly stressful to that person. It is the failure to accept real situation. Statements like: "It can't happen to me" fall into this category.

Example: The failure to recognize the death of a loved one, or students who fail to find out their test grades!

2. Repression: It is the blocking of unpleasant memories from conscious awareness. Not being able to recall a threatening situation, person, or event which it amounts to selectively remembering instances. It occurs without the conscious awareness or intention of a person.

Example: A person almost drowns as a child, but can't remember the event even when people try to remind him — but he does have a fear of open water! [Many fears and phobias]

3. Displacement: It is a complex defense mechanism. In this defense mechanism, an individual shifts his feeling of hostility from the person who is the stressor to some other target. It is the redirection of an impulse onto a safer substitute target. Directing emotions and behavior towards objects or people that aren't the real cause of worry to feel safe.

Example: An individual who was severely reprimanded by his boss and ridiculed in front of his colleague may not be able to show his anger to the boss, but may come back home and show his frustration to his spouse. Another example could be of someone who hates his or her mother, may repress that hatred and direct it instead towards women in general.

4. Projection: This is the most often observed defense mechanism used for ego protection. Remember how a mother reacts to a small child falling down? She hits or kicks the floor, blaming the floor to be the reason for the child to fall, just as an effort to bring back the smile on the baby's face. It is the tendency to see your own unacceptable desires in other people. Unacceptable feelings are attributed to someone else. Blame others or things for your failure. Using others as scapegoats, blaming the teacher's poor teaching skills for student's failure etc fall in this category. Fate and bad luck are the other two often projected defense mechanism.

Example: A faithful husband finds himself terribly attracted to the lady next door. Rather than acknowledge his own feelings, he becomes increasingly jealous of his wife, constantly worried about her faithfulness.

5. Reactionformation: In this defense mechanism, the individual protects himself from developing a dangerous behavioural pattern by exhibiting the opposite behavior. This is what Anna Freud called "believing the opposite". Changing an unacceptable impulse into its opposite. A feeling that produces anxiety is transformed into its opposite. Reaction formation helps an individual to demonstrate socially acceptable behavior. Concealing your anger with kindness, Pinching and pulling the cheeks of someone you like are all falling in this category. This defense mechanism mainly works at the unconscious level and the individual does not have much control over it.

Example: "I hate Mom" becomes "I really love Mom a lot!!!". The individual will often go above and beyond in their expression of love in order to alleviate feelings of guilt and anxiety.

6. Regression: A very significant defense mechanism considered in psychology for protecting the ego of the individual, always happening at unconscious level. It is a movement back in psychological time when one is faced with stress. A person reverts to a previous phase of psychological development when encountered with stress. For example using child-like behavior when we are stressed by something. When we are troubled or frightened, our behaviors often become more childish or primitive.

Example: A child may begin to suck their thumb again or wet the bed when encountered with a stressor. Someone may start howling, swearing and throwing things when agitated, which are not the regular behavior of the individual. We often observe in movies when people encounter severe physical violence, they curl up in the fetal form.

7. Rationalization: Here the person justifies his maladaptive behavior by giving logical explanation to it. It is the cognitive distortion of "the facts" to make an impulse more acceptable. Justifying your irrational behavior. This happens very much at the conscious level. We do it often enough on a fairly conscious level when we provide ourselves with excuses. Many of us are quite prepared to believe our lies. Of course we have heard the story of "Fox and the sour grapes "!

Examples: A student who is not able to compete for academic ranking in a class of very bright students rationalizes by saying "Any way I am not in this rat race". Another example could be "I entered the one way from wrong side only because my regular road was crowded and I had an interview to attend in time".

8. Sublimation: It is the provision of socially acceptable ventilation an undesirable feeling. It is the transforming of an unacceptable impulse, whether it is sex, anger, or fear, into a socially acceptable and productive form. So someone with a great deal of hostility may become a hunter, a butcher, a football player, or a mercenary. It is positive defense mechanism, where an individual will channelize his anger or any other negative feelings into something productive like a piece of art, poem, book etc.

Example: When an individual is very angry, he goes to gym and practices kick boxing. According to Freud, all positive creative activities were sublimations mostly of the sex drive.

9. Substitution: In this case, an individual replaces an unattainable goal with an attainable goal to pacify himself and relieve disappointment.

Example: A person who can't sing well becomes a Tabla expert because he is connected to music and he excels in a musical instrument.

10. Altruism: Way of dealing with stressors by going out of the way and helping others and dedicating oneself for the betterment of others. By practicing altruism, the person derives a vicarious pleasure of seeing others happy.

Example: A widow or spinster taking up NGO work and helps the poor and needy to deal with the problem of loneliness.

11. Anticipation: This is a defense mechanism where the stressors are dealt by anticipating the consequences and feelings associated probable future events and planning realistic solutions for them.

Example: Planning for retirement and booking an old age home facility in anticipation of insensitive future behavior from their children.

12. Compensation: When an individual encounters a real or imaginative personal shortcoming, the individual reacts in defense though this defense mechanism. The individual tries to draw attention away from the defect by striving hard to get a noticeable and praiseworthy attribute. This defense mechanism has negative as well as positive consequences. Over compensation will lead to an individual trying to hide his inferiority feeling by devaluating anyone who comes in front of him.

Example: A physically weak and non-attractive student may compensate by being number one in academics. An employee who does not have required skill set for his job may compensate by being very nice and pleasant to all in the office to camouflage his weakness.

Strength of Psycho Analytical Theory

This theory has application in management studies. It contributes to four areas:

i. Creative Behavior

ii. Dissatisfaction

iii. Group Development

iv. Leadership and influence

Limitations of Freud's theory:

The theory is untestable, as there is no means of measuring: the unconscious objectively. The study sample of Freud was mainly upper class Austrian women, which is biased and the results may not be applicable globally. His theory viewed women as inferior beings, which again is not acceptable. The strongest argument against this theory is that it did not give room for prediction of future behaviors. Besides there was too much emphasis on early childhood experiences in personality formation.

An advertisement using some of the concepts of Id for consumer appeal

2. Type Theories of personality:

1) Hippocrates 4 humors:(Hippocrates, Friedman, Sheldon)

Aims to classify people into distinct categories which are mutually exclusive. Hippocrates 400 BC and Galen, 140/150 AD classified 4 types of "humors" in people. Each type was believed to be due to an excess of one of four bodily fluids, corresponding to their character. The personalities were termed "humors". (humors are bodily liquids, like the vitreous humor in the eye)

CHARACTER	HUMOR	FLUID	CORRESPONDING BIG 5 TRAIT
Irritable	Choleric	Yellow Bile	Agreeableness
Depressed	Melancholic	Black Bile	Neuroticism
Optimistic	Sanguine	Blood	Openness to Experience
Calm	Phlegmatic	Phlegm	Neuroticism

2) Sheldon's Somato type: Physiognomy Personality Types: William Sheldon has propounded three types of personality based on the human anatomical or physical structure of persons and psychological characteristics. Physical size of the body influences the human behaviour and temperaments. The personality types are.

a) **Endomorph:** Certain characteristics of personality and behaviour associated with the body type are friendly, concern to people, helping others in troubles, very slow reaction to stimuli. They seek comfort; have strong inclination to delicious food, etc. The persons who possess these personality characteristics, are liked by all. (endomorphs are plump and developed). They are relaxed, tolerant, peaceful, comfort living and sociable

b) **Mesomorph:** Persons having moderate physical characteristics are known as Mesomorph. The body is strong and tough. Some of the personality characteristics of this type are: seeks physical adventure, enjoys body building, feels restless, shows high aggression and self-assertiveness, likes to take risk and develops competitive spirit. The person is liked by virtue of his physique.(Lean, muscular). They are active, assertive, rigorous, argumentative and competition oriented.

c) **Ectomorph**: Ectomorph body type is characterized by a thin and flat chest. The person is intelligent, feels shy and avoids social contacts. However, he is typically anxious, ambitious, and dedicated to his work. He is quick to react and hypersensitive to pain and pleasure. (Quick, fragile, assertive, rigorous, combative) People retain their personality of this type even after they change body type for whatever form

Sheldon's Somatotype	Character	Shape
Endomorph [viscerotonic]	relaxed, sociable, tolerant, comfort-loving, peaceful	plump, buxom, developed visceral structure
Mesomorph [somatotonic]	active, assertive, vigorous, combative	muscular
Ectomorph [cerebrotonic]	quiet, fragile, restrained, non-assertive, sensitive	lean, delicate, poor muscles

Sheldon, using a correlational study, found that many convicts were mesomorphic, and they were least likely to be ectomorphic (Sheldon et al 1949). Organisational implication of this theory is that the typical personality type can help in career choices based on the somato types.

3) Friedman's Type A& B:

Type A personality is defined by Friedman and Rosenman as aggressively involved in a chronic, incessant struggle to achieve more and more in less and less time, and, if required to do so, against the opposing efforts of other things or other persons. They have defined Type B personality as rarely harried by the desire to obtain a wildly increasing number of things or participate in a endless growing series of events in an ever decreasing amount of time.

Type A: Try to do more things but end up not finishing them perfectly

Type B: do a few things in the same time span, but complete them perfectly

Strengths of Type theory

- classify people into distinct categories
- simple applicability
- person-centered

Weakness of the theory

- over-simplistic
- Quantitative nature

4) Carl Jung's Extrovert & Introvert personality types:

This theory uses analytical psychology approach. According to this theory, personality is developed as a process of creativity. An individual's personality is a mixture of 4 factors: Thinking, Feeling, Sensation, and Intuition. From these four, two personality characters viz "Extrovert and Introvert were evolved. Extroverts are sociable reality oriented performers, where Introverts are guided by their own thinking and less risk taking. They are less interactive too.

This is one of the most useful theories applicable to organisational psychology. It can be applied in job designing, leadership styles, training and development, Organisational Development etc. An introvert performs better in repetitive jobs. Extroverts perform better in dynamic and people oriented jobs.

3. Trait theory of personality:

This is one of the most significant theoretical areas in the study of personality. Trait theory uses two different methods of research:

- Idiographic approach: defines traits by studying individuals in depth and focuses on the distinctive qualities of their personalities (Gordon Allport)
- Nomothetic approach: studies groups of people in the attempt to identify personality traits that tend to appear in clusters. This approach uses the statistical technique called factor analysis (Raymond Cattell)

a) Allport described three different types of traits:

Golden Allport identified around 4000 odd words used in the English dictionary which describe different personality types. These traits are categorized in to 3 types.

1. **Cardinal traits**: These are the traits which dominate an individual's entire life span. Traits that are so much a part of an individual, that you can define the person by the trait. This character directs an individual most of the activities. Allport believed that cardinal traits are rare and it tends to develop much later in life. Power hungers, Altruism etc. are such cardinal traits.

   Example: Honest Abraham Lincoln, Kindhearted Mother Theresa etc.

2. **Central traits**: They are the general characteristics that form the basic foundation of a person's personality. Major characteristics of our personality which can exist in 5 to 10 numbers in any one person (such as: sensitivity and generosity, honesty, sociability).

These traits are quite generalized and enduring, and these are the traits that form the building blocks of our personality. Allport found that most people could be characterized by a fairly small number of central traits.

3. **Secondary space traits**: These traits are not always exhibited by individuals. They are less generalized and far less enduring traits that affect our behaviors in specific circumstances. Examples could be getting restless while waiting in a queue, dress style preferences, dislike for modern art etc.

Cardinal traits are most pervasive; secondary traits least pervasive.

b) Raymond Cattell :

Cattell reduced the list of 4000 traits as identified by Allport to 16 key personality traits. He began his work by identifying certain obvious personality traits, such as integrity, friendliness, and tidiness (1950, 1965, 1973, and 1982). He called these dimensions of personality surface traits. Cattell then obtained extensive data about surface traits from a large number of people (nomothetic approach).

Statistical analysis of these data revealed that certain surface traits seemed to occur in clusters or groups. Cattell theorized that these clusters indicated a single underlying trait.

Cattell derived a list of 16 primary or source traits that he considered to be at the center or core of personality. He listed each of these traits as a pair of polar opposites which he called 16PF. The personality assessment test is often used in employee testing and selection. It is also used in career counseling.

The 16 personality traits

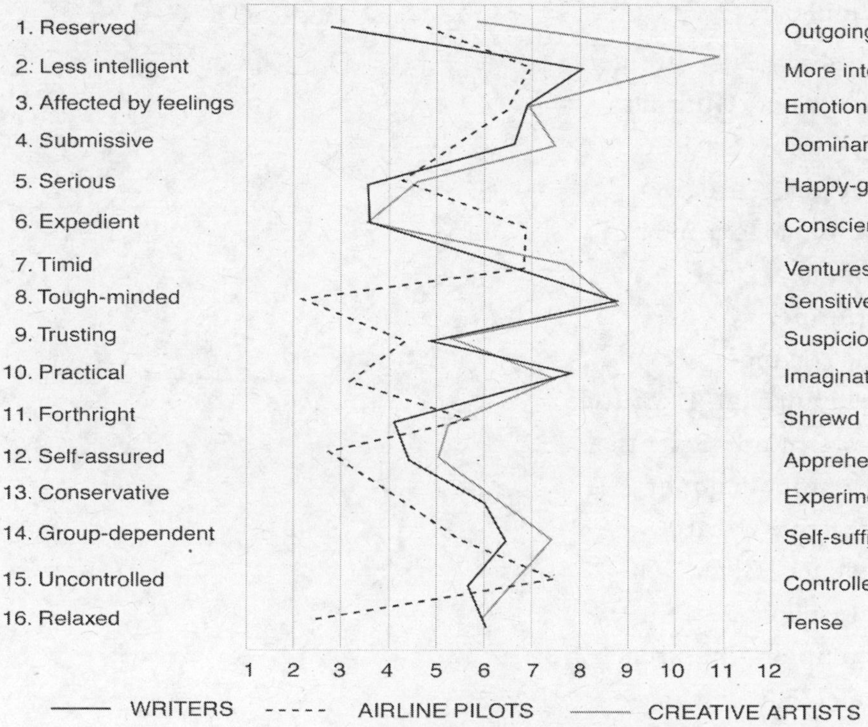

Personality Tests Can they identify the real you ?

Personality assessments are now ubiquitous. In a global recession, many firms want to hedge their bets and cannot afford to pick the wrong people.

Tighter profit margins also mean working under more stress and companies want to make sure their employees get on. Disagreements are costly and inefficient.

In the US alone, there are about 2,500 personality tests on the market. One of the most popular is called the Myers-Briggs Type Indicator or MBTI. Used by 89 of the Fortune 100 companies, it has been translated into 24 languages and has been adopted by governments and military agencies around the world.

"Myers-Briggs is the most successful psychometric out there and deservedly so," says Rachel Robinson of the consultancy firm YSC in central London.

"It has been a fantastic vehicle for people to think about themselves and how others are different."

Perhaps its attraction lies in its seductive simplicity - according to the MBTI, we all conform to one of 16 character types.

But that simplicity is precisely what makes some people sceptical, or even suspicious.

The 16 **MBTI types** are sometimes given shorthand tags - though not by MBTI itself. For example:

- ISTJ - Inspector, Duty fulfiller
- ESTJ - Supervisor, Guardian
- ISFJ - Protector, Nurturer
- ESFJ - Provider, Caregiver
- ISTP - Crafter, Mechanic
- ESTP - Promoter, Doer
- ESFP - Performer
- ISFP - Artist, Dancer
- ENTJ - Fieldmarshal, Executive
- INTJ - Mastermind, Scientist
- ENTP - Inventor, Visionary
- INTP - Architect, Wizard
- ENFJ - Teacher, Giver
- INFJ - Counsellor
- ENFP - Champion, Inspirer
- INFP - Healer, Idealist

"There is something about the wish to put everything in neat little boxes so that we can manipulate them and make them serve our purposes that is quintessentially corporate America," says American author Annie Murphy Paul.

Her 2006 book, The Cult of Personality, claims personality tests are leading us to miseducate our children, mismanage our companies and misunderstand ourselves.

Like many personality tests, MBTI is based on the work of Carl Jung, the Swiss psychiatrist who, together with Sigmund Freud, laid the foundations of modern psychology. Jung developed the idea of opposed pairs of character traits which are present in all of us and suggested that in each pair we each have a natural preference.

It came into being thanks to an awkward relationship between a woman and her future son-in-law. Katherine Briggs, a wealthy housewife from Washington DC, realised Clarence Myers was a good catch when her daughter Isabel brought him home from college. He seemed like a nice young man, but his way of thinking was so alien to her that she turned to books for help.

Jung's Psychological Types fascinated her and became what she described as her "Bible". Soon, Isabel was infected by her mother's enthusiasm. Over two decades, the pair became avid "type watchers".

Jung only identified eight personality types, but Isabel Briggs Myers eventually doubled that number. Everybody can be described by four letters chosen out of a total of eight, she says.

To the uninitiated, it can look a bit like alphabet soup, but the first category is relatively straightforward - are you E or I? Extrovert or Introvert? The second is a choice between S or N - Sensing or Intuitive - which means some interpret the world by collecting data through their senses, others make intuitive leaps.

Then are you predominantly a T or and F? A thinker or somebody more governed by their feelings? And, finally, are you J or P? According to the blurb in the booklet, Judging types prefer to "regulate and manage their lives" whereas Perceivers favour spontaneity.

There are plenty of websites devoted to pigeonholing celebrities. Apparently, Shakespeare was an INFP and Margaret Thatcher is listed as an ENTJ. The Queen, "data driven" Condoleezza Rice and the "information carnivore" Hillary Clinton are all ISTJs.

Madonna's rebellious streak and talent for self-promotion makes her an ESTP. Jung may have dismissed such classification as "nothing but a childish parlour game"

Employees often sense that management is looking for a particular type for a specific post. A Sydney- based executive who used to work for an international bank, admitted to cheating on the test at the start of her career when she was desperate for promotion.

"I don't believe that corporations value diversity and I wanted to be a senior manager," she said. "I knew they wanted either an ESTJ or an ISTJ and I am an ENTJ so it didn't take a lot to fiddle with the answers. But I was conscious that I was doing it."

The investigative writer and self-proclaimed "myth buster by trade" Barbara Ehrenreich, who has been a strong critic of personality testing for years, thinks employers have a greater tendency to worry about whether a candidate is I or E, than P or J.

"You will be told that no one type is better than another and you should be spontaneous in answering the questions," she says.

"But, in reality, they are not looking for introverts. Even if what you are doing is looking at figures all day. They want everyone in the environment to be perky and positive and upbeat at all times."

According to Susan Cain's recent bestseller, Quiet: The Power of Introverts In a World That Can't Stop Talking, introverts are just as high achievers.

Felicity Lee, a chartered occupational psychologist, says it is perfectly possible for introverts to try to act like an extrovert, but it will be more tiring for them.

American and Canadian culture tends to put a higher value on the qualities of extroverts than some other cultures do, Lee says. She also thinks a bias towards extroversion exists in the UK.

But she says being an extrovert, does not necessarily mean a person does extroversion well.

Yet these days more employees are expected to work in teams - to "groupthink" to use the jargon - and possibly communicate effectively with people on the other side of the world whom they have never met. There is a perception that extroverts are better at this.

The Myers Briggs Foundation discourages the use of the test for hiring and firing, seeing it primarily as a means of getting employees to think about how they interact with colleagues and work as a team.

"We don't like its use for selection because it's not an assessment of skills and abilities," says Jeff Hayes from the San Francisco-based Myers-Briggs publishing company, CPP.

"But we can't police that in every circumstance because it is used all over the world."

Source :BBC News magazine, July 6, 2012
http://www.bbc.co.uk/news/magazine-18723950

c) The five-factor theory (OCEAN) of personality by **McCrae and Costa** (1997)is the most recent addition to trait theory. According to this theory, the human personality can be explained under five domains viz:

1. Openness to Experience – Creative & willing to try new things. Individuals, who have active imaginations, are attentive to their inner feelings and have a tendency to enjoy art, new intellectual experiences, and ideas. People with two levels of openness tend to be less receptive to new ideas and less willing to change their minds.

2. Conscientiousness – Reliable, responsible, thorough, dependable, hard-working. Individuals who are purposeful, organized, thorough & plan-full and have tendency to show self-discipline, act dutifully, and aim for achievement. They are similar to type "B" personality people. A person with low levels of conscientiousness tends to be similar to type "A" people.

3. Extraversion – Outgoing, social, active, talkative. Individuals who are sociable, talkative, energetic, assertive, gregarious & have a tendency to seek stimulation and the company of others. The

opposite is introversion, whose people are less sociable, less talkative, less assertive and more reluctant to start relationships

4. Agreeableness – Easy to get along with, pleasant, sympathetic, warm, cooperative. individuals who are fundamentally altruistic, sympathetic, kind, affectionate, good natured, cooperative, trusting & have tendency to be compassionate rather than antagonistic towards others. They are generally compatible. The opposite of this would be disagreeableness.

5. Neuroticism – Emotional stability: a personality dimension that characterizes someone as calm, self-confident, secure (positive) versus nervous, depressed and insecure (negative). An extremely neurotic person tends to be unable to control his/her emotion.

Activity: Observe your clothing preferences. Do they differ from those of your friends? What personality traits might explain why your preferences are different from those of other people?

Acronym: OCEAN

4. John Hollands Personality Typology theory (1997):

This is a theory of career and vocational choices based on personality types. This theory and its model are extensively used to identify the interest of an individual for a particular profession. According to this theory, individuals are attracted to a given career because of personalities and numerous variables that constitute their backgrounds. One chooses his career for satisfying his preferred modal personal orientation. Six modal orientations and respective occupational environments are listed by Holland. The theory assumes that all individuals can be categorized into any of the six models of orientation.

RIASEC model of Holland

R: Realistic: They are independent minded individuals with high practical orientation. Individual who falls in this modal with tools and machines and does not prefer an occupation with high level of social activities like teaching, counseling etc. Values practical things and likes to work with tangible things.

Ex: Astronaut, carpenter, dentist, driver, surgeon, physical educationist etc.

I: Investigative: These people are scientific, with an intellectual bend. They often introspect and they are very inquisitive. They enjoy research.

They are good in understanding scientific and math problems. They give a lot of importance to facts and figures. They tend to avoid jobs which need persuasive skills like that of a sales person or a leader.

Ex: Computer programmer, Lawyer, Psychologist, Researchers etc.

A: Artistic: They consider themselves to be expressive, original and independent. They have good intuitive skills. They have high artistic abilities like creative writing, drama, crafts, music etc. They are spontaneous and open minded. They do not prefer very systematic and orderly activities. They also do not like repetitive activities.

Ex: Film maker, fashion designer, poets, theatre artists etc.

S: Social: They are very friendly, kind and trustworthy people. They give high importance to helping people and working for a social cause. They will avoid jobs which largely makes use of tools, machines and equipments. They like tasks which will involve team work. They will shine in the professions of teaching, counseling, nursing or providing information.

Ex: Teacher, counselor, baby sitter, NGO worker, nurse, special education etc.

E: Enterprising: They are highly adventurous people. They are energetic, sociable and ambitious people. They like to lead and persuade people and sell things and ideas. They avoid jobs that demand careful observation and scientific thinking. They will be good in politics, leadership roles and business.

Ex: Politician, CEO, secretary, management consultant, recruiter, international relations.

C: Conventional: They are good followers. They value precision of job and accuracy. They are very orderly, like to work with numbers, records etc. They do not like ambiguous, unstructured activities. They can take up any back end job where record keeping, documentation and handling numbers are involved.

Ex: Accountant, bank teller, book keeper, math teacher, financial analyst, market research analyst etc.

The RAISAC test gives a fair idea of an individual's orientation towards a specific career of interest.

5. Social learning theory (Albert Bandura) OR Role Model Theory

Learning according to Albert Bandure is mainly due to observation. Bandura suggests that there are three aspects to motivation:

1. External reinforcement (as in operant theory)
2. Vicarious reinforcement – the observation of other people being rewarded or punished for their behaviour
3. Self-reinforcement – gaining internal satisfaction from an activity, which therefore motivates the individual to behave in a similar way in the future.

Pros and Cons of Trait theory:

Trait theory, especially the Big 5 model, is able to describe personality very distinctly.

Cross-cultural human studies find good agreement for the Big 5 model in many cultures

Appear to be highly correlated not only in adulthood, but also in childhood and even late preschoolers. Gender and birth order seem to have high correlation with Big 5. Women generally score high on Agreeableness and Neuroticism. First born individuals are generally more Conscientious and less Agreeable. On the flip side, it is understood that the five domains are not mutually exclusive. There is negative correlation between Neuriticism and Extraversion. Moreover, big five does not account for all the personality traits which are very common like Sense of humour, Thriftiness etc.

- It also does not give explaination on why traits develop
- Trait theory does not clearly explain issues connected to transient and long lasting traits

PERSONALITY ASSESSMENT

Assessment is a process of making judgments that are to be used for improving the product, the process and even the goals themselves.

Assessment is a more wider term than the measurement. Measurement denotes quantity but assessment denotes quality too.

Personality assessment is a process of making judgment on the various personality traits of an individual that are to be used for improving the personality of the individual being assessed. A Personality assessment measures those relatively enduring aspects of an individual which distinguish them from other people, making them unique.

Why assessment of personality?

- To understand the personality of individual
- To modify personality if necessary
- Career Planning
- Team Building and Management Development Activities
- Help managers forecast who the best bet for a job is to effectively manage the people.
- Helpful in hiring decisions
- Most common method: self-reporting surveys
- Observer-ratings surveys provide an independent assessment of personality – often better predictors

Personality Traits:

Enduring characteristics that describe an individual's behavior

Methods of personality assessment

1. **Subjective method:**
   — Autobiography
   — Case history
   — Questionnaire
   — Interview
2. **Objective methods**
   — Situational test
   — Q test (Forced Choice)
3. **Projective tests**

A person responds to ambiguous stimuli to reveal hidden emotions and internal stimuli. Projective tests reveal the central aspects of personality that is hidden in the unconscious mind of an individual. The unstructured nature of projective tests elicits the hidden desires, inner fears and complexes. It can give endless list of possible responses.

Psychologists present ambiguous visual stimuli to individuals and they are asked to explain what they see in the stimuli. Unconscious concerns, thoughts, opinions and fears are projected by the individual and those will then be interpreted and understood by the psychologist.

Projective tests helps an individual to showcase his personality attributes, which otherwise would have not been noticed during interview. Test takers are not aware of the psychological interpretation of the responses, and hence chances of faking a response are minimal. Moreover, this kind of tests will reveal latent aspects of personality, which was never observed by the individual himself.

Some of the famous projective tests are as follows:

- **Rorschach IB Test**

Developed in 1921 by Swiss psychiatrist Herman Rorschach, this test consists of 10 inkblots. These are used to measure intellectual and nonintellectual personality traits. During the test, individuals are asked to state what the inkblots look like to them. Responses are scored by psychologists using pre-determined categories. These tests are used for diagnosing mental illness, for personality description and behavioural prediction.

- **TAT**

Thematic Apperception Test (TAT) was developed by Henry Murray. This consists of 20 black and white pictures which are deliberately drawn in an ambiguous way. After seeing the picture, a story is to be told by the individual, based on what he understood from the picture. The story is then interpreted by the psychologist, who will look for revealing statements and projections of the individuals' subconscious mind.

Though it is a popular projection test, the varying scoring patterns and procedures makes the use of TAT more or less restricted to clinical utility.

4. Personality inventories :

It is a printed form consisting of a set of statements or questions applying to human behavior. The questions have close ended answers and they are hence objective in nature.

Some of the most commonly used inventories of personality are Cattelles 16PF, NEO PI by Costa &McCrae, based on five factor model of personality traits, Myers Briggs Type Indicator (MBTI), Minnesota Multiphasic Personality Inventory (MMPI) etc. MMPI has 567 statements, which is mostly used in clinical conditions for testing an abnormality.

Given below are the brief descriptions of two such personality inventories:

a) Myers Briggs Type Indicator (MBTI):

Most widely used instrument in the world. It is a personality test that taps four characteristics and classifies people into 1 of 16 personality types. It is based on Carl Jung's Theory & Raymond Cattell's 16 traits. It is a Self-Report Instrument which is non-judgmental. It is constructed based on the research on normal population.

PERSONALITY TYPES described under MBTI:

- **Extroverted vs. Introverted (E or I)**
- **Sensing vs. Intuitive (S or N)**
- **Thinking vs. Feeling (T or F)**
- **Judging vs. Perceiving (P or J)**

Dimensions of MBTI

Extraversion **Introversion**

Interest Orientation

E ←——|——→ **I**

Outer world of actions, Objects and people | **Inner world of ideas and concepts**

Sensing **iNtuition**

Perception

S ←——|——→ **N**

Immediate reality and Direct experience | **Inferred meanings and relationships**

Thinking **Feeling**

Judgement

T ←——|——→ **F**

Reliability of logical order -cause and effect | **Priorities based on personal importance and values**

Judgement **Perception**

Environment Orientation

J ←——|——→ **P**

Judging attitude – Control of events and Systematic planning | **Spontaneity- curious, awaiting events and adapting to them**

For example:

- Visionaries (INTJ) – are original, stubborn and driven.
- Organizers (ESTJ) – realistic, logical, analytical and businesslike.
- Conceptualizer (ENTP) – entrepreneurial, innovative, individualistic and resourceful.

Application of MBTI

MBTI® can be used effectively for self-awareness and counseling. It can also be used in training and development. But it should *not* be used as a selection test for job candidates. It helps us to learn to capitalize on strength of self & others. It helps us to supplement & augment areas that one may overlook.

b) Big 5 of personality/ OCEAN by Costa &McCrae

The view that all personality traits can be distilled into five big ones:

- **O**penness
- **C**onscientiousness
- **E**xtroversion
- **A**greeableness
- **N**euroticism

What each of these traits stand for?

O: Openness: Is the individual smart or not?

C: Conscientiousness: Can I count on the individual?

E: Extroversion: Can I bully the individual or will the individual bully me?

A: Agreeableness: Is the individual warm and pleasant or cold and distant.

N: Neuroticism (Reversal of Emotional stability): Is the individual sane and predictable or insane and unpredictable?

	Low Scores	High Scores
Openness	Down to earth Uncreative Conventional Uncurious	Imaginative Creative Original Curious
Conscientiousness	Negligent Lazy Disorganized Late	Conscientous Hard Working Well organized Punctual
Extroversion	Loner Quiet Passive Reserved	Joiner Talkative Active Affectionate
Agreeableness	Suspicious Critical Ruthless Irritable	Trusting Lenient Soft hearted Good natured
Neuroticism	Calm Even Tempered Comfortable Unemotional	Worried Temperamental Self conscious Emotional

How Do the Big Five Traits Predict Behavior?

Research has shown OCEAN to be a better framework in comparison to MBTI. Certain traits have been shown to strongly relate to higher job performance:

Highly conscientious people develop more job knowledge, exert greater effort, and have better performance and are less creative. They are very structured in thinking and have a high level of commitment to organization. But they are poor in adapting to organizational change. Emotional stability or low neuroticism is related to job satisfaction and low stress levels. People with high scores of neuroticism tend to make quick decisions.

Extroverts freely express their feelings and they tend to be happier in their jobs and have good social skills. Extroversion is a good predictor of leadership as they easily take charge of situation and are more assertive.

But they tend to be impulsive and tend to be absent from job. Employees who score high on Openness are the people who are more creative and can be good leaders as creativity is essential for leadership. They are more comfortable to ambiguity. They readily accept change and are more adaptable. Agreeable people are chosen first from among many people while forming groups. They are more compliant. They are better suited for jobs which demand interpersonal skills like customer relations. Agreeable people are poor negotiators and hence it can affect their earnings from the job.

While employing managers, screen for the Big Five trait of conscientiousness will be very fruitful to help in hiring organized and responsible individuals.

Activity: On a scale of 1 to 10, rate yourself on all the five dimensions of OCEAN based on what you think of yourself.

Difficulties in assessment of personality:

1) **Complex nature of the personality of the individual:** An individual who is being assessed is capable of employing hundreds of ways to evade being assessed. Even if he co-operates willingly with the best of his intentions, he may be unable to tell about the elements hidden in his unconscious mind.

2) **Nature of assessment instrument:** In personality assessment there is no starting point (Zero) for reference. No child is born with zero personality. This creates difficulties in the exact assessment of personality. Above all, tools of assessment of personality are not very exact, reliable, and valid in terms of their result.

3) **Complex nature of assessor of personality:** Subjectivity of the person who assesses can also influence assessment. Even when the same person assessing the same individual at different intervals under the same conditions, results may differ. It is also observed that when two or more persons assess the same person, results may not be identical.

Article: CEO Modifies His Personality To Lead People Better

David Kirchhoff's enthusiastic, hard-charging personality helped him become CEO at age 40 of a global firm with 54,000 employees. But some of the traits that propelled his rapid career ascent did not serve him well as head honcho.

"My stock in trade was always being passionate with a tendency sometimes to prove my worth by being a forceful presence who would immediately say, 'This is the right answer,'" said Kirchhoff, 46, chief executive of Weight Watchers International. "That's how you get noticed."

After six years as CEO, Kirchhoff has learned to give others a chance to bask in the limelight. He realized he needed to change when he participated in a 360-degree feedback exercise with his management team in 2009.

"The message I got from them is 'pipe down,'" said Kirchhoff, author of "Weight Loss Boss." "The comments I got were, 'You shouldn't feel the need to be the smartest guy in the room' and 'Don't be the loudest guy in the band.'"

Learning To Listen

Responding to such blunt feedback proved pivotal to Kirchhoff's evolution as a leader. Humbled by the input, he knew he needed to stop dominating meetings and step back so others could showcase their smarts.

"I'm an 'E' (extrovert) on the Myers Briggs (personality assessment) so I tend to problem-solve out loud in groups," he explained. "I get excited and animated. But I didn't appreciate that I was sucking the oxygen out of the room."

When his managers gave presentations, Kirchhoff would often interrupt after the first slide and say, "This is the issue I see." After taking his team's feedback to heart, he began to withhold his thoughts and let others talk.

Kirchhoff admits that changing his behavior hasn't been easy. But he has alerted his lieutenants to let him know when he reverts to his old ways.

"There's no one on my team who's particularly shy about pulling me off to the side and being direct and honest with me," he said. "I'm a much better listener, but I'm not perfect."

Planning To Talk Less

Because Kirchhoff works in a business devoted to behavior modification, he understands the importance of self-awareness to improve results. He's constantly looking for warning signs that he's interrupting people who want to speak; when he catches himself lapsing into bad habits, he shifts into listening mode.

In the past three years, he has undergone more 360-degree feedback programs with his staff, and the results are better. Kirchhoff now goes into meetings thinking, "I need to get the most out of my team." This reminds him to keep quiet and make succinct comments when appropriate, rather than talk so much that others decline to share their ideas.

Source: *Investors business daily 17/ 5/ 2013 , http://news.investors.com/ management-managing-for-success/051713-656514-weight-watchers-ceo-kirchhoff-conquers-bad-habits.htm*

WORK RELATED ASPECTS OF PERSONALITY:

Major Personality Attributes Influencing OB

- Locus of control
- Machiavellianism
- Narcissism
- Self-esteem
- Self-monitoring
- Risk taking
- Type A personality
- Authoritarianism
- Self efficacy
- Need for achievement/ Achievement orientation.

Locus of Control

The degree to which people perceive control over a situation being internal or external is called locus of control these behaviors are significant to managers.

Internals

Individuals who believe that they control what happens to them. People believe that internal factors (their skills and abilities) are the determinants of their destiny. Own actions and behaviors are major and decisive determinants of job outcomes.

Externals

They are individuals who believe that what happens to them is controlled by outside forces such as luck or chance, other people or organisational factors. They believe that outside forces are responsible for what happens to them and around them and they do not think their own actions make much of a difference.

Organisational Implication of Locus of Control

a) Absenteeism: Internal LOC people tend to take less leave because they believe that their health is under their control, and even when they are not well they can manage to do some amount of work.

b) Employee turner: There is higher tendency among the internal LOC to quit the job because they tend to take action based on their beliefs.

c) Job satisfaction: Internal LOC are more successful and satisfied in jobs.

d) Decision making style : External LOC tend to use intuitions for decision making whereas internal LOC tend to use more facts and information before making a much deliberated decision, as they want to have control over their decisions.

e) Social interaction: Internal LOC are more sociable and tend to use social relationships for their improved esteem.

Machiavellianism(Mach)

Based on the writings of Niccolo Machiavelli who advocated a psychologically detached and unemotional behavioral approach by individuals to organizational participation in meeting their personal objectives. The term Machiavellianism refers to the degree to which an individual puts effort to gain control over organizational tasks.

It is the degree to which an individual is pragmatic, maintains emotional distance, and believes that ends can justify means. The primary focus is on obtaining and using power as a means to further one's own ends, regardless of its impact on others. Machiavellians would be prone to participate in organizational politics. They are also adept at interpersonal game-playing, power tactics, and identifying influence systems in organizations.

Machiavellian:

A pragmatic, emotionally distant power-player who believes that ends justify the means.

High Machs are manipulative, win more often, and persuade more than they are persuaded. They use others to get ahead in life. They are not swayed by friendship, emotions and don't hesitate to lie.

High Machs will flourish when they have one to one interaction with others. They work best when there are minimal rules and regulations. They also thrive well when emotions distract low mach people, they capitalize on that.

Narcissism:

A high Narcissist has a high sense of self importance. The expectto be considered superior without commensurate achievements. They often need excessive admiration and praise. They are pre occupied with fantasies of very high level of power and success. They are generally very arrogant and show high self-importance. They tend to talk down to people who do not praise them and they treat them as inferior people. They tend to be less effective in their jobs.

Advantage for organisation:

Narcissist leaders are driven and they go to any extent of personal sacrifices to achieve the goals. Since they are not very sensitive to others, they are able to take tough decisions without any remorse as during the time of retrenching employees

Self-Monitoring

A personality trait that measures an individual's ability to adjust his or her behavior to external, situational factors. Individuals can be high or low in self monitoring based on their ability to adjust to situational demands. High self monitors observe others around them and their behavior to adjust their own behavior to suit the situation. They are successful in performing roles which are not similar though they show high level of behavioural inconsistency. They will have specific purpose friends who will help them perform well in a specific activity. They avoid situations which put them in bad mood. They have a striking balance between public, personal and private selves. High monitors conform more and are more likely to become leaders. They are more successful in managerial positions where individuals are required to play multiple and even contradictory roles.

Low self monitors tend to act from internal states rather than from situational cues. They show consistency in their behavior and are less likely to respond to work group norms or supervisory feedback. Their friends are not chosen for meeting any specific purpose. They take time to fit into a situation. Low self monitors are not as vigilant to situational cues and act from internal states rather than paying attention to the situation.

Correct understanding of the type of self monitoring of subordinates will help the managers to communicate, motivate and elicit the required work out of them. It was found that though high self monitors are good performers and often they become leaders, they have less commitment to the organization.

Self-Esteem (SE)

An individuals' degree of liking or disliking themselves is known as self esteem. It is very much connected to an individual's desire to succeed. An individual with a high desire for success is a person with high self esteem. Positive self-evaluation leads to higher job performance. They believe that their strengths are more important than their weaknesses. They tend to choose risky and challenging jobs. They prefer their pride over monetary gain. They don't have a tendency to do things for pleasing others. They are free thinking, independent and are satisfied with higher order of needs in need hierarchy. High self-esteem people are high performers and are more satisfied with their jobs. People with low self esteem will also have low job satisfaction, low desire for success, and fear for challenging jobs. They do not give up an opportunity to please others. They are critical of others, generally repressed and blame others for their failure.

Risk-Taking / Risk propensity:

People differ in their ability to take chances. This is closely connected to the time taken for decision making. High risk-taking managers make quicker decisions with minimum information. They operate well in smaller and more entrepreneurial organizations. Low risk-taking managers are slow in decision making and need large amount of information to help in decision making. They perform well in larger organizations with stable environments

Authoritarianism:

Authoritarian personality: is a generic term used to describe an individual who has strong belief in the legitimacy of established mechanisms of formal authority and views obedience to authority as necessary. This concept refers to a belief that there should be status and power differences among people in organization. They have certain negative beliefs about the work and workers. They compel obedience to authority. They adhere to conventional values and do not give room to new ideas. They prefer stable and structured work environments which are governed by clear rules and procedures. They are conservative.

Authoritarian leadership style is not a preferred leadership style and once the leader is understood to have an authoritarian leadership style, introspection and solicited feedback to improve the leadership style will do a lot more good to the motivation level of subordinates and hence the organisational performance.

Self efficacy :

Has strong belief in one's own ability to deal with events and challenges. High self efficacy results in better performance of the employee. Self-Efficacy is the belief and the expectations of one's ability to accomplish a specific task effectively. Self-efficacy may stem from prior experiences, behavior models (observing success in others),persuasion and assessment of current physical & emotional capabilities.

High Sense of Self- Efficacy	Low Sense of Self-Efficacy
View challenging problems as tasks to be mastered	Avoid challenging tasks.
Develop deeper interest in the activities in which they participate.	Believe that difficult tasks and situations are beyond their capabilities
Form a stronger sense of commitment to their interests and activities	Focus on personal failings and negative outcomes.
Recover quickly from setbacks and disappointments	Quickly lose confidence in personal abilities

Achievement orientation:

It is the desire to accomplish something difficult, to overcome obstacles and to attain high standards. Employees with high motivation would want to overcome obstacles quickly. They believe that success or failure is because of their actions. They prefer jobs with moderate difficulty. They work hard on projects which holds personal advantage and not otherwise. Prefer jobs with rapid performance feedback, have direct relation between effort and reward. They are more suitable for supervisory or managerial jobs. There are higher proportions of high achievers in the entrepreneurial category.

Test your knowledge

Multiple Choice questions:

1. The Big Five model of personality uses all of the following basic personality dimensions except
   a. Extroversion
   b. Perceptiveness
   c. Conscientiousness
   d. Openness to experience
   e. Locus of control.
2. An individual with an external locus of control is
   a. A chameleon, able to change to fit the situation, manipulative
   b. Maintains emotional distance, and believes that ends can justify means.
   c. Intellectually rigid, judgmental of others, deferential to those above, and exploitative ofthose below.
   d. Prone to blame a poor performance evaluation on his boss's prejudice, his co-workers, or other events outside his control.
   e. Believes that he can turn the world.
3. Which of the following is true about Type 'A' personality?
   a. They eat rapidly
   b. They are not impatient
   c. They don't have a sense of urgency
   d. They do not reveal their accomplishments
   e. They can relax without any guilt.
4. Which of the following is a characteristic of a Type 'B' personality?
   a. They are relaxed
   b. They are moving
   c. They keep walking
   d. They are achievement oriented
   e. They are restless.

MODEL QUESTIONS

Section – A

(Each question carries 2 marks)

1. What do you mean by super-ego? Explain.
2. Define and give meaning of personality.
3. Explain the Type A and Type B theory of personality in brief
4. Explain extroversion and introversion traits of personality in brief
5. What is personality assessment? Why is it important in organization?
6. What do you mean by Id?

SECTION – B

(Each question carries 5 marks)

1. How does the study of personality help in understanding organizational behavior?
2. What is meant by personality assessment? What are various methods of assessment of personality? Explain in brief.
3. Explain the Dynamic theory of personality? With example
4. Name the different theories of personality and give brief explanation for each theory.
5. What are the various dimensions of MBTI? Explain.

SECTION – C

(Each question carries 15 marks)

1. Explain the psychoanalytic approach to personality
2. What is personality? What are its determinants? Which of them, you feel, are more important in shaping personality and why?
3. Write notes on (a) type theory and (b) trait theory of personality
4. Write short note on.
    - i. locus of control
    - ii. Openness to Experience
    - iii. Agreeableness
    - iv. Self monitoring
    - v. extroversion
    - vi. introversion

5. Explain the Big 5 theory of personality in detail.
6. Explain the work related aspects of personality or explain the personality characteristics in an organization.

REFERENCES

1. R.K.Sharma & Shashi . K Gupta, Management and behavioural process, Kalyani Publishers, New Delhi, ISBN 81-272-0001-8.

FIGURE SOURCES

https://encrypted-tbn1.gstatic.com/images?q=tbn:ANd9GcTuhdr-oZB9M6tvwK92TjqCB5Mv3SzsUNvkSG1UJJXjoxE7LGBG_g

◈◈◈◈

Read More on the Web

Ones personality is a difficult thing to define, and even more difficult to justify. Ones personality colours the way he/she perceives the world. There are numerous reasons to why a person is who he/she is. How one behaves is ingrained into his/her being, which is why people say," do not react on first impulse". Our first impulse is that ingrained pathway we follow, one that isn't always suited to a given situation. Our personality is the prime reason we react the way we do. For example, a person who has grown up in a household with little financial security will always be careful about money, even if he/she grows up to be very wealthy. He/she will always think twice before he purchases something, even if that thought process is rendered unnecessary by his/her current economic status.

Of course, in some cases it can go the other way too. The same person could become overconfident in his status and end up landing in the same situation he sought to escape. Then again, this could be attributed to different causes that had altered his personality and way of thinking his/developing stages.

Usually, our personalities go hand and hand with our learning and development graph, be it positive or negative. The way a person behaves is a dynamic thing and is very often determined by the circumstances that surround him/her. However, his personality- ingrained and difficult to break- remains more or less constant, without the influence of major mental or physical trauma.

However, during a person's development, a lot of things can go wrong, leading to something psychiatrists call personality disorders. These disorders range from simple to downright disturbing, with varying levels of severity. From an organizational viewpoint, knowing an employee's personality determines the type of job he/she'd be the best at. Also, when early signs of severe personality disorders are seen, it can take evasive action, if necessary.

A few examples of personality disorders could be:

- **Obsessive Compulsive Disorder:** whose effects can range repeating a certain task a fixed number of times all the way to excessive hoarding and the preoccupation with violent and anti-social thoughts.
- **Narcissistic Personality Disorder:** This is also called megalomania and is typically severe egocentrism. It is typically a defense against some shame. Some of the symptoms include an elevated image of oneself, a fragile self esteem, etc.
- **Stockholm syndrome:** Where a person develops certain affections towards ones captor (in any sense) but typically in a 'captor' situation. A famous example is the Patty Hearst Case, who eventually assisted her captors in a bank robbery that they were orchestrating.
- **Diogenes syndrome:** also known as Senile Squalor Syndrome is characterized by extreme self neglect, social withdrawal, compulsive hoarding and the lack of shame. This person exhibits near catatonia.
- **Stendhal syndrome:** Also called the Florence syndrome, whose symptoms range from tachycardia, dizziness, fainting and even hallucinations in the face of particularly beautiful art, or even while confronted with immense beauty in the natural world.

- **Split personality/ multiple personality disorder:** where there are two or more distinct identities that alternatively control the person's behavior, along with memory impediments. The other personality could be of a different age, sex, religion, etc.
- **Capgras delusion/syndrome:** this is a delusion a person holds in which he/she believes that a close person (family, friend, spouse) has been replaced by an identical looking imposter. This delusion sometimes manifests itself in severe cases of schizophrenia (a mental disorder characterized by the breakdown of thought processes and by a deficit of typical emotional responses.)

One of the most widely used treatment for many disorders, particularly for depression and other anxiety disorders is psychoanalysis. The aim here , is to release repressed emotions and experiences; to make the unconscious, conscious. Psychoanalysis was founded by Sigmund Freud. The basic assumptions made for the same are:

- Psychoanalytic psychologists see psychological problems as rooted in the unconscious mind.
- Manifest symptoms are caused by latent or hidden disturbances.
- Typical causes include unresolved issues during development, or trauma.
- The treatment focuses on bringing up the repressed conflict to consciousness where the client can deal with it.

Due to the nature of defense mechanisms and the inaccessibility of the determining forces operating in the unconscious, psychoanalysis in its classic form, is a lengthy process often involving 2 to 5 sessions per week for several years. The analyst typically is a 'blank screen', disclosing very little about themselves in order that the client can use the space in the relationship to work on their unconscious without interference from outside.

The psychoanalyst uses various techniques as encouragement for the patient to develop insights into their behavior and the meanings of symptoms, including ink blots, parapraxes (minor errors made, a slip of the tongue), shows latent associations and motives) free association, interpretation (including dream analysis), resistance analysis (patients either directly or indirectly oppose changing their behavior or refuse to discuss, remember, or think about presumably clinically relevant experiences), and transference analysis (the redirection of feelings and desires and especially of those unconsciously retained from childhood toward a new object).

Sources and References

http://www.simplypsychology.org/psychoanalysis.html
http://en.wikipedia.org/wiki/Patty_Hearst
http://listverse.com/2007/10/13/top-10-bizarre-mental-disorders/
http://en.wikipedia.org/wiki/Diogenes_syndrome
http://en.wikipedia.org/wiki/Hypochondriasis
http://en.wikipedia.org/wiki/Stendhal_Syndrome
http://en.wikipedia.org/wiki/Body_dysmorphic_disorder
http://en.wikipedia.org/wiki/Schizophrenia
http://en.wikipedia.org/wiki/Obsessive%E2%80%93compulsive_disorder
http://en.wikipedia.org/wiki/Dissociative_identity_disorder
http://en.wikipedia.org/wiki/Narcissistic_personality_disorder

CHAPTER 4

LEARNING

Learning Objectives of the Chapter

- Definition & Meaning of Learning
- Theories of Learning- Classical conditioning
- Operant Learning, Cognitive Learning and Observational Learning
- Principles of Learning- Motivation
- Reinforcement
- Punishment
- Extinction
- Whole versus part learning and learning curve
- Short term and long term memory
- Ways to improve memory

Introduction:

Human beings behave in a socially acceptable manner based on encountering a variety of experiences in life. These skills of adjustment to the society requirements are derived from the process of learning. Learning is essential not only to mankind, but also for any living being to adapt to the living situations to make living comfortable. Memory helps one to remember varied things, incidents, location, concepts etc for helping in managing the daily routine as well as for future planning. This chapter deals with concepts of learning and memory which are crucial for an individual

Definitions of learning

Learning is – "A relatively permanent change in an organism's behavior or behavioural potential that occurs as a result of experience"

According to Stephen P. Robbins, "learning is a relatively permanent change that occurs as a result of experience"

Generally, learning is described as the process of having one's behavior modified, more or less permanently, by what he does and the consequences of his actions or by what he observes

Characteristics of learning:

1. Temporary change in behavior can't be termed as learning
2. Learning can result from *vicarious* or direct experience.
3. Behavioural changes occurring due to maturation process is not a part of learning.
4. Learning is not necessarily always positive. Ex: Bad habits learned through learning process.
5. Learning is transferable.
6. Change in behavior should be relatively permanent.
7. Learning is reflected in behavior.
8. Change in behavior should occur as result of experience, practice or training.
9. Practice and experience must be reinforced for learning to occur.
10. Learning is a continuous (improvement) process.

Approaches to learning:

Learning approaches basically describe the conditions under which learning takes place and it to helps theorize the process of learning. The general categorizations of learning approach are: Surface approach and Deep approach

Surface approach: In this approach the learner considers learning as a task and the intent is to just complete task requirements. Without understanding the core concept, the learner memorises the information. The task is seen as an external imposition on the learner.

Deep approach: In this approach the learner intends to understand the meaning of the object at hand. The learner interacts actively with the content, relates newly learned ideas to his previous knowledge and everyday experience. The learner tries to examine the conclusion drawn in the context and seeks alternate solutions.

Learning domains:

Learning domains are the areas in which learning takes place. There are 3 learning domains identified, which are not mutually exclusive and they often overlap each other. They are *Cognitive, Affective* and *Psychomotor* domains. Many a times, one domain draws input from other domains for completion. For example, psychomotor development (Ex: Learning driving) needs proper knowledge and understanding of the vehicle mechanics (cognitive development). Therefore, learning can't be considered to belong to any particular domain. Familiarity with learning domains helps in identifying intended outcome of learning.

a) Cognitive domain:

In education process, Learning basically focuses on the cognitive domain, as cognition is *to know* and hence it is a part of seeking knowledge. Learning at the cognitive domain operates at 6 levels, viz. Knowledge, Comprehension, Application, Analysis, Synthesis and Evaluation. By and large, cognitive learning is evaluated at schools.

b) Affective Domain :

The learning situation affects the feelings, interests, emotions and attitudes of the learner. Ex. a learner shows more affinity towards a subject because of more exposure in that field. Thus, learning in the Affective mode includes the changes in interest, attitude and values of the learner, which leads to better societal adjustment of the learner. The core of affective domain is the degree of internalization, which is the extent to which the feelings or emotions are incorporated in the personality of the learner. Affective aspect of learning is less observable and hence less rigorously measured.

c) Psychomotor Domain :

In this domain, learning happens under the supervision or guidance of an expert or skilled person.

Ex: Swimming skills can be acquired under the direct supervision of a coach, who is skilled in swimming. Physical and art education fall in this category of learning domain.

Factors affecting learning:

It is necessary to understand different factors affecting learning to understand why the extent of learning differs between different learners. Factors affecting learning can be categorized into *Personal factors, Environmental factors and learning method related factors.*

a) Personal factors :

These factors can be altered to improve the learning process. Proper understanding of these factors will help the teachers and parents of the learner to understand and guide the learner in the right direction. Some of the important personal factors are:

1. **Sensation and Perception:** The five sensory organs receive the stimuli and helps in perception of various stimuli. Faulty sensory organs will affect learning and knowledge acquisition. Ex: Defective vision will reduce learning efficiency and there by lack of inclination towards studies.

2. **Fatigue and boredom:** Fatigue is the mental or physical tiredness that impairs the efficiency to work and learn. Boredom is the lack of desire or aversion to work or learn. Boredom creates fatigue thereby reducing the students' efficiency to learn.

3. **Mental state of the learner:** Desirable mental state enhances learning. Happiness, joy etc favors learning and negative emotional conditions like stress, tension and mental disturbance etc reduces learning efficiency.

4. **Interest of the learner:** A subject, a field, topic or situation that interests the learner can be understood by the learner faster. Ex: An individual who has interest in botany, vegetation and nature

will learn the scientific names of the plants much faster than others who do not have such interest.

5. **Motivation:** Motivation generates the desire in an individual to do something or learn something. Motivation sustains learning.

   Motivation for learning could be intrinsic i.e., from within Ex : An individual learns how to make a model of automobile engine which pollutes the atmosphere relatively less, so that he can make a working model, which makes him happy. Motivation for learning can be extrinsic also. Learning takes place for an external reason. Going by the same example, if the individual learns to make a model of the engine with commercial viability, income coming out of selling the patent etc, it becomes extrinsic motivation. Extrinsic motivation can take the form of reward and punishment, praise and blame.

6. **Age and maturation:** Learning can't take place till the individual is mature enough to learn, though some young children learn much faster compared to children of that age. Though mental age increases with chronological age, it stops at the age of 16 and after that mental maturation happens, which helps in solving difficult problems.

7. **Intelligence:** IQ has a positive correlation with learning. Though high IQ learners learn fast, the complete learning experience may be affected by learners interest, motivation attitude etc.

8. **Attitude:** Favourable attitude of the learner makes the learning easy and fast.

b) Environmental factors:

External environmental factors which affect learning are connected to the individual's interaction with family, teachers, colleagues etc. Some of the major external factors that affect learning are:

1. Natural, Social and Cultural surrounding:

Climatic conditions can affect learning. Ex: High temperature and humidity can reduce learning efficiency. Since early morning hours are relatively less hot and humid, complicated and difficult tasks can be learned with less difficulty during that time.

Social surroundings include atmosphere of home, school etc. Size of the family, birth order of the individual, non conducive learning conditions like poor ventilation and lighting at the place of learning, frequent visits of guests, poor teaching methods of teacher, non friendly behaviour of the people at place of learning etc can hamper learning.

Cultural surroundings also impact learning. Ex: In a modernized culture set up, emphasis for learning will be more related to information technology as against an agriculture based community, where the stress is more on learning skills that are required to suit the community needs.

2. Learners relationship with the teacher, parents and peers:

Teachers teaching style has a bearing on students learning. An authoritarian teacher will create a hostile learning climate while a democratic teacher will create a participatory learning climate, wherein learning is better.

Healthy parental relationship will lead to a congenial learning climate. A disturbed family atmosphere like the separation of parents, death or other traumatic events in the family or among friends is detrimental for learning.

Peer group relationship, if healthy can contribute immensely to learning. Class room learning can be augmented by promoting healthy class discussions and debates.

3. Influence of media on learning:

Both print (text books print outs of learning modules) and non print media (Electronic media like audio tapes, films and videos) have an influence on learning. Non print media generally facilitates learning much faster than print media in certain cases. Ex: Audio tapes for learning languages are more effective than print media.

c) Learning methods:

If the right choice of learning method is used, it can improve learning. Effective learning methods promote memory. Some of the most effective methods of learning are discussed below:

1. Whole Vs Part learning:

Whole learning is learning something completely, from beginning to end. Here, various tasks, concepts, skills etc are learned at a stretch. Ex: Memorising a poem completely. Part learning is learning in bits and pieces of an entire learning item, little at a time. Another suitable example will be learning all the concepts of HR and performing them together as situation demands v/s learning in parts about selection, recruitment, placing, induction, training and development et.al. The choice of whole vs part learning depends entirely on the length or quantum of learning material, type of learning material and the mental age of the learner. Whole learning is recommended for more bright and mature students and when learning material is not too long. Slow learners, average learners and young learners can adopt part learning for effectiveness.

2. Mediating method:

When whole learning is adopted, sometimes the length of the learning material as well as unusual words and phrases in the learning material will hinder smooth learning. To reduce this problem, a modification in the whole method is adopted wherein difficult words and phrases are mastered first by intensive study. It is not part learning method and here the students do not lose the sight of relationship between parts.

3. Spaced V/s unspaced learning :

This learning method is based on Learn - Rest - Learn style. This is also known as distributed learning, wherein the learner learns for some time, takes a break and learns again. Ex : A chapter, which needs 7 hours to completely learn, is learned for two hours at a stretch and then with a break of half an hour again another learning stint of two hours etc. Unspaced learning is when learning is continuous and without a break. Ex: A lesson is learned completely in 7 hours without a break. Shorter study periods with breaks in between are best suited for young students. When the learners' intelligence, motivational level and interests are high, unspaced learning is more effective.

4. Recitation method of learning:

In this learning method, the learner reads the learning material many times and recalls the content without looking at the content. In this method, the learner checks his own ability by reciting to himself what is learned. This method saves a lot of study time, as the learner is sure of how much is learned and gives a chance for the learner to correct any errors.

5. Memory systems:

Individuals will have varied capacity to memorise things. It largely depends on mental imagery and the retrieval capacity of the individual. Recall is an indication that learning has taken place.

6. Laws of association:

When students learn meaningless or disconnected materials (as in the case of part learning), there is a tendency to quickly forget it. When a student uses whole method and logical association, learning is enhanced and it is not forgotten easily. Speed of learning is connected to method of learning. Associative learning has long term impact in learning.

Laws of association influence learning and recall. Association can be by way of law of continuity, where in, events that occur in close proximity to each other in time or space are readily associated with each other and recalled easily. Ex: When we hear the whistle of train, we know that the train is reaching the station and the travelers get ready to board the train.

Association can be by way of *law of similarity.* According to this law, similar events and facts are linked up together in such a way that one easily recalls the other. Ex: Colour red reminds you of a rose and an apple because both are red in colour.

Association can be by law of contrast where in the contrasted characters get associated with each other in such a way that the thought of one recalls the thought of the contrasting item. Ex: Seeing an obese person can bring the thought of a slim model.

Different ways of association can improve learning and memorization. For example, use of acronyms like VIBGYOR, PODSCORB (Planning, Organizing, Directing, Staffing, Coordination, Reporting and Budgeting) etc helps us to learn and memorise the concepts.

Activity: Sripal was selected in a prestigious college for business management studies because of his previous academic performance as well have his performance in the selection process. His performance in the new college was not upto the mark and it kept declining. What could be the reasons of his poor performance? Help him get back to his original academic performance

Learning theories

Learning takes place in varied forms. The basic process of learning can be understood under Observational learning & Experimental learning. Observational learning happens when an individual learns by observing behaviours and the consequences of the behaviours of others. Experimental learning has characteristics of experimentation. Under this two forms of learning are dealt with, Viz, Classical condition and operant conditioning.

Theories of Learning:

A) Observational Learning/Social learning

B) Classical conditioning

C) Operant Learning

D) Cognitive Learning

A) Classical conditioning (Ivan Pavlov, Russian Psychologist)

Classical conditioning is a process of learning where you associate one event with another desired event resulting in a specific behavior. This learning process occurs through associations between an environmental stimulus (unconditioned stimulus) and a naturally occurring stimulus (conditioned stimulus). It is a type of conditioning/ learning where an individual responds to some stimulus that would ordinarily not produce such a response.

Pavlov's Experiment

Pavlov, while conducting several experiments on dogs on various digestive reflexes found out that salivary reflexes could be initiated by stimuli which are initially completely neutral after conditioning it. He conducted an experiment on a dog and tried to relate dog's salivation and the ringing of a bell. A system was made to measure the amount of saliva secreted by the dog. When Pavlov introduced the dog to a piece of meat, the dog showed an evident increase in salivation. When he withheld the presentation of the meat and merely rang a bell, the dog had no salivation. Then Pavlov moved ahead to connect the meat and the ringing of the bell. After repetitively hearing the bell before getting the food, the dog began to salivate as soon as the bell rang. After a while, the dog salivates immediately at the sound of the bell, irrespective of the food not being offered. In effect, the dog had learnt to respond (Salivate) to the bell.

From the above description certain concepts of Classical conditioning can now be introduced.

Unconditioned reflex or response- Salivation in response to food is a natural process, unlearned response- (It's a reflex)

The food, because it elicited the unconditioned response automatically was called unconditioned stimulus.

Repeated presentation of bell followed by food - led the dog to salivate in response to the bell alone - Conditioned response.

Therefore this emphasized that response (Salivation) was dependent upon a stimulus (Bell) other than the natural one (Meat).

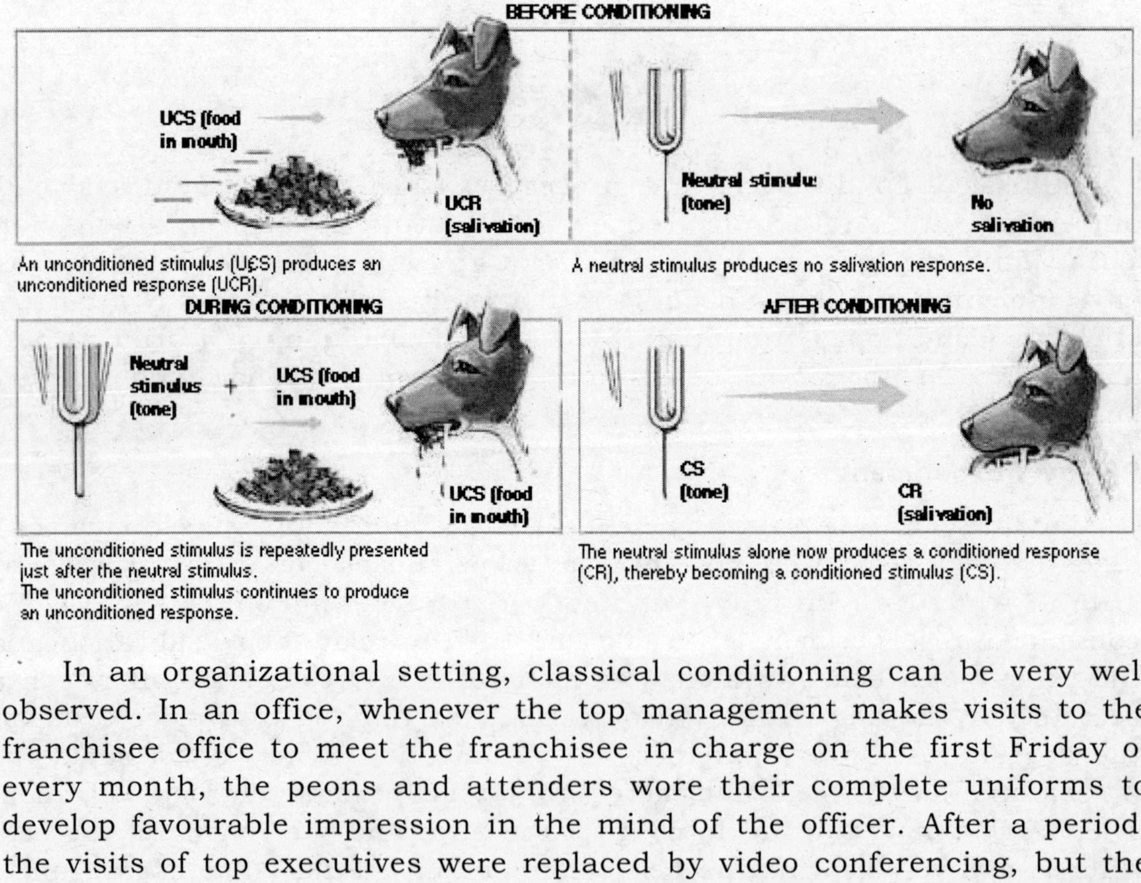

In an organizational setting, classical conditioning can be very well observed. In an office, whenever the top management makes visits to the franchisee office to meet the franchisee in charge on the first Friday of every month, the peons and attenders wore their complete uniforms to develop favourable impression in the mind of the officer. After a period, the visits of top executives were replaced by video conferencing, but the attenders continued wearing the full uniforms on all first Fridays of the month.

Classical conditioning is passive. It is more of a reflex action which is elicited in response to a specific event. But most of the time, in an organization, individual behaviours are not always reflexive. It is emitted, not elicited. It is more voluntary in nature. Employee behavior in organization has better connect with operant conditioning.

Practical application of classical conditioning:

A good example of a practical application of this learning theory is often found in training pilots in adjusting altitudes while flying a plane. During the training period, a warning system is used to alert the pilot if the plane drops below the critical altitude level. Whenever the level drops, the warning light blinks. Over a period in time, the pilot learns to adjust the altitude whenever the light blinks, even without the help of the trainer.

Criticism of this theory

- It considers learner the learner as a passive element
- It presents a tiny part of complete human learning.
- Skinner, another psychologist felt that more complex behaviors cannot be understood by classical conditioning alone as human behavior also operates on the surrounding.

B) Operant conditioning/ Reinforcement conditioning/ Instrumental conditioning. (B.F. Skinner)

This is a modified behavior theory by B.F. Skinner. Unlike in case of classical conditioning, in which the response to stimuli is entirely external, operant conditioning also takes into cognizance of the internal aspect of the organism.

According to Stephen P. Robbins, Operant conditioning is a type of conditioning in which desired voluntary behavior leads to a reward or prevents a punishment. Operant Conditioning refers to process in which our behavior produces certain consequences and our future behavior is dependent on those consequences (Learning through rewards and punishment). Some of the consequences are positive and the behavior is repeated and learned. Behaviour which brings negative consequences are suppressed. Strengthening the behavior is termed as *reinforcement* and suppressing the behavior is called *punishment*.

Skinner demonstrated his theory by conducting an experiment using a rat in a box known as "Skinner box". A rat was put in the cage and was allowed to move around freely. Accidentally when the rat pressed a lever inside the box, a food pellet was released. Every time the rat pressed the lever, food pellet was released. This reinforced the learning in rat that if it is hungry, it can press the lever (action) and food pellet (reward) will be given to it. If the reward is withheld repeatedly, the learned behavior extinguishes itself.

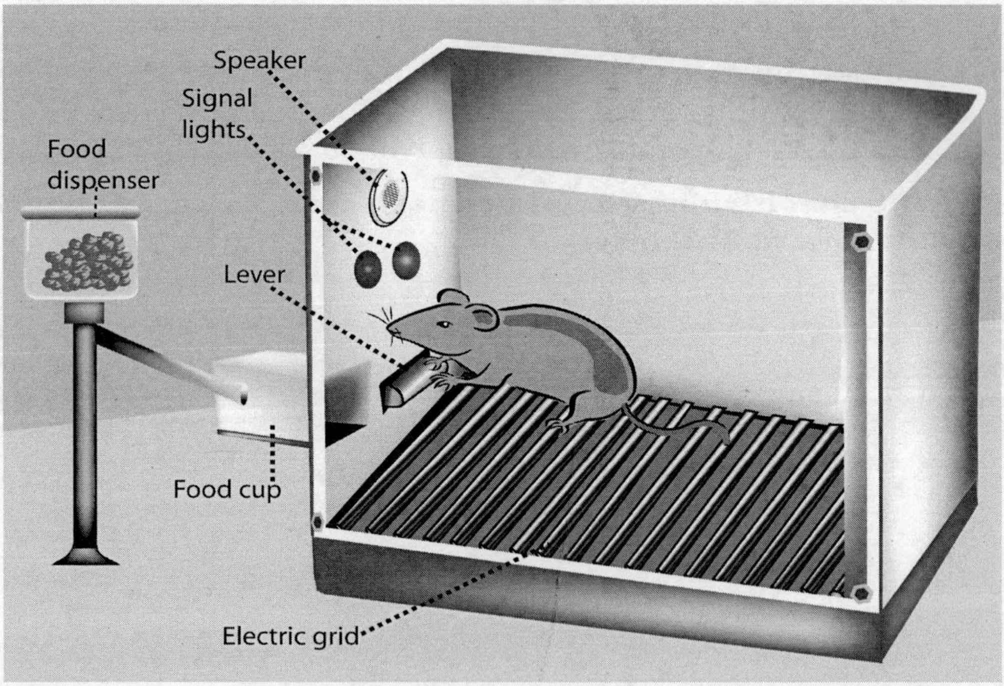

We are more likely to repeat behaviors in which we have had pleasant experiences. For example - A student might prefer doing a combined study if his results in exams are good after doing combined studies, and vice versa . We are less likely to repeat behaviors, if our experiences were not pleasant for example - If a student has not scored well because of combined studies he is less likely to have combine studies and will prefer individual Studies.

We can find examples of operant conditioning at work all around us. Consider the case of children completing homework to earn a reward from a parent or teacher, or employees finishing projects to receive praise or promotions.

Therefore, researchers call this theory as operant because it operates on the environment and it also has much greater impact on human learning.

Operant conditioning in an organizational setting:

Most of the employee behaviours can be attributed to operant conditioning. For example, if the administration staff of an organization is made to work over time during a busy season of business, with a promise that overtime will be rewarded, the staff will immediately follow the instruction. But if they are not compensated for their additional work, chances are that the employees will find excuses for not staying overtime during the next peak business season. Another example of operant conditioning is the college principal announcing attendance bonus on college sports day to ensure improved attendance of staff members.

Practical application of operant conditioning theory:

1. Helpful in good habit formation
2. Helps in breaking bad habits.
3. Effective innovation in the teaching learning process like programmed instruction , which is based on reinforcement

C) Cognitive theory of learning

Cognition ("Cognoscrere") in Latin means to know or to perceive. In cognitive approach, learning is considered as the inner psychological functioning of the learner, like perception, attention, memory etc. In this theory, teaching is considered to be a process of developing an understanding or insight in the learner. Cognitive theory refers to a process where an individual learns the meaning of various objects, events and learned responses based on the meaning assigned to stimuli. Learners are conscious about how they learn. The learner first perceives the stimuli/ problem in totality finds the relationship between the elements of stimuli or problem and comes up with a strategy to solve the problem. Learning is the "change" in cognitive structure. Cognitive learning theory emphasizes on transfer of knowledge from someone who knows (expert) to a person who does not know (learner). As per this theory, learning is a process of connecting different pieces knowledge to something more meaningful and memorable.

How does cognitive learning happen?

First, people use past learning from experiences and act upon present one (for example an employee having a bad past experience in his previous job as he worked as a call center executive thinks twice before taking up any other call center related job)

Second, people make choices about their behavior (For example, same employee taking up other job)

Third, people recognize the consequences of their choices (For example, the same employee thinks of his performance in the other job as a marketing executive)

Finally people evaluate those consequences and add them to prior learning, which affects future choices (Finally, the same employee decides to take up the marketing job after learning from his past experience as a call center executive)

Positives of this theory

1) It is relevant in modern managerial routines.
2) Most motivation theories center around the concept of cognition- Expectations, attributions, locus of control, all of these are cognitive concepts requiring attention while motivating employees.

D) Social learning theory (Observational learning)- (Bandura)

Social learning theory explains how individuals learn via observation and experience. Social learning theory talks about the capability of an individual to learn by watching people, who are generally termed as models.

The individual imitates those models whose behavior leads to a successful outcome. The important models for individuals are their parents, peer group, teachers, superiors in the workplace, movie and TV artists and others. Social learning emphasizes on cognitive, behavioural and environmental determinants of behavior. Social learning theory is an extension of operant conditioning.

Bobo doll experiment by Albert Bandura in 1961 and 1963

In connection to social learning theory, Bandura conducted a Bobo doll experiment to study patterns of behavior connected to aggression. He divided 72 children in 3 groups of 24. Group 1 had an adult who showed aggression by hitting the bobo doll hard, pinching it and other violent behaviours. Group 2 children were allowed to play with other interesting toys for 2 minutes and were taken out of room and this was to build up the frustration of children. Group 3 children were not exposed to any aggressive or non-aggressive adult and were kept as control group.

Bandura came to the conclusion that children who were unprotected from the aggressive model acted physically and verbally aggressive much more than the children who were guarded from the aggressive model.

The experimenters found that children watching adult behavior were inclined to think that this kind of behavior was correct, thus reducing the child's aggressive inhibitions. Due to this reduced aggressive inhibitions in children, they tend to act aggressively in future situations.

Bobo doll experiment

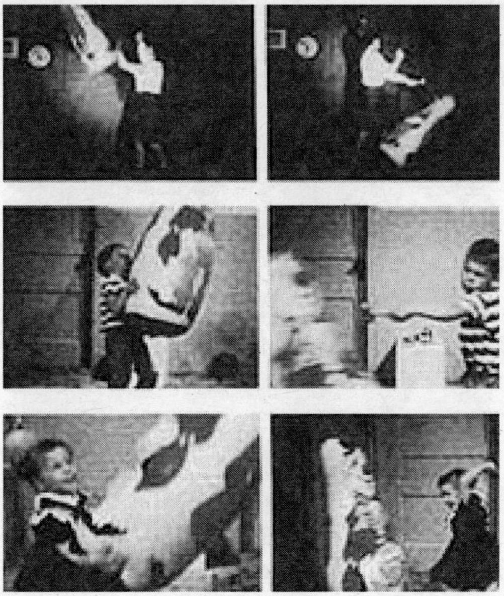

Source : Bobo Doll Experiment - Simply Psychology.

An individual achieves knowledge by watching carefully as to what happens to their model. This is popularly known as Vicarious Learning. A learner learns tactics, knowledge and skills through vicarious Learning.

Process of observational learning

ATTENTION-extent to which one focuses on others actions

RETENTION-extent to which one remembers others actions

PRODUCTION PROCESS- Our ability to act on the memory representations.

REINFORCEMENT PROCESS- The extent to which one repeats the above behaviours

Importance of Observational learning in Organizations:

1) This learning method can be used for cross cultural training of expatriates by showing them the proposed foreign destinations video, work set up, other cultural aspects etc.

2) Employee always acquires Job skills by observing successful peers to be the best performer and gain recognition.

3) This kind of learning can happen informally and in a much unarticulated manner. Ex :As a student you might not go up to a student to ask him his or ways of learning but eventually you start imitating their ways and put them into practice if your results turn out to be good after imitating a top student in class.

People with High Sense of Self-Efficacy	People with Low Sense of Self-Efficacy
Take up tough problems as tasks to be mastered.	Avoid challenging tasks.
Cultivate profound interest in the activities in which they take part.	Stuck with the mindset that the task at hand is too difficult to be dealt with.
Enthusiastic and committed to the task at hand.	Dig their own grave by only focusing on negative results and personal failures.
Recover quickly from setbacks and disappointments.	Quickly lose confidence in personal abilities

Critiques of this theory-

- According to Worthman and Loftus (1992), Bandura's study was immoral and shameful as the subjects were forced to react in an aggressive manner. Hence, they were trained to be aggressive.
- In addition to the previous point, biological minds put forth the fact that the social learning theory has put the individual's biological state in the dark by being oblivious to the distinctiveness of an individual's DNA, brain development, and learning differences.

Principles of learning

Principles of learning are deduced from learning theories. It is important to learn principles of learning because it is useful for managers to impart skills and knowledge to employees and to also to adopt methods which can make employees learn better. It's a part of motivation to check what works and what does not work for employees to perform.

1) **Principle of effect:** According to this law, when a modifiable connect between stimuli and response is made and it is followed by a satisfying outcome, the strength of the link between stimuli and response increases. It in other words is the concept of motivation. Motivation is basic and without motivation learning becomes meaningless. Ex: A student should have a basic motive behind attending college to reach the goal of getting good marks and getting a good job for his learning to be more effective.
2) **Law of intensity:** This is connected to the previous law. This law states that, higher is the intensity of satisfying outcome/ reward, greater is the learning. Greater the reward, faster and surer is the learning. Also, shorter the time gap between expected response and reward, stronger is the learning.
3) **Law of practice:** If the things being learnt are repeated time and again, it gains permanence in the learners' memory. Making students to write imposition to write the answer many times is based on this principle. It goes with the adage that "Practice makes man perfect"
4) **Law of readiness:** The learner should have the willingness to learn and only then will the learning be effective. The student should have the felt need to learn, only then will he learn.
5) **Law of Reinforcement:** The effort to cultivate or strengthen desirable behavior. For example, appreciation could increase a

student's performance in college. Reinforcement can be Positive or Negative.

Positive Reinforcement: The process by which people learn to perform acts that lead to desirable outcome is known as positive reinforcement. For example, in organizations employee usually find it pleasant and desirable to receive monetary bonuses, paid vacations and various forms of recognition.

Negative Reinforcement: The process by which people learn to perform acts that lead to avoidance of undesirable consequences is known as negative reinforcement. For example, an employee will definitely want to avoid unpleasant events such as probation, termination, rejection etc at workplace.

Punishment and extinction:

Punishment: The effort to eradicate or remove undesirable behavior either by applying a negative or positive consequence. For example, if an employee has been irregular to his work place, he might have to face the brunt of a salary cut (punishment). If an employee has exceeded his leaves at workplace there will be a reduction in pay of the particular day he missed.

Extinction: It is the situation where unconditioned stimulus and conditioned stimulus are no longer paired and therefore the strength and frequency of learned behavior diminishes. The process where the reward is withheld for a long time after the behavior has occurred and when the behavior dies out it is called extinction. Ex: A subordinate goes to a superior for some relaxation on his reporting time. Once or twice the manager obliges and employee gets the benefit, and he makes it a habit to always ask for exemption. Once the manager starts refusing such requests, he will stop going to the manager with such requests.

Schedules of reinforcement:

Reinforcement by and large has a close connect to eliciting an expected response from the employees in an organization. Psychologists have identified many contrasting schedules of reinforcement (rules governing the timing to give rewards). Managers need to be aware of the time span involved in rewarding the employees. The most effective reinforcement is just after the expected response is received.

1. **Fixed interval schedule:** are those in which the reinforcement is given to an employee at a fixed interval of time. For example: Individual receiving salary on the 10th of every month.

2. **Variable Interval Schedule:** are those in which a variable amount of time has to pass between the administrations of reinforcement. For Example: Your first promotion comes after 3 years, second promotion comes after 7 years

3. **Fixed Ratio Schedule:** are those in which reinforcement is administered the first time the desired behavior occurs after a specified number of such actions have been performed. For example: A piece rate incentive system is a fixed ratio schedule. Network marketing- suppose, members of sales staff know that they will receive a bonus for each $1000 worth of goods that they sell. Immediately after receiving the bonus their performance will slack. But as their sales begin to approach $2000 in the next level at which reward is expected, performance will once again improve.

4. **Variable Ratio Schedule:** are those in which a variable number of desired responses must elapse between the administrations of reinforcements. For Example: Slot machine gamblers can never tell which pull of the handle will win the jackpot and they are likely to keep on playing for a long time. Another example is that of sale persons working on commission basis. Sometimes the sales person makes a sale after entertaining two customers, but sometimes to make a sale the sales person will have to deal with 20 prospective customers.

The first two relate to the time taken to perform or to complete the task and the last to relate to the number and targets achieved by the employees. The performance is at the highest and remains consistent in variable interval schedule and variable ratio schedule as the employee is anticipating reinforcement for his performance/behavior.

Learning Curves: A learning curve is a diagrammatic portrayal of the amount learned in relation to time. The learning curve shows the amount learnt on the Y axis and on the passage of time on the X axis.

Certain attributes are the same on all learning curves. One of them is the initial spurt. In the beginning, the rate of learning shows a spurt. In the beginning of the learning process, the subject is well motivated and shows a massive surge of effort.

Another feature of the learning curve is the learning plateau. At some point of time in the learning process, there is a leveling in the levels of improvement, a plateau. The process of learning is marked by breaks and involves rising from one plateau to another.

Escalating from one plateau to another is called organization of learning. Organization of learning is acquired when the learner finds a new and more effective way of completing particular tasks.

Disorganization of learning is a step down in performance. This happens when the subject is torn between two or more alternative methods of tackling a task.

The last attribute of the learning curve is the end spurt. The end spurt is comes before by fatigue which sets in with time. When the training session draws nearer to an end, and the subject becomes aware of this, there occurs a revival in interest and an effort to learn more.

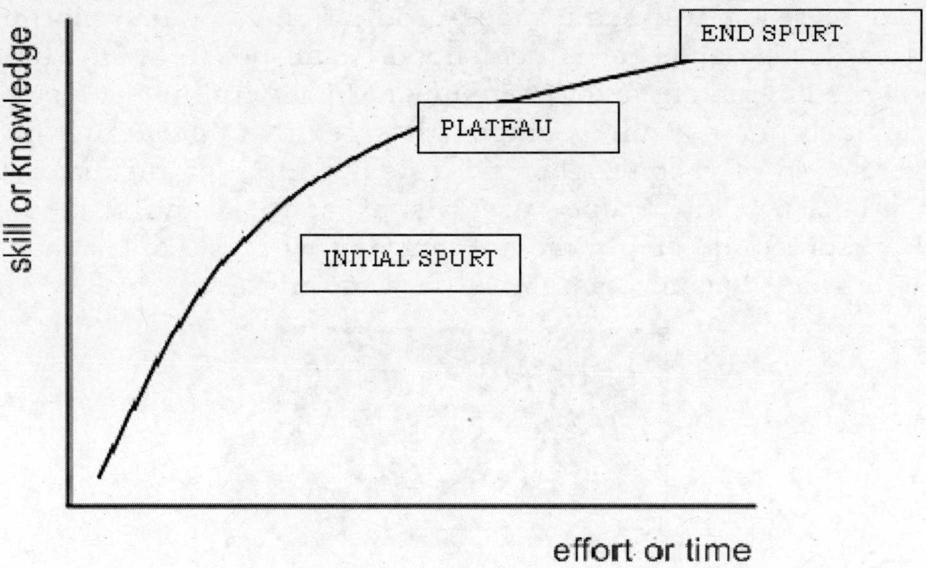

Image: Learning Curve

Application of learning to organizational psychology

1. Employees Discipline
2. Reduced Absenteeism
3. Developing Training Programmmes
4. Creating Mentoring programmes
5. Self-Management

Toyota uses social learning theory in professional excellence in training

Toyota established the Global Production Center in July 2003 to efficiently train large numbers of shop-floor experts to support an increasing number of production sites worldwide. Key to this effort is the wholesale conversion of implicit knowledge into explicit "standardized knowledge," using digital technology to create visual training materials.

The GPC "best skill training area" is 8,000m^2. Here, up to 130 trainees hone their skills on approximately 400 specially developed work tables and pieces of simulation equipment. In practicing "element work," trainees gain the ability to perform each task within a standardized timeframe, which is essential to maintaining tact time* to keep an assembly line flowing smoothly. In the global pilot production area, workers from overseas plants can practice assembling the new model so they will be optimally prepared to instruct their teams back home. This cuts preparation time to a fraction of the up to 1-year period previously needed to reach full-scale mass-production for same-platform model changes. It also aims to reduce support man-hours by one half, thereby easing the burden on factories in Japan. Image training is also important, particularly for assembly stages that require operations outside the worker's field of vision — behind a door panel, for instance. To rapidly gain proficiency, the trainee uses visual manuals and off-line or "static" skill practice to develop a mental image of what his or her hands will be doing during "dynamic" assembly on a moving line.

Beginning about a decade ago, Toyota has applied its digital engineering technology, known as V-comm, to help enable nearly simultaneous model changes at widely dispersed plants around the world. Now, GPC is augmenting this capability to reduce preparation time and minimize the need to send personnel to overseas sites to supervise training for new-model assembly.

GPC offers not only a dedicated V-comm room, but also offices for project preparation and a global pilot production area.

Source: The Official Website of Toyota Motor Manufacturing, Kentucky

Memory

Memory is the act or an instance of remembering or recollecting. The term Memory is very important if learning has to take place. It places a wider role in individuals' capacity to store any kind of information and put it into execution of any task.

Definitions of memory:

1. "Memory is the process of maintaining information over time" (Martin 2005)
2. "Memory is the general ability, or faculty that enables us to interpret the perceptual world to help organise responses to changes that take place in the world". (Eliasmith 2001)
3. Memory is the means by which we draw our past experience in order to use this information in the present (Sternberg, 1999)

Memory is the cognitive system for storing and retrieving information. Memory has 3 main stages Viz *Memory encoding, Storage/ Retention and Retrieval*

1. Memory encoding :

Sensory receptors receive the input and this needs to be converted in to a form that the system can understand. The information is changed or encoded in 3 different ways.

a) **Visual (Picture form):** Visual coding happens when the learner visualizes or sees the information. Examples: maps, paintings, pictures. Ex: Identifying a concept in the text book as the last paragraph in the page.

b) **Acoustic/ (Sound form):** The learner encodes the input from the sensory stimuli in the form of sound. Ex: An individual repeats the words/ numbers in a list to encode it.

c) **Semantic (Meaning):** Some one remembers an item /concept by understanding the meaning of it. This is done by transforming sounds or visual images into recognizable words Ex: Red traffic light means to stop.

2. Memory storage: This concerns the kind of memory storage. The place of storage of information, the duration of storage, how much can be stored at any time and what kind of info can be stored.

There are two kinds of Memory:

A) Short Term Memory - Also called "working memory" because it is what is being currently processed, it can hold what is said in 1.5-2 seconds and lasts for 15-20 seconds and then is forgotten. Items in short term memory(STM) are not fully processed as in the Long Term Memory (LTM). Adults can retain around 7 items in their STM. The coding system used in STM is *Acoustic* i.e.; repeating and rehearsing. For example if a phone number you hear is repeated many times, you are activating your short time memory. Information which is in STM form is forgotten easily. With new stimulus input, the earlier information gets erased in STM. The storing capacity of STM can be improved marginally by "Chunking", where the information is combined together.

B) Long Term memory - A system for permanently storing, managing, and retrieving information for later use. Items of information stored as long-term memory may be available for a lifetime. The coding system used in LTM is *Semantic.* This means to say that if a concept is clearly understood by the learner, it has long term memory impact. The information stored in LTM can be stored for a life time. The Storage capacity of LTM is not known. It could be months or years.

Encoding in the LTM: how we store information to remember it later.

In Long term memory there are three filing cabinets to store memories

Semantic— Semantic memory contains meaning of words and concepts. It stores general facts and information (learned items) Eg: 2+2=4, the earth is round, capital of India is New Delhi etc

Episodic— This contains personal experiences of LTM. We remember our past through episodic memory. It stores specific information with personal meaning (personal experiences) Eg-Accidents, surprises, achievements, awards etc

Implicit— It contains information you never intended to remember (random facts, "stupid stuff you know") Eg- While attempting a marketing paper you wouldn't have thought about a brand name to write as an example but you write it because the name just pops up in mind without you intending to think of that brand name while studying. Another example is, whenever you stand waiting for bus in a particular bus station, you may be nervous, without knowing why you are nervous. This is connected to your sub conscious mind.

Ways of Encoding in the LTM:

a. By meaning: remember overall meaning but not small details (Example—after a long story you remember the main point or moral)

b. Non-verbal: coded in non-verbal images—like smells, tastes, sounds (Examples— a familiar voice on the phone, the smell of a rose, the shape of Florida)

c. Verbatim—word for word memories—mostly very familiar things. (Example—the Pledge)

3. Memory Retrieval:

This means getting information out of storage. If we are not able to remember something, it is due to poor retrieval. STM is stored and retrieved sequentially, where as LTM is stored and retrieved by association.

Memory process

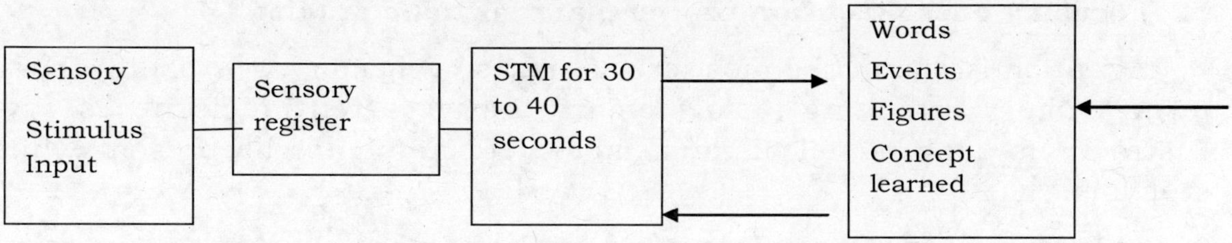

A memory process starts with the external stimuli being received by the sensory organs. The sensation received through sensory stimuli is held for few seconds in certain sensory receptors. Information is passed through the sensory register to short term memory. In short term memory, information is held for 30 to 40 seconds. Some part of the information stored in STM is processed as a rehearsal buffer. Rehearsal is repeating items of information silently or aloud. This is an active process of transferring materials from STM to LTM. The more an item is rehearsed, the more are the chances of it to be stored in LTM. From here, the information is passed on to LTM, where it is categorized and stored for years. If a piece of information is not processed in this manner, it is forgotten. Retrieval involves getting the required information whenever it is wanted.

Forgetting – It is the failure of memory. It means to cease or fail to remember; be unable to recall. Forgetting can happen due to a variety of reasons. Some of the theories of forgetting are as follows.

Decay theory - passing of time decreases the strength of the memory, especially if not recalled for a long while. Memory traces gradually fade with the passage of time. Memory traces are like the negatives of a photo film. As long as the negatives are intact, the photos come out properly.

Interference theory - As per this theory forgotten memories are neither lost or damaged, but misplaced due to the proliferation of many more memories. Interference from other information causes memories to be mixed up or pushed aside. Ex: Students tend to forget the subjects learned in the 1st year when they are in the 3rd year.

Amnesia (neurological amnesia and functional amnesia) refers to difficulty in learning new information or in remembering the past. Amnesia is caused in extreme cases due to many factors such as psychological factors (Mental factors, post traumatic stress etc)

Ways to improve memory.

1. Focusing ones attention on the material to be studied.

Attention is one of the most crucial parts of memory. To solidify short-term memory into long-term memory, active attention is necessary. Distractions such as televisions, music etc must not be present while studying.

2. Don't take a big bite, unless you can chew it.

According to Bjork (2001), studying the material over scheduled session's gives you the time you need to sufficiently process the information. It is a known fact that students who study meticulously and regularly score much better than students who study a day or two before the exams.

3. Organize the information into simpler formats while studying.

Group similar concepts, key words and terms together. Format your notes in such a way they are easily readable.

4. Make use of mnemonic devices to easily register information.

Mnemonic devices strengthen recollection powers of students. A mnemonic is used to easily remember information. The best example would be to associate a term that needs to be remembered with an item that is very familiar. Useful mnemonics are those that are used for positive imagery, humor or novelty. Coming up with a rhyme, a joke or a song helps in remembering a certain segments of information.

5. Practice reciting the information studied.

Encoding what you study into long-term memory helps in recalling information. Elaborative rehearsal is the best encoding technique known to mankind. The best example of this technique: reading the definition of a key term, studying the definition of that term and then reading a more detailed description of what that term means. The ability to recall information will reach unprecedented levels after repetition of the above exercise.

6. Connect the given information to things already in the brain.

Relating new information with things you already know helps in recalling the information during the time of requirement. By connecting new ideas and earlier memories, you can exponentially increase the chances of remembering recently learned information.

7. Make pictures of the concepts to improve memory and recall.

Visualizing the concepts greatly enhances the recalling power. Charts, photos, poster etc in textbooks help the student understand the concept better by helping them visualize. Pictures should be created when visual pictures are not provided and will help in a better understanding of the concept. Make figures, graphs or charts in your notes which are related to your study.

8. Explaining the concept to another person.

Orating the material loudly considerably improves the memory. It is a known fact that a student, who teaches the concept has a better understanding of the concept, hence improves memory. You are advised to use this approach in your own studies by teaching different concepts and information to a friend or study partner.

CLOSING CASE

Smarter than ever?

Adapted from Monitor on psychology, American psychological association, March 2013, Vol 44, No. 3

Over the past century, the average IQ in industrialized countries has risen to keep pace with the complexity of modern life. IQ researcher James Flynn discusses why those gains have occurred psychological assocu

Over the past 100 years, Americans' mean IQ has been on a slow but steady climb. Between 1900 and 2012, it rose nearly 30 points, which means that the average person of 2012 had a higher IQ than 95 percent of the population had in 1900.

Political scientist James Flynn, PhD, of the University of Otago in New Zealand, first discovered those astonishing IQ gains nearly 30 years ago. Since then, the steady rise in IQ scores in the United States and throughout the developed world has been dubbed the "Flynn effect."

What has caused these changes?

The three things that stand out are: first, formal schooling. That clearly has to be involved in the huge gains in vocabulary and general information we see in America since 1950 — vocabulary subtests of the IQ tests have risen by 17 points over those 50 years. If you project that back to 1900, a period for which we don't have adequate data, that would be 34 points, or two standard deviations. So that's a lot of vocabulary. It means that people today on average know enough vocabulary to mimic the speech of only the cultural elite of 1900.

The second factor is what Alexander Luria discovered when he tested rural Russian peasants in the 1930s. He discovered that pre-scientific people can't take the hypothetical seriously. That is, if you pose to them questions like, "There is snow at the North Pole; where there is snow, bears are white; what color are bears at the North Pole?" they would say, "Well, I've only seen brown bears. And only if a person came from the North Pole with testimony would I believe that the bears there are white."

They were addicted to the concrete world, not the world of hypotheticals. And that of course has a big impact on a whole range of tests. If you look at Raven's, where the gains have been so huge, the test consists of all hypothetical questions about symbols that are well removed from concrete reality.

Luria also asked his subjects about classification, such as, "What do dogs and rabbits have in common?" In 1900, a person would say, "You use dogs to hunt rabbits." Today you say, "They're both mammals." And that gets the question right.

In the past, people's minds were utilitarian. They weren't interested in hypotheticals or in classifying things together. But today people have "donned scientific spectacles," they have scientific habits of mind.

In 2000, the Supreme Court decided that it was cruel and unusual punishment under the U.S. Constitution to execute someone who was lacking moral competence, and that one of the standards for doing this was low IQ scores on Wechsler and Stanford Binet and other tests. And I thought, well look here, there are going to be people on death row who took a test that was 10 or 20 years out of date, and whose IQs have been inflated by three or six or nine points.

Let's say there's a guy on death row, and at school he was tested on the old WISC, which was normed back in 1947 and 1948. If he was tested in 1972, just before the new test came out, then the test would inflate his IQ by seven points. And a person who normally had an IQ of 68 would have 75, and would now be eligible for execution. So I've been very active in trying to educate the judicial community.

Initially, it was very tough going. People had the notion that an IQ score was fixed. It just told you what the person's IQ was — they don't realize that it's a relative score and that sometimes people are being compared with the previous generation.

Finally, there's the wealth of visual images in the modern world. I think that is responsible for improvements in mapping skills and improvements in looking at three-dimensional figures and how they rotate.

Questions:

1. Do you think Flynn effect is applicable to Indian population as well? Why? Why not?
2. According to you which other factors could cause Flynn effect?
3. What are the social advantages and dis advantages of Flynn effect in India?

Test your knowledge:

Multiple choice questions:

1. Permanent change in behavior happens as a result of
   a. Learning
   b. Perception
   c. Personality
   d. Groupthink.
2. Operant conditioning focuses on
   a. Psychological learning
   b. Rewards and punishments
   c. Extinction
   d. Discipline
   e. None of the above.
3. Classical conditioning is also known as
   a. Cognitive learning
   b. Respondent conditioning
   c. Operant conditioning
   d. Action Learning
   e. None of the above.

4. Which among the following is correct about stimulus-response conditioning?
   a. It is Learned
   b. It is Perceived
   c. It is Acquired
   d. It is Reinforced
5. Which of the following involves punishment & reinforcement?
   a. Social learning
   b. Cognitive learning
   c. Classical learning
   d. Operant learning
   e. Administered Learning.
6. In Classical Behaviorism, association of which of the following is true?
   a. Stimulus and Response
   b. Response and Stimulus
   c. Modeling
   d. Self-efficiency
   e. Stimulus and Stimulus.
7. Classical conditioning was the outcome of:
   a. Thorndikle's experiment
   b. Bandura's experiment
   c. Pavlov's experiment
   d. Bartlett's experiment
8. Getting birthday gifts is an example of which reinforcement schedule
   a. Variable ratio
   b. Fixed ratio
   c. Variable interval
   d. Fixed interval

MODEL QUESTIONS

Section–A

(Each question carries 2 marks)

1. What is meant by cognitive theory?
2. Define Memory.
3. What is the difference between forgetting and amnesia?
4. What is difference between negative reinforcement and punishment?
5. Define learning and learner.

Section–B

(Each question carries 5 marks)

1. What are various forms of classical conditioning?
2. What is meant by reinforcement? What are the various strategies of reinforcement?
3. Is punishment necessary evil? Explain with suitable example.
4. What strategies can be employed under operant conditioning to modify the behavior of subordinates? Discuss with the help of suitable examples.
5. Define the term learning. What is its impact on employee behaviours?
6. Explain the difference between STM & LTM.

Section–C

(Each question carries 15 marks)

1. Define learning? What are its various distinguishing features?
2. Explain the theories of personality.
3. What are the key characteristics of observation learning? Why is it considered as social learning?
4. What is operant conditioning? How is it different from classical conditioning?
5. Describe various principles of learning in details.
6. Name four different schedules of reinforcement. Describe how each may be used in organization.
7. Explain the techniques for improving memory.

REFERENCE

1. Stephen. P Robbins, Timothy A. Judge & Seema Sanghi, Organisation Behaviour, 13 th edition, ISBN: 978 81 317 2121 6 , Dorling Kindersley, Pearson education, 2009, pp 57 to 67.
2. McLeod, S. A. (2011). *Bobo Doll Experiment - Simply Psychology.* Retrieved from http://www.simplypsychology.org/bobo-doll.html.

FIGURE SOURCES

https://encrypted-tbn3.gstatic.com/images?q=tbn:ANd9GcTjvgjz_ip0FJDCeQu9BRedLh-mPbJAzAOVjMWsJaIozkGmsQz1_Q

http://courses.washington.edu/psii101/images/pavlo_dog.jpg

https://encrypted-tbn1.gstatic.com/images?q=tbn:ANd9GcSrH6djT1XuueqEYqyDAzMXghtUnbXxxlZr8IlErYx-SgIcyN25

https://encrypted-tbn2.gstatic.com/images?q=tbn:ANd9GcSD5Dwapu8yKS03ORZHKNdRAhX_BNTQKZTsyO1kuTn_In6N66nf

http://www.simplypsychology.org/bobo-doll.jpg

http://cwabacon.pearsoned.com/bookbind/pubbooks/gradeaid_ab/chapter5/medialib/FIG5_14.JPG

◈◈◈◈

Read More on the Web

Every day is filled with new experiences that we go through, and that influences what, and the way we learn. Learning is a complicated process. The most interesting link it has here is to sleep and to dreaming. No one knows all the purposes of sleeping and dreaming, although lack of sleep can be lethal. Sleep-deprived rats do okay for a week or two, and then their appetites increase dramatically. Even when they get all they want to eat, their weights decrease, their body temperatures become unstable, and then they die. Humans who are sleep deprived behave abnormally and hallucinate. Coming back, napping after learning something new could help you commit it to memory - as long as you dream, scientists say. They found people who dream about a new task perform it better on waking than those who do not sleep or do not dream. Dreams, therefore, may be an indication that your brain is working on a problem on many levels, and it may portray the brain's effort to keep learning, even as we sleep.

Dreaming could also be the way of the mind, more the subconscious, telling us that we might've missed something. It aids us in problem solving. In a study, Boston, 99 volunteers were trained for an hour to make their way through a complex virtual three dimensional puzzle as quickly as possible. Then, half of them were allowed to sleep for about an hour. The other half stayed awake, reading or relaxing.

During the resting period, the subjects were interrupted or awakened and asked to describe their thoughts or dreams. After the resting period, the participants were asked to again tackle the maze. Those who hadn't napped showed no improvement or did even worse after the break. Nappers who were rested but didn't report any maze-related dreams did better but showed only marginal improvement. However, four nappers who reported dreaming about the maze showed a startling improvement, cutting their completion time in half. The difference in scores before and after sleeping was 10 times higher for the maze dreamers than those who hadn't dreamed about the task, according to the findings. Notably, the dreamers had all performed poorly on the test prior to dreaming about it.

Sleeping essentially lets the chaos of life sink in so that we can make some sense of it. It gives the mind a break where it isn't constantly under the onslaught of new information; because we can't process something if were simultaneously taking in something else. Getting yourself to dream about something is difficult; but once it is achieved, you're at an advantage. Dreaming is terribly hard to control. The sleeping brain has its own set of rules, which is why our dreams are so difficult to understand and interpret. The most important rule the sleeping mind has here is that it focuses on what it deems to be the most important. It is difficult, but with practice, you can make your mind dream about what you want it to dream about. The trick here is convincing your brain that that particular event or bit of information is very important and takes precedence over other inputs. One way to do this is to constantly think about the same and focus on it; and before you sleep, still your mind allow it to wander- but around the same topic.

Dreams answer two questions.

- "What do I care about?" and
- "Why do I care?"

It does take a roundabout route to try to tell us what the scene is exactly. Dream analysis is a constantly evolving science and is difficult to apply given the number of variables it operates with. For a simple example, the simple act of lock picking in a dream could signify the need for approval from someone. A tunnel could signify death (in the dream) or even a trying circumstance.

The brain makes associations between new and old information and past experiences. Learning in one area is taken and applied to another area. Freud also hypothesized that dreams provide gratification for suppressed desires, and allow repressed emotions and experiences to express themselves. So, a healthy mind brings its emotional experiences to handle the stress of the day and forges new mechanisms to deal with the same if it recurs. Dreams however are fleeting. It is highly unlikely that one will remember exactly what one dreamt of, simply because the conscious mind immediately takes precedence over the subconscious as soon as one wakes up. So, the theory of lucid dreaming was formulated.

To understand Lucid Dreaming, we need to first understand how a dream works. We dream mostly in the Rapid Eye Movement (REM) phase of our sleep, when brain activity is high and resembles that of being awake. Now, the body paralyzes itself to prevent harm, because, as studies have shown, when one moves certain centers of the brain are activated; similarly, when one is thinking of moving (like in a dream), the same centers are activated, which may lead to actual movement. Anyway, people are more likely to remember the dream if they're awakened during the REM stage. Following that thread, a lucid dream is one in which you know you're dreaming. This typically happens when the dreamer encounters something strange, causing them to stop and question reality. They then realize that they're dreaming.

The problem here is that, in high level lucidity, one knows that they're dreaming, and are able to control what they see to an extent, but they are essentially paralyzed, bar their eyelids (which is how volunteers in studies signify, with pre arranged movements, that they are dreaming lucidly). This makes them unable to react to threatening circumstances in their mind, even though they know that they are in no danger. The inability to move sometimes causes panic. Willfully entering lucid dreaming is therefore not advisable, especially when your frame of mind isn't stable, because your mind forces you to witness all the irregularities you see in a dream (which could be violent); and many a time, we can't take it. Imagine being trapped in your body with no way to control anything physically but with your mind. But once control is learnt, it is possible to use it as a therapeutic tool- to fight nightmares, and counter certain things that are bothering you.

Sources and References

http://subliminalmanipulation.blogspot.in/2010/09/heres-fun-test-to-check-how-perceptive.html

http://news.harvard.edu/gazette/1996/02.08/ResearchLinksSl.html (the link between sleep, dreaming and learning)

http://news.bbc.co.uk/2/hi/8638551.stm

http://well.blogs.nytimes.com/2010/04/22/learning-while-you-dream/?_r=0

http://www.livescience.com/9874-naps-dreams-boost-learning-study-finds.html

http://www.susanblackmore.co.uk/Articles/si91ld.html

http://en.wikipedia.org/wiki/Dream (for extra reading)

http://science.howstuffworks.com/life/inside-the-mind/human-brain/lucid-dreaming.htm

CHAPTER 5

WORK RELATED ATTITUDE & MOTIVATION

Learning Objectives of the Chapter

- Meaning
- Components and nature of attitude
- Factors influencing the formation of attitude
- The types of attitudes connected to work place
- Meaning of prejudice
- Meaning, concepts, applications and theories of motivation

OPENING CASE

ALBERTSONS WORKS ON EMPLOYEE ATTITUDES

Albertsons is a huge grocery and drug company. It has more than 2,400 supermarkets and its Osco and Savon brands make it the fifth-largest drugstore company in the United States. In a typical year, shoppers will make 1.4 billion trips through its stores.

Albertsons competes in tough businesses. Wal-Mart, in particular, has been eating away at its market share. With revenues flat and profits falling, the company hired Larry Johnston to turn the business around.

Johnston came to Albertsons from General Electric. And it was while he was at GE, that Johnston met a training specialist named Ed Foreman. Foreman endeared himself to Johnston when the latter hired Foreman to help him with a serious problem. At the time, Johnston had been sent to Paris to fix GE Medical Systems' European division. The division made CT scanners. Over the previous decade, four executives had been brought in to turn the division around and try to make it profitable. All had failed. Johnston responded to the challenge by initiating some important changes—he made a number of acquisitions, he closed down inefficient plants, and he moved factories to Eastern European countries to take advantage of lower labor costs. Then he brought in Ed Foreman to charge up the troops. "After we got Ed in," says Johnston, "people began to live their lives differently. They came to work with a spring in their step." In 3 years, the division was bringing in annual profits of $100 million. Johnston gives a large part of the credit for this turnaround to Foreman.

What is Foreman's secret? He provides motivation and attitude training. Here's an example of Foreman's primary program—called the Successful Life Course. It lasts 3 days and begins each morning at 6 a.m. The first day begins with a chapter from an inspirational handout, followed by 12 minutes of yoga-like stretching. Then participants marched up a hill, chanting, "I know I can, I know I can." This is followed by breakfast and then a variety of lectures on attitude, diet, and exercise. But the primary focus of the program is on attitude. Says Foreman, "It's your attitude, not your aptitude that determines your altitude." Other parts of the program include group hugs, team activities, and mind-control relaxation exercises.

Johnston believes strongly in Foreman's program. "Positive attitude is the single biggest thing that can change a business," says Johnston. He sees Foreman's program as being a critical bridge linking employees with customers: "We're in the business of the maintenance and acquisition of customers." And with so many shoppers going through his stores, Johnston says this "provides a lot of opportunities for customer service. We've got to energize the associates." To prove he's willing to put his money where his mouth is, Johnston has committed $10 million to this training. By year-end 2004, 10,000 managers had taken the course. They, in turn, are training all 190,000 Albertsons "associates", with the help of tapes and books.

Foreman claims his program works. He cites success at companies like Allstate, Milliken & Co., and Abbott Labs. "The goal is to improve mental, physical, and emotional well-being," he says. "We as individuals determine the success of our own lives. Positive thoughts create positive actions."

Questions

1. Explain the logic as to how Foreman's 3-day course could positively influence Albertson's profitability.
2. Johnston says, "Positive attitude is the single biggest thing that can change a business." How valid and generalizable do you think this statement is?
3. If you were Johnston, what could you do to evaluate the effectiveness of your $10-million investment in Foreman's training program?
4. If you were an Albertsons' employee, how would you feel about going through Foreman's course? Explain your position.

Source: *Based on M. Burke, "The Guru in the Vegetable Bin," Forbes, March 3, 2003, pp. 56–58.*

http://www.forbes.com/forbes/2003/0303/056.html

Introduction:

The study of attitude has always been an active area of research in social psychology. Attitude has application in varied areas of study like perception, learning, motivation, interpersonal skills, prejudice, discrimination, conformity, compliance etc. Since attitude influence behavior, it is an integral part of organizational psychology.

What is Attitude ?

Attitude is a hypothetical construct which can be inferred only through the behavior of an individual. It is an evaluative statement, either positive or negative about objects, people or events. It mirrors how one feels about something or someone. It is not permanent and it can be developed by means of many factors.

Definition of Attitude

"Attitudes are learned predisposition to respond in a consistently favorable or unfavorable manner with respect to a given object"

- Fishbein and Ajzen (1975)

"Attitude is defined as a mental and neutral state of readiness, organised through experience, exerting a directive or dynamic influence upon the individual's response to all objects and situations with which it is related"

- Gordon Allport (1935)

"Attitude is a psychological tendency that is expressed by evaluating aparticular entity with some degree of favor or disfavor"

- Eagly and Chaiken (1993),

Different Forms of Attitude

Attitude towards self is called ***Self Esteem***

Unfavorable attitude towards a particular person or group is called ***Prejudice***

Favourable attitude towards others is called ***Interpersonal attraction***

Attitude towards one's job is called ***Job satisfaction***

Components of attitude: ABC's of attitude

Attitude reflects in the feelings, beliefs and inclination to act in a particular way. Consider this example. A student *believes* that eating almonds will improve his memory power because he has heard this from his grandmother and he feel that it is true. Hence he eats almonds everyday (*takes action*). The following three components constitute attitude.

ABC's of Attitude

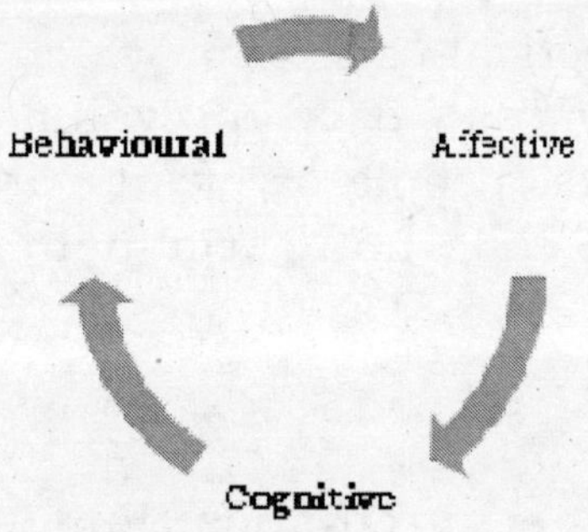

Cognitive Component (what you believe)

This refers to the beliefs, values , ideas or information about the object or situation. When you form a favourable or unfavorable opinion on the basis of information about the object, it is the cognitive component. It is the storage component where the organized information about the attitude object is stored in the form of belief, thoughts, opinions and ideas. For example, one may believe that learning psychology will help him to understand others in a better way, which will make his life easy. In reality, this may or may not be true. Cognitive component is the key to attitude formation. This sets the platform for the other two components of attitude.

Affective / Emotional component (how you feel)

This refers to the feelings and emotions evoked by a particular person, object or event. For example, the news that your office management has decided to increase the pay package by 20% will evoke a feeling of happiness among employees. Such feelings can vary in intensity. It may not evoke the same degree of happiness to all the employees. Affective component is a prominent component of attitude formation.

Behavioural component (how you are predisposed to act)

It is the tendency or predisposition to act in a particular way based on ones beliefs and feelings. This behavioural tendency may not exactly predict one's behavior. Behavioural intention may be only a verbal indication than the actual behavior. This means to say that you may verbally express your thoughts on a particular issue, but sometimes you may not take an action based on that. For example, if you think that your boss is unethical and you feel that you can't work under him, you may want to leave the job (behavioural disposition) but you may not leave the job until you get a better opportunity. (behavioural action). This is the only component in attitude which can be observed directly.

Nature of attitude

1. Attitudes are the feelings and beliefs of individuals or groups of individuals.
2. Attitudes are directed towards self, other people, objects, or ideas.
3. Attitude may lead to behaviour or action.
4. Attitudes can be of varied degrees and can be from very favourable to very unfavorable.
5. Attitudes are long enduring, though they can change.
6. All individuals, irrespective of their status or intelligence, hold an attitude.
7. There can be many number of elements in forming an attitude.

Why study Attitudes in organizational psychology?

1. Attitudes form a part of social cognition and help an organization to evaluate stimuli and categorise them as positive or negative.
2. Attitudes affect the employee behavior and they help in predicting employee behavior though an attitude does not necessarily produce the expected behavioural characteristics always.
3. Attitude helps people to express their central values and beliefs.
4. Attitudes help employees to build and maintain self-esteem.

Factors affecting formation of attitude

Individuals acquire attitude from several sources. The major classification of factors affecting attitude formation are

1. Learned attitudes
2. Attitude formed through social comparison
3. Genetic factors.

The most important sources of acquiring attitude are Social learning by means of direct experience with the object, associations, Indirect learning like vicarious learning. Social comparison in the form of family, neighbourhood, economic & social positions and mass communication also contribute to attitude formation. The latest in the category of factors contributing to formation of attitude are Genetic factors.

1) Learned attitudes

a) Direct experience with the object: Attitudes can develop from a personally rewarding or punishing experience with an object or situation . Employees form attitude about jobs from their previous experiences. For example, if any employee gets a promotion after 2 years of his stay in the company, the rest of the employees are likely to believe that they may also get a promotion after 2 years of their service. Direct experience can have different learning situations/processes. They are explained below.

b) Classical conditioning- One of the basic process underlying attitude formations can be explained on the basis of learning principles. Classical conditioning generates an affective or emotional component by pairing objects with stimuli that generate emotional responses. The same classical conditioning processes that made

Pavlov's dogs salivate at the sound of a bell can explain how positive or negative attitudes are formed on an otherwise neutral stimuli. It is natural tendency for people to develop associations between various objects and the emotional reactions that accompany them. For example, if the classes are over at 3 pm everyday, students are so conditioned to leave the class room at 3 pm and would not want to sit for any extra time. Similarly, a positive attitude can be developed towards a particular perfume because a favourite model wears it. Another good example of attitude formation in classical conditioning is one's experience in a fast food joint that caused food poisoning. Next time when the sign board of that fast food joint is seen, the person may have nauseating feeling.

c) Operant conditioning is another learning process which underlies attitude formation. Attitude that are reinforced, either verbally or non-verbally, tend to be maintained. Conversely, a person who states an attitude that elicits ridicule from others may modify or abandon the attitude. If parents of children constantly praise them for good performance in academics, that behavior is reinforced and children develop a positive attitude towards studies. Agreement or disagreement from others will form the attitude in this case.

d) Vicarious learning/observational learning can also contribute to attitude formation. In case of vicarious learning a person learns something by observing others, especially when the individual has no direct experience with the object about which the attitude is held. Through vicarious learning processes, children develop the prejudices of their parents. Children who are exposed to negative conversation between parents about a particular place will develop negative attitude about the place even without seeing the place. We learn attitude vicariously through television, films, and other media. For instance movies that glorify violence reinforce positive attitude regarding aggression.

2. Social comparisons :

a) Family and peer groups

A person couldl earn particular attitudes through imitation of his/her parents. If the parents have a positive attitude towards an object or situation and if the child admires his parents, he is likely to adapt the same attitude even without being told. An attitude towards the oppose gender, religion, tolerance or prejudice, education, occupation political parties and almost all areas where attitude is capable of expression are due to us either accepting or rejecting the attitude held by the members of our family. Attitudes are also acquired from peer groups in schools, colleges and organisations.

b) Neighbourhood

The locality we live in has a certain composition in terms of cultural facilities, religious groupings, and ethnic differences. There are chances to accept the opinions of our neighbours or deny them and possibly rebel.

c) Economic status and occupations

The economic and occupational positions of an individual also contribute to attitude formation. People from high or low economic background have chances of developing an attitude in accordance to their status. Likewise, occupation like software engineer, doctor, lawyer, and teacher may all have attitude in accordance to their job.

3. Mass Communications

Mass communications media like TV, radio, newspapers, and magazines provide large quantities of information. Mass media users use media constructively to cater to the thinking and taste of the audience. The audience selectively observes the content of the media based on what they want to observe. Messages used in mass media tries to change the attitude of people towards a certain product or service. For example, advertisement of Kent water purifier may develop a favourable cognitive and affective component . (The individual understands the advantages of drinking purified water and develops a positive feeling towards it). This will lead to a desirable buying behavior for the company (The individual purchases the water purifier). Another example is Glaxo Smith Kline (GSK) trying to change the attitude of consumers about Horlicks as a health drink to Horlicks as pleasurable nourishment by introducing vanilla, chocolate and honey flavours.

4. Genetic factors: There are some inherited general dispositions which make a person see things in a positive or negative light. For example, attitudes involving gut level preferences like preference for coffee over tea may be more influenced by genetic factors. High or low need for seeking information, Consciousness of social status etc., are also passed on genetically. Researchers assert that about 30% of employee job satisfaction can be attributed to genes.

Activity : Describe a situation where you developed an attitude on a product or service based on your exposure to the advertisement about the product or service in the media

Changing others attitude:

Attitudes of individuals can be changed in varied ways:

1. Self-perception
2. Cognitive dissonance
3. Persuasion
4. Exposure & associative learning (Classical & Operant conditioning)
5. Co-optation

1. Self-perception :

An attitude can be changed by self-perception if the attitude is initially very weak or less important for the self-concept. According to Self-perception theory by Daryl Bem(1965), when we have no (or very weak) prior existing attitude on a particular issue, we can infer our own attitude from observing our own behavior. This means to say that we attribute attitudes to ourselves from the observation of our own behavior. This attribution can be for internal or external causes. Ex : We freely express our opinion on particular issues, like inflation or ozone layer depletion.

2. Cognitive Dissonance:

Cognitive dissonance is a mental state when individuals behave in a way which contradicts their existing attitude that creates a feeling of discomfort. When people carry out an action which is incongruent to their original attitude, this knowledge creates an internal imbalance or dissonance. Ex : A pro environmentalist will feel upset if he has to use many plastic bags and he has to throw away that, littering the environment, say during a picnic. To reduce the discomfort or dissonance arising out of difference in his attitude (pro environmentalist) and his behavior (using and throwing plastic bags in jungle), he will modulate his attitude by coming to a conclusion that " it is ok to dispose the plastic bag once in a blue moon, as I don't do it on an everyday basis". Here, people may alter their attitude in order to better align them with their behavior. They may alter the behavior also, sometimes, to reduce the dissonance.

Cognitive dissonance can be used for a change in attitude of people if we have a clear opinion of the issue at hand or it is very important to us.

This cognitive dissonance is an unpleasant stage and individuals are internally motivated to resolve it. To resolve the internal disturbance, individuals will try and rationalize the behavior by using a number of cognitions and thus resolve the discrepancy. If no explanation is available, the individual will have no choice but to change the attitude so that it is incorporated in the behavior/ action they have performed. Reduction in dissonance leads to change in attitude.

3. Persuasion

It is a cognitive way of bringing a change in the attitude of an individual. While the above two form an attitudinal change via an internal discrepancy, persuasion brings an attitudinal change via external message. The core idea of persuasion is how people react to messages intended to make them change their mind. In persuasion, attitudes can be changed by a persuasive message which may take a Central (systematic route) or the Peripheral route. The central route is taken when people are motivated and pay attention to the content of a message and people are influenced by strength and quality of the arguments. When people are unwilling or unable to analyse message contentthe peripheral route is taken. In this people do not pay much attention to the content . Attention is paid to the attraction of communicator and the amount of information presented.

Persuasion can be positive as well as negative.

Negative persuasion is when fear is induced for non-compliance. It works best when quick results i.e. attitudinal change is expected. Effective forms of bringing a change in attitude when coping strategy or advice is also offered. Examples: Cigarette smoking ban or restriction, along with a coping strategy of providing information of de addictive measures. Drinking and driving penal measures are another example of negative persuasion.

Positive persuasion amounts to inducing good feelings for attitudinal change. Reward given to students for 100% attendance will generate positive persuasion for further behavioural change of attending more and more classes.

4. Co-opting

Co-opting is a very effective method of attitudinal change. Here, the employees who are dissatisfied with the situation are made to take part in things to improve the situation. For example, an employee who constantly complains about the quality of food served in the office canteen will be made a member of a committee which looks into quality of food served in the canteen. Once the employee understands the practical difficulty of the situation, it is most likely that he would change his attitude.

Types of Job related attitudes

Job related attitudes are evaluative tendencies towards aspects of work, which are based on clusters of feelings, beliefs and behavioral intentions. Individuals possess many different attitudes towards work. The main work related attitudes are: Job involvement, Job satisfaction, Organizational commitment, Employee engagement and Work motivation

a) Job involvement :

A relatively new addition to organizational psychology. One of the general definition of Job involvement is *" Job involvement measures the degree to which a person identifies himself psychologically with his job and considers his perceived performance level important to self-worth."* (G.J Blau and K. R. Boal)

Employees with high level of job involvement identifies with job in a better way. High job involvement reduces absenteeism and attrition rate. Hence the level of the involvement of the employee towards his job should be kept at high. In case of low job involvement, the reason for the same should be analyzed. The common reasons for low job involvement could be exhaustion, routine activities without any excitement and motivation, low salary etc.

b) Organizational commitment

It is the worker's feeling and attitude towards the entire organization.

Organization commitment is defined as a state in which an employee identifies with a particular organization and its goals, and wishes to maintain membership in the organization.(Blau&Boal)

The difference between job involvement and organizational commitment is that, job involvement deals with level of employee involvement with the specific job where as organizational commitment is the employees involvement with the entire organization.

It depicts the level of connection an individual has towards the organization. Employees who are less committed to the organization feels less connected to the organisation. Individuals with high levels of organizational commitment have a "we" feeling and they regard themselves as the partners of the company.

Organisations with employees of high level commitment have greater productivity. Such organizations will have lesser absenteeism and turnover. Organisational commitment is a better indicator of employee turnover than job satisfaction or job involvement, as in certain cases the employee may be happy with the job but not with the organisation.

Research work suggests that Japanese workers have a higher level of commitment than the U.S. workers.

In the current scenario, organizational commitment as a concept has taken a back seat, as the trend of job hopping is more prevalent in organizations.

c) Job satisfaction

Job satisfaction is the positive and negative feeling and attitude of an individual towards his job. It describes how happy an individual is with his/her job. A person who is highly satisfied with the job will have a positive feeling towards the job. A dissatisfied person will have negative attitude towards the job. Job satisfaction is not the same as motivation or aptitude, although all these terms are connected.

Definition

" Job satisfaction is the extent to which people like (satisfaction) or dislike (dissatisfaction) their jobs" Spector (1997) .

Job satisfaction can be intrinsic or extrinsic. Intrinsically satisfied employees will consider only the kind of work they do and the tasks linked to it and they are happy about it. Extrinsically satisfied workforce will consider conditions of work like compensation, operational conditions, conveniences, superior etc.

Determinants of job satisfaction

1. **Equitable rewards:** As per scientific studies, irrespective of the kind of industry, 80% of the employees deem compensation and rewards as a major factor of job satisfaction.
2. **Challenging work:** Employees would want to have opportunities to prove their skills. Jobs that do not provide different way of thinking make the job boring.
3. **Good working conditions:** Good working conditions like suitable ventilation and lighting should be provided to the employees. Individuals should feel comfortable in the operational environment.

Congenial work environment psychologically lifts the employee morale.

4. **Favorable Organization Climate (OC):** Employees join organizations with different backgrounds. The diversity at the work place must be favorable to everyone. Climate refers to the shared views of the employees in an organisation. OC must be flexible enough to favor good communication and must aid high interpersonal relationships.

5. **Supportive colleagues:** This forms an integral part of job satisfaction for many colleagues. Some employees do not focus only on monetary benefits, but they seek favorable relationship created by the co-workers.

d) Employee engagement :

This again is a relatively new term in the field of organizational psychology.This is a combination of an employee's job involvement, satisfaction and enthusiasm towards the job he or she is currently doing. Employee Engagement is a condition of emotional & intellectual association that workers have in an organization. Employees feel engaged when they find special and personal meaning in their work and derive motivation from their work, get positive inter personal support and work in a competent work environment. Highly engaged employees are committed and focused.

There is an intrinsic link between employee engagement, customer loyalty and profitability. According to Sunil Kumar, VP HR, Vertex, "when an employee connects with the organization emotionally, it impacts their attitude towards the company's clients and there by improves customer satisfaction and service levels". Research studies indicate that companies with employees having high level of engagement have higher level of customer satisfaction.

The following diagram shows the components of employee engagement:

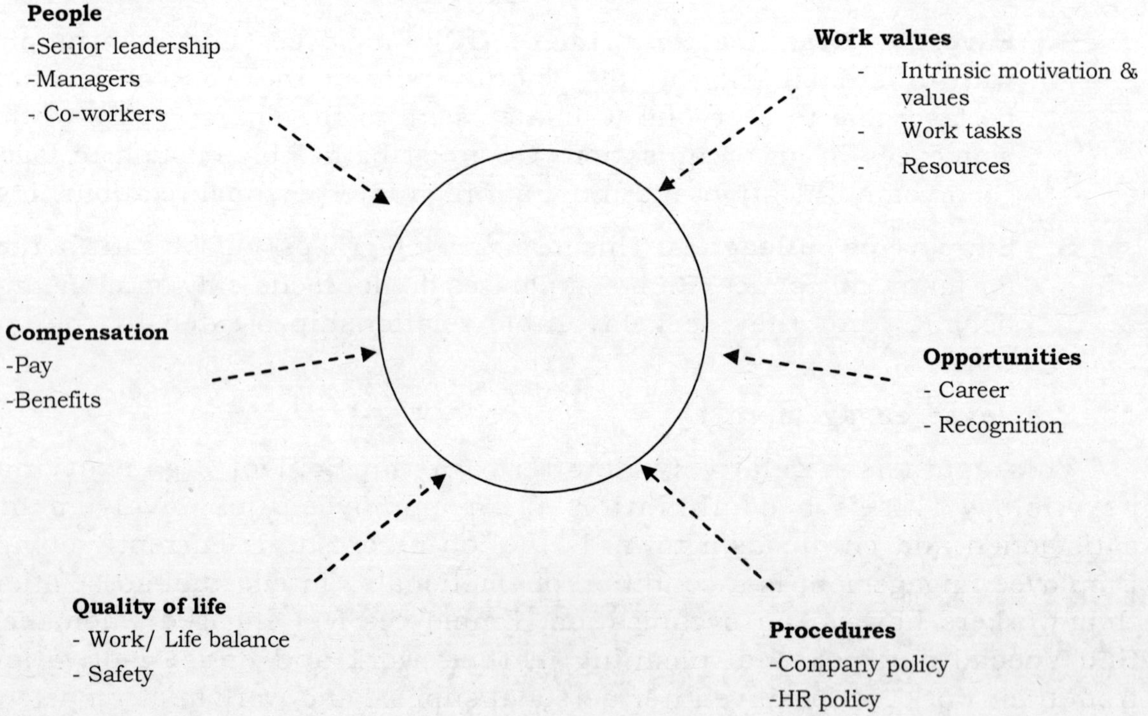

AT&T Re-Engages 'Plateaued' Employees

There will always be employees who reach a plateau and start looking for new challenges. AT&T re-engages and retains "plateaued" employees with a program called Resource Link, which functions as an in-house temporary service. Through this program, employees with diverse management, technical or professional skills "sell" their skills to different departments for short-term assignments.

Prejudice: Negative attitudes towards others

A negative attitude an individual holds towards another based on his or her membership in a particular group is referred to as Prejudice. Prejudice can be against the following groups :

Prejudice based on age

There is a stereotyped thinking that older workers are too stubborn in their ways to train and that they will tend to be unwell often and are accident prone. This prejudice is not founded on accurate information. Some of the recent studies show that organizations tend to have tremendously positive experiences with older work force. They have good skills, are highly devoted to doing their jobs well, and have stupendous safety records.

This kind of prejudice can have a negative impact for star performers too. It is a known fact that the top level management of many organizations are aged above 40 years. A star performer, who reaches that level in his 30s may be looked upon as being less competent due to lack of required age and related experience

Prejudice Based on physical condition

Certain physical conditions tend to be the focal point of widely held prejudicial attitudes. People with ectomorphic physical features (thin body structure) are generally considered to be lacking in physical stamina and most of the time rejected in job interviews citing this as a reason. Other physical conditions (e.g., blindness, disfigurement, physical paralysis) are said to have a negative impact on job selection due to prejudice attached to that.

Prejudice based on sexual orientation

Sexual orientation of an individual often becomes a bias in thinking in the organisations. Prejudice against gay men and lesbian women are always found in many organizations, though that may not have any job related repercussions. Researches indicate that about two-thirds of CEOs from major companies note that they are unwilling to position a homosexual on a top management committee.

Prejudice based on race and national origin

Some nations discriminates employees from not so well developed nations. They are generally minority groups in the organisation. For example , an Indian employee filed a case against Matsushita company of Japan for discriminating him against Japanese and Caucasians. Some of the developed countries like United States have Equal Employment Opportunity Commission to enforce fair employment opportunities to all races with fixed percentage intake for employees of varied nations like thePhilippinos and Hispanics.

Prejudice against Women

It is a general notion that women employees are incapable of taking up all the tasks a male employee does. There is prevalence of powerful gender stereotyping. Though there can be jobs which are meant exclusively for male employees due to the special nature of specific jobs that needs physical stamina, most jobs do not demarcate a male employee from a female employee in terms of the job description. In spite of this fact, it is a known fact that there exist a "glass ceiling" where women employees growth is restricted to certain levels in an organisation. Though the situation is slowly changing with more women employees joining the workforce, there is an alarming disproportion of number of female to male CEOs across the world. Recent statistics reveal that there are only 10% of female CEOs cross the world.

Activity : Understand your own hidden prejudice on gender and race by taking a test at http://www.understandingprejudice.org/iat/index2.htm

Motivation

Among all the factors of production, human resource is the most important factor due to the reason that when all other resources are the same, productivity can be greatly altered by altering the human factor. Motivation is the concept employed in altering the performance of an employee by varied means to fulfill certain organizational objectives. A motivated employee gives the best possible performance which is beneficial for the organisation. Similarly, a demotivated group of employees can impede the growth of an organisation.

The word Motivation is derived from the Latin *movere*, which means "to move".

Motivation is a psychological phenomenon which is generated within an individual. Employee performance can be predicted by the level of motivation of employees. The following formula gives the connect between motivation and employee performance:

Performance = *f*(Ability* Motivation)

The components of motivation as described by Arnold are *Direction* – what a person is trying to do, *Effort* – how hard a person is trying, *Persistence* – how long a person keeps on trying to do what is expected out of him.

Definition of motivation

According to Vance, 'Motivation implies any emotion or desire which so conditions one's will that the individual is properly led into action.'

According to Dubin, 'Motivation is the complex of forces starting and keeping a person at work in an organisation.

Nature of Motivation

Motivation is an inner feeling that makes the person work more. It is concerned with channelizing the employee effort towards achieving organisationobjectives and missions. Every individual needs some form of motivation. It is a continuous and complex process. Motivation produces target directed behaviour.

2 types of factors that influence motivation are:

Intrinsic –They are the self-generated factors (responsibility, autonomy, scope to use and develop skills and abilities, attractive and challenging work, opportunities for progression etc). In comparison to extrinsic factors, they have a deeper and longer-term effect in the behavior of employees

Extrinsic - These are the factors which are outside the realm of the job by itself. It includes those what is done for people to motivate them (rewards, promotion, punishment) . Extrinsic factors have an instant and potent effect, but it is not long lasting.

Importance of Motivation

1. Motivation brings out untapped energies, both mental and physical.
2. It brings down the cost of production by increasing employee efficiency.
3. Motivation boosts novelty and creativity in thinking
4. It reduces absenteeism and employee turnover by improving loyalty towards the organisation.
5. When the employees are motivated in the organisation, it improves the image of the organisation and improves employer branding.
6. Finally, an organisation with motivated employees will have better and harmonious industrial relations.

Types of Motivation

Positive motivation: This deals with motivating the workforce with positive motivation techniques like promotions, augmented pay, providing fringe benefits, ESOPS, recreation facility etc. These methods are aimed at improving employee's performance.

Negative Motivation: In negative motivation, the employees are motivated by using negative motivation techniques like punishments, demotions, pay cut, punishment transfers etc. The idea behind using negative motivation is to make the employees realize that their performance is not on par with the organisation's expectations so that they work towards improving their performance.

Financial motivators: The economists advocate financial motivators as most potential motivators. It includes increased wage and salary, bonus, other fringe benefits etc. Importance of money as a strong motivator was emphasized by many traditional management thinkers like Abraham Maslow, Herzberg and Alderfer. Money as a motivator acts better with young employees, who may have young children whom they may have to educate and those who have many more financial commitments.

Non–financial motivators: Non financial motivators take the form of better status in the organisation, recognition, participation in decision making, job security etc.

Ways of motivating employees in an organisation

We can broadly classify the ways of motivating employees in to 4 categories. There are many theories of motivation which fall under each category. Let us examine those categories and their respective theories.

1. Motivating employees through meeting human needs
   a. Need hierarchy theory of Maslow
   b. Achievement model of McClelland
   c. ERG theory of motivation by Alderfer
2. Motivating employees through job design
   a. Two factor theory of Herzberg
3. Motivating employees through performance expectations
   a. Expectancy and valence theory by Victor Vroom
4. Motivating employees through equity
   a. Equity theory by Adam.

1. a) Abraham H. Maslow's need hierarchy theory:

Clinical psychologist Abraham Maslow propounded the theory of hierarchy of needs. According to him, people have a complex set of unmet and exceptionally strong needs and these sets of needs can be arranged in a hierarchy. It is assumed in this theory that once the unmet need is fulfilled, its motivational importance declines and the next set of needs emerge. As per the theory, lower sets of needs should be met before considering higher level needs. The theory divides the set of needs in to 5 groups viz physiological, safety/security, affiliation, esteem/ego and self-actualization. Maslow classified physiological and safety needs as lower level needs and affiliation, esteem and self-actualization as higher order of needs. Higher level needs are satisfied internally whereas lower level of needs is met by external means. Following are examples of different levels of needs in the hierarchy:

1. *Physiological needs* - Include hunger, thirst, air, shelter, sex, sleep, etc.
2. *Safety needs* - Include absence of pain, fear, protection from unfavourable events, and protection from other emotional and physical harm.
3. *Affiliation/Social needs:* This include acceptance, friendship, love, work group, family, affection, relationships, etc.
4. *Esteem needs* - This includes self-respect, autonomy, achievement, recognition, mastery, status, attention, dominance, prestige, designation etc.
5. *Self-Actualization needs* - This include the drive to reach one's full potential, self-fulfillment, seeking personal growth, challenging assignments etc.

Maslow's need hierarchy is well accepted by practicing managers due to its simplicity and logical application. This suggests types of behaviours to fulfill different levels of needs. Managers need to satisfy higher level needs whereas assembly level workers need to satisfy more of lower level of needs. This theory suggests that rewarding an employee with the same kind of motivator may have diminished importance in motivating an employee, as the perceived value of the same kind of motivator diminishes after that particular set of needs are fulfilled .

1. b) Achievement theory by McClelland

David McClelland proposed the "Learned needs" model of motivation. This theory has particular relevance to industrial enterprises, as achievement in itself has maximum importance for success or failure of an enterprise.

McClelland postulated that every individual has three particularly important needs. Need for Achievement, Affiliation and Power. This could vary in degree between individuals. Of the three needs, McClelland focused maximum on *nAch*.

Need for Achievement (nAch) : It is the need to achieve, drive to stand out, and strive to succeed.

Need for Power (nPow) : This is the need to make other people behave in a way you want them to .

Need for Affiliation (nAff) : It is the need for friendly and pleasant interpersonal relationship.

Employees with high *nAch* will perform better when they perceive that their probability of success is at least 50%. They dislike mundane jobs. They select moderate goals which are neither too easy nor too difficult to attain. They set their own goals and like the challenge of making tough decisions. They undertake calculated risk taking and they get achievement satisfaction when they stretch themselves a little to achieve a relatively difficult goal. If they achieve the goal , they want the credit for the same and if they lose, they are ready to accept the blame. They prefer tasks which provide immediate feedback. For them, goals are very important and they want to know whether they are doing well and hence seek feedback for their goal directed activity. They are aware of their abilities and limitations and they value their services to an organization and charges them accordingly. They are less likely to stick to an organization which do not pay them well. They value money as a symbol of their efficiency and achievement.

High *nAchs* generally tend to be low in affiliation *(nAff)*. To measure achievement motivation, McClelland used Thematic Apperception Test (TAT) as it catches the pre conscious motives of the people.

1. c) ERG theory of Alderfer

Maslow's need hierarchy theory was reworked by Clayton Alderfer to synchronize it with empirical research. Clayton Alderfer redefined need hierarchy theory and formed the needs into three core groups : *Existence* (Physiological and safety needs of Maslow), *Relatedness* (Social needs of Maslow), and *Growth* (Self esteem and Self actualization needs of Maslow). This modified theory of Alderfer is known as ERG theory of motivation.

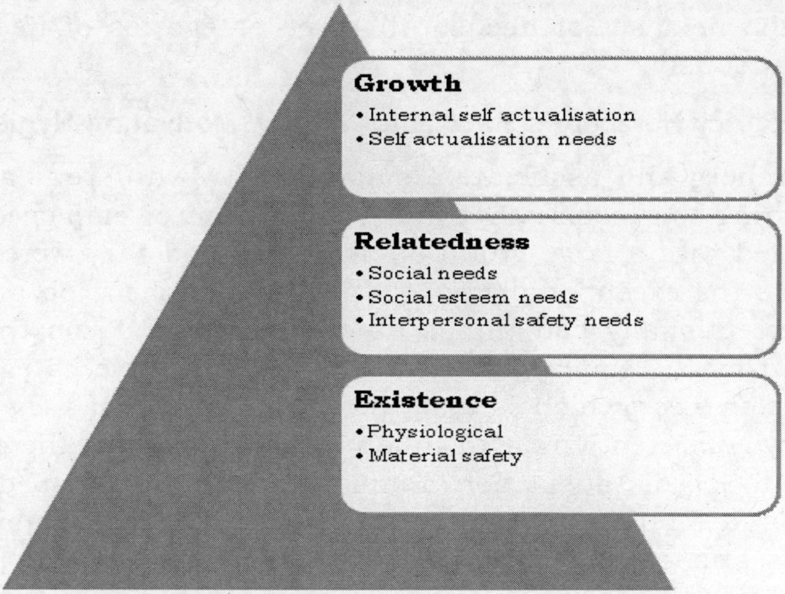

- **Existence needs-** These include the need for fundamental material necessities as in the case of physiological and physical safety needs.
- **Relatedness needs-** These include the individual's need for maintaining good interpersonal relationships with family, peers or superiors, getting public recognition and fame etc. Maslow's social needs and external component of esteem needs form this class of need.
- **Growth needs-** These include the need for personal development, growth and advancement. Maslow's self-actualization needs and intrinsic component of esteem needs form this category of need.

How do you satisfy ERG needs?

Existence : Existence need can be met by providing basic amenities like good lighting and ventilation in the work place, drinking water, sanitary facilities, canteen, job security, insurance, health programs, time off etc

Relatedness need : This can be met by providing good team work, quality supervision, social events etc

Growth needs : This can be fulfilled by providing challenging jobs, autonomy, interesting work, participation in decision making etc.

Unlike Maslow, Alderfer never assumed that the need hierarchy was rigid and that it was not necessary for one set of need to get satisfied, to go to the next set of needs. All three categories of needs may co-exist simultaneously.

2. Frederick Herzberg's Two factor theory/ Motivation-Hygiene theory

Herzberg and associates considered two different approaches while considering the factors that affect motivation of employees. Research was conducted with a large group of employees and they were asked what they felt were the exceptionally good things about their job and what they felt were exceptionally bad things about their jobs. From the exhaustive list provided by the employees, Herzberg developed two categories and formed *Two factor theory*which is also known as *motivator – Hygiene theory*. One category consistently related to job satisfaction while the other consistently related to job dissatisfaction. Employees who are satisfied in the job listed intrinsic factors like recognition, advancement, responsibility, achievement etc. Dissatisfied employees listed extrinsic factors like pay, supervision, working conditions, rules and regulations etc. The theory postulates that two sets of factors - *Motivators* and *Hygiene* are responsible for job satisfaction and job dissatisfaction.

Motivator factors:

Intrinsic job related factors like the work itself, recognition, career advancement, responsibility and authority etc form the motivator factors. They are largely internal to the individual. They provide job satisfaction to the employees. These factors motivate the employees to perform better and improves their loyalty to the company. They have a long lasting effect on employees.

Motivating Factors are:-

1. Achievement
2. Appreciation for achievement
3. Increased accountability
4. Opportunity for Growth and advancement
5. Creative and challenging Work

Hygiene factors :

These factors prevent employees from dissatisfaction but their presence is not motivating. The hygiene factors help employees to avoid unpleasantness but do not motivate them to take more interest in the work. When hygiene factors are provided, it creates a positive environment for motivation and prevents job dissatisfaction. They are largely extrinsic in nature and they are related to job/work conditions. When employer does not provide sufficient hygiene factors, it leads to employee dissatisfaction. However, if they are provided, they do not guarantee job satisfaction. Some of the hygiene factors are as noted below.

1. Company's HR policies
2. Supervision
3. Working environment
4. Interpersonal relations with colleagues, subordinates and superiors
5. Salary
6. Job Security

Motivators instill a sense of motivation among employees to work better. Motivators improve the efficiency and productivity of employees. Frederick Herzberg believed that motivators are essential to provide job satisfaction. It also helps in maintaining high level of job performance.

3. Victor Vroom's Expectancy/ VIE theory

Valence is the degree of preference of an individual towards an expected outcome. Valence is hence the amount of value an individual perceives in a particular outcome.Valence is more than one or positive when an individual preferes an outcome. When the individual is indifferent about the outcome, the valence is zero.

Instrumentality is the extent or degree to which the first level outcome is likely to bring second level outcome.

Expectancy is the probability that a particular action will lead to desired outcome. It ranges from 0 to 1. If an individual finds zero probability of an action bringing in the desired outcome, he wont put effort to take the action.

Expectancy relates to the effort to be put to get the first level outcome where as Instrumentality relates first level outcome to second level outcome.

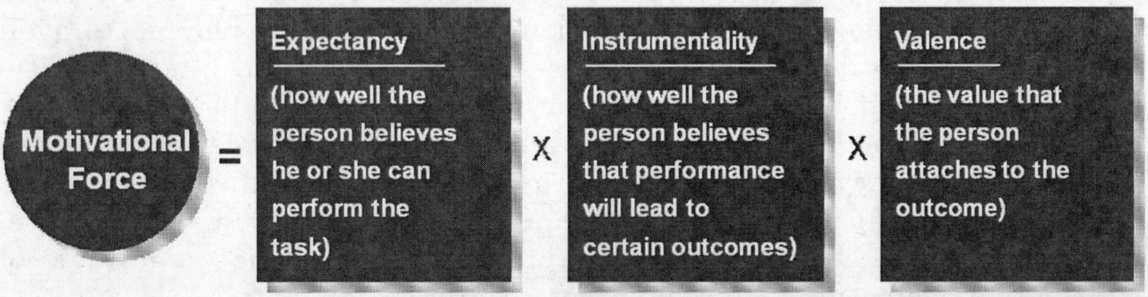

For example, if an employee desires promotion, depending on the strength of desire to get the promotion *(Valence)*, he may perform well thinking high performance will get him promotion *(Expectancy)*. Importance or weightage of high performance in getting the promotion is *instrumentality*.

According to the VIE theory, an individual will weigh the 3 aspects before he decides to put an effort to achieve a particular target.

4. Stacy Adams' equity theory

This theory stems from the sense of people's justice and fairness. All workers seek a fair balance between the effort put in a job and what we obtain out of it. Adam referred these as inputs and outputs. Inputs, in this context are an employee's educational qualification, experience, special skill sets etc. Outputs are salary, bonus, benefits, designation, recognition etc.

Inputs		Outputs
Qualification, Exertion, Faithfulness, Hard work, Loyalty, Skill, Ability, Compliance, Flexibility, Tolerance, Grit, Passion, Trust in the boss and superiors, Providing support to colleagues and subordinates, Personal sacrifice, etc	=	Financial rewards - Pay, Salary, Expenses, Perks, Benefits, Pension Arrangements, Bonus and commission Intangibles - Recognition, Designation, Praise and Thanks, Interest, Responsibility, Opportunity to travel, Training etc development, sense of achievement and advancement, promotion, etc.

According to the equity theory, a person's motivation depends on the degree of equity that they perceive in the work situation. Perception of fairness will be often based on the comparison of our own situation in terms of inputs and outputs with other 'referents' (reference points or examples) in the organization. Employees are influenced by contemporaries, friends, and partners in the organization while establishing certain benchmarks. Employees regularly compare their input output ratio with the input output ratios of relevant others. The comparison may also extend to other organizations for similar jobs. When an employee perceives inequity in input out ratios of self and others, "Equity tension" occurs which creates anger and tension in the individual, leading to resentment. The extent of demotivation is proportional to the perceived inequality between inputs and the expected outputs. When he perceives that he is over rewarded for his effort, it may lead to guilt. Equity tension motivates a person to correct it. This is done by an under rewarded person reducing the quantity or quality of output and reducing his commitment to the job and the organization. An over rewarded person will either work hard to compensate the feeling of guilt or discount the value of the extra reward to maintain balance.

This theory highlights the value of social comparison in motivation. It also recognizes the role of cognitive processes in motivation.

What should be the managerial actions to keep employees motivated in the organization?

1. Endow the employee with more valued rewards according to the employee needs and perceived value. For example, establish a

suitable reward and incentive system keeping in mind the needs of the majority of employees.

2. Change the values of the person towards available rewards. For example, if the company gives group rewards or team based pay, often seen in case projects in IT companies, consider educating the employees on benefits of group rewards so as to bring in a change in their value system.

3. Improve the employees' perception of the linkage between behavior and reward. This can be done by casual conversation with the employees about what could be the probable outcome of a particular level of performance like a pay hike, promotion etc.

4. Impress on the employees the reality of the behaviour-reward association. Employees should be made aware of the paying capacity of the organization. In case of the inability to pay according to market standards, employees should be informed about when in the future they will be rewarded accordingly.

Application of motivation theories in the organizational context

1. Leverage the Maslow's need hierarchy by instituting employee recognition programs to satisfy the esteem and self-actualization needs of managers. For meeting the physiological needs of shop floor employees by giving break for lunch and tea. Provision of good safety and security practices like security guards, CCTV camera etc will make employees feel safe at the workplace. Social needs of employees can be met by having team activities and other social events in the work place.

2. ERG theory can be effectively used by fixing challenging tasks for employees with high *nAch i.e.,* employees with high achievement motivation so that they feel satisfied in the job. The ERG theory follows *frustration- regression* principle. According to this principle, if higher order of needs like growth needs are left unfulfilled, the employee may regress to lower level of needs, which may be relatively easier to satisfy. For example, if the high achiever's growth needs are suppressed, he will regress to lower level need of socializing with colleagues more often than needed and wastes his time. Early warning signals of losing such a star employee should be identified by the management and the need to provide for his growth needs for retention of such employees should be undertaken.

3. As per the expectancy theory, employees will put effort in work commensurate to the perceived value of a reward. Hence use a mixed bag of traditional and contemporary compensation strategies to motivate employees from the expectancy theory perspective.
4. Equity theory explains why employees can be happy and motivated with their work situation one day and with same work condition, can get demotivated if they learn that a colleague is enjoying a better reward–to–effort ratio. Hence, as much as possible the organization should strive hard to give a sense of fairness to all employees when it comes to reward–to–effort ratio.
5. From the two factor theory of Herzberg, it can be understood that employee motivation factors are not extrinsic factors, but is very much connected with the satisfaction derived from the job itself. Hence, to motivate an employee, the job itself should be challenging and interesting and there should be scope for job enrichment. From this theory, the importance of job design, job enrichment, job enlargement, job rotation etc can be understood.

CLOSING CASE

Trendz enterprises is a stockist of fashion apparels which is one of the well run firm. They have rules in place and have manuals for reference. The procedure manual of Trendz stated that backorders must be filed number wise by the invoice number appearing on Trendz's purchase order to its suppliers. When a customer called to check on an item that was backordered, it was time-consuming for the employee of the firm Mr Jacob to locate the orderform.The customer had forgotten the invoice number of its backorder . Hence it was next to impossible to check through the pile of back orders to get the right back order of the customer. Understanding the difficulty faced by employees whenever such a case happens, Jacob decided to file the backorders in alphabetical order of supplier's name. Jacob was feeling very happy and proud about the work he did , which removes the practical difficulty of locating back orders.

In a weeks time, his branch manager MrSanyalneeded a backorder invoice to answer a query a customer had about his order. Mr Jacob easily gave the form as the invoice was filed alphabetically under the name of the account. Mr Jacob was expecting MrSanyal to compliment on his practical thinking. However, MrSanyal told Jacob that although it was a good idea to have the filing in alphabetical order and the invoice had been easily located, his filing system for backorder invoices did not conform to company procedures. MrSanyal asked Mr Jacob to revert to the old system of invoice filing. Mr Jacob was very depressed and disappointed about the whole episode. He knew that he is only making the system inefficient by reverting back to the old system. Never the less he followed the instruction of his supervisor .

Question

1. Will Mr Jacob be motivated to try other methods of improving the efficiency of the job in the future? Explain.

Test your knowledge

Multiple choice questions

1. According to 2 factor theory, which among the following is a hygiene factor ?
   a. Recognition
   b. Sense of achievemnt
   c. Good pay package
   d. Personal growth
2. Equity theory focuses on
   a. How employees should work in a given situation
   b. What are the employees expectations on outcome of a given action
   c. Employees perception of fairness at work
   d. None of the above
3. Which of the need category of Alderfer is most important for an entrepreneur?
   a. Existence
   b. Growth
   c. Relatedness
   d. None of the above
4. Which of the following is included under law of learning?
   a. Law of exrcise
   b. Law of understanding
   c. Law of readiness
   d. Law of gravity
5. Which are the animals used by Skinner in studying operant conditioning?

a. Cats & monkeys
b. Dogs & porcupines
c. Rats & Pigeons
d. Snakes & Tigers

6. Extinction is connected to
   a. Law of intensity
   b. Law of repetiotion
   c. Law of use & disuse
   d. None of the above
7. Consequenses of an action that discourages the repetiontion of the particular behaviour is
   a. Extinction
   b. Positive re inforcement
   c. Negative reinforcement
   d. Operant conditioning
8. The famous " Bobo Doll experiment " was conducted by
   a. Skinner
   b. Bandura
   c. Pavlov
   d. Freud

MODEL QUESTIONS

Section – A

(Each question carries 2 marks)

1. What are attitudes?
2. What are the function of attitudes
3. What is ABC model
4. What is job satisfaction
5. Can attitudes be formed?
6. What are values? Give two examples of attitude
7. Define attitude
8. What is social learning
9. What is self awareness

Section – B

(Each question carries 5 marks)

1. Explain how attitudes are formed?
2. Write two contemporary theory of motivation
3. Write the influence of persuasion and job satisfaction
4. What are the needs for goal setting?
5. Write a note on organizational commitment
6. Write the application of motivation
7. What is managing diverse work force
8. Is emotional intelligence in workplace a boon or bane defend your stand
9. How can prejudice and groupism effect organization
10. Write the attributes of job satisfaction

Section – C

(Each question carries 15 marks)

1. How is attitudes formed ?what is the contribution of social learning in organizational development
2. How is genetic factor influencing the attitude of a person give relevant examples
3. Write in detail the contribution of concepts and application towards motivation building
4. What is organizational commitment? What all could be the barriers of organizational commitment
5. Explain the reasons for frustration? How can emotional intelligence influence in reducing this problem
6. Write in detail the contribution of contemporary theories of to organizational psychology
7. State the Role of direct learning and genetic factors in relation to work and framing the attitudes in organization

References

1. G.J Blau& K. R. Boal, "Conceptualizing how job involvement and organizational commitment affect turnover and absenteeism" , Academy of management review, April 1987, p 290.

2. www.expresscomputeronline.com "Employee Engagement", SupdiptoDev.

3. www.soundviewexecutivebooksummaries, Vol-27, No-6 Part -2, June 2005.

4. Hellreigal& Slocum, "Organisational behavior", Thomson learning, ISBN 981- 243 -547. P 117-139.

FIGURE SOURCES

https://encrypted-tbn3.gstatic.com/images?q=tbn:ANd9GcQyerJh_G0zjYOB7Zktn0M-fh4fLw4HAHGMRAWzUnJe5IRR6kf8Pg

◈◈◈◈

Read More on the Web

A job attitude is a set of evaluations of one's job that constitute one's feelings toward, beliefs about, and attachment to one's job. So, a person's attitude is directly associated with the effectiveness and success on the job. There are four basic people in business today, and they can be best categorized by their attitudes:

- **Job Lovers:** they love their job. But the flipside to this attitude is that the person gets too attached to the same and invests too much. As a result, they are often blind to new opportunities, personal and professional.
- **Job Doer:** people who view a job as the means to an end. They enjoy things like vacations, pride in their work and financial security. Here, there is place for growth.
- **Job Hater:** they are constantly concerned with ordering people around, complaining and criticizing. A person with this attitude wastes time on negativity, and often misses positive opportunities.
- **Job what? :** These people perpetually have the query, "why am I here?" They are often tardy, do not work on time and spend more time on personal issues. Their potential is buried by the lack of caring and activity.

There are many factors that affect the categorization of these types of people. Some variables could be the working conditions, task significance, supervision, stress, autonomy, promotional opportunity, skill variety and identity, pay, social relationships, co worker relationships , feedback, workload, company policies, politics, groups, benefits, work life balance, client attitudes and finally the job itself.

The structure of attitudes can be described in terms of three components:

- **Affective component:** this involves the person's feelings/emotions about the attitude object. For example ("spiders" being the attitude object): "I am scared of spiders".
- **Behavioral component:** the way the attitude we have influences how we act or behave. For example: "I will avoid spiders and scream if I see one".
- **Cognitive component:** this involves a person's belief or knowledge about an attitude object. For example: "I believe spiders are dangerous".

This model is known as the "ABC Model of Attitudes".

Also, attitudes are reinforced by constant repetition, just like our mind is conditioned by lies. So, if one constantly says, "I hate studying this subject", he/she will end up conditioning the mind to hate that subject, hence closing the mind off to any inputs related to the same subject.

B: Motivation

Motivation is defined as the process that initiates, guides and maintains goal-oriented behaviors. Motivation is what causes us to act, whether it is getting a glass of water to reduce thirst or reading a book to gain knowledge. The term motivation is frequently used to describe why a person does something. Motivation has three major components:

- **Activation:** This involves the decision to initiate certain behaviour. The initiation could be intrinsic or extrinsic.

- **Persistence:** This is the continued effort towards a goal even in the face of certain obstacles.
- **Intensity:** this is the concentration and vigor that goes into pursuing a goal.

Intrinsic motivations are those that arise from within an individual while extrinsic motivations are those that arise from outside an individual and often involve some sort of appreciation or benefit to the individual in question. An organization needs to inculcate motivation on both fronts. Extrinsic motivation is easy. Intrinsic motivation can arise only if the employee truly believes that he/she is happy in his/her position, and therefore gets motivated to perform better, by his/her own choice. Motivation can, therefore, cause a person to orient himself and his behavior along a certain course of action, be it negative or positive.

According to BJ Fogg's Behaviour Model (Stanford University), behaviour modification has three core motivators, each with two sides. Core motivators apply to everyone and are integral to the human mindset and the "why".

- **Sensation:** pain/ pleasure
- **Anticipation (of):** fear/hope
- **Social cohesion:** rejection/ acceptance.

Motivation has close ties with the Need Hierarchy as we know. Every person tries to move up the hierarchy and the above behaviour model can be linked to the same as well. Motivation hence is not a personality trait, but is a very situational adaptation; even though ones personality does play a huge role on ones motivating factors.

Sources and References

http://www.careerealism.com/job-attitudes-types/
https://wikispaces.psu.edu/display/PSYCH484/11.+Job+Satisfaction
http://www.simplypsychology.org/attitudes.html
http://psychology.about.com/od/mindex/g/motivation-definition.htm
http://www.behaviormodel.org/motivation.html
http://www.motivationhacker.com/motivation-is-situational-not-a-personality-trait/

CHAPTER 6

GROUP BEHAVIOUR, POWER & POLITICS

Learning Objectives of the Chapter

- Definition & nature of group
- Function & formation
- Benefits & costs of working with others
- Emerging team concept
- Groups & teams
- Effective teams
- Social influence
- Individual power
- Bases of power
- Implication
- Dependency
- Managing power
- Organisational politics – Power in action
- Productive use of organizational politics
- Ethics in organizational politics

OPENING CASE

Perils of Team Work

(Article adapted from The Wall street journal, September 29th 2004., http://online.wsj.com/article/0,,SB109641717999730825,00.html)

A civilian worker at one of the nation's largest Air Force bases who was working for a general, watched on a team was formed to come up with a better system to handle the mail.

Mail to the base included letters from multi-starred generals and directives that had deadlines. The "process improvement team," also known as a PIT, had a roster of middle managers, mostly civilians, who spent the better part of a month coming up with a plan.

But instead of streamlining the process, they complicated it. "I was horrified," said the woman. "There used to be eight steps; now there are 19." Each piece of official mail was viewed by a greater number of managers before getting to its intended recipient, she says, enabling the mail to be lost at home or in the bathroom, or covered with spills from someone's breakfast. Even ponies could have delivered it faster. The lag between the first manager who saw a piece of mail and the person who had to act on it was two weeks, she said.

Questioning the team would have amounted to heresy, so she kept quiet until a year later, when her general emerged from his office and bellowed, "What the hell is happening to my mail?" Once enlightened, he changed everything on the spot.

"So many things that a team comes to consensus on are monumentally goofy," says the civilian worker. But she adds that she is nonetheless a "true believer in teams." Her current job at the base: teaching interpersonal communication, including how teams can work together better.

Unfortunately, despite plenty of research cautioning against the knee-jerk idolatry of teams in the workplace, these group efforts are still sacrosanct. Sure, no company could survive without teams, but many companies could prosper without some of them. Teamwork's underlying assumption is that two heads are better than one, with the math looking something like this: 1 head + 1 head = 2 heads. In reality, teamwork looks more like a multiplication function: 1 head x 1 head = 1 head. Worse, consider what happens in a team full of half-wits: half-wit x half-wit = one-quarter wit.

The shortchanging is similar to the group think illustrated by the so-called Abilene Paradox. In that parable about how individuals reach agreement, a family is happily playing dominoes when someone comes up with the bad idea of going to Abilene for dinner. Everyone thinks all the others believe it's a good idea, so they set aside their opposition to the long, hot, dusty trip to get lousy cafeteria food, and they go anyway.

Amy Edmondson, a professor at Harvard Business School, says that teams represent an effort to pool diverse skills and knowledge, but they typically fail in three ways. First, people don't recognize that the interesting and relevant information they possess is interesting and relevant, so they don't share it. Second, people often overlook the fact that colleagues have opposing interests. ("Layoffs? They can't come from my group.") Third, people withhold information deliberately.

Teams often work better when they have at least some conflict, particularly if there is more than one dissenter, says Michael Useem, a professor at the University of Pennsylvania's Wharton School. "A single devil's advocate or whistleblower faces a really uphill struggle," he says. "But if you have one ally, that is enormously strengthening."

Just don't expect Carmen Johnson, a manager with a telecommunications company, to be one of those dissenters. She routinely toes the line if a superior on a team wants to do something a certain way. When she's asked for her opinion, she says, "I give it hesitantly, watching for the most powerful on the team to give approval because if they don't, I've got to change my story real quick."

On the other hand, some teams are tyrannies dressed up as democracies. When Jim Stagg was a graphic designer 10 years ago, he was part of a five-person team that worked well together. But after one team member left, the boss found a replacement candidate he was determined to hire. His question to the others: "Do any of you see a reason NOT to hire the candidate?"

Despite the team's pleas for more candidates and more time to reach a decision, the boss's choice was hired. And within a year, most of the rest of the team had resigned.

At the other end of the spectrum, team democracy can seem like anarchy. Derek Kirk, an aerospace-company technician, attended a management meeting with a psychologist to assess emotional problems among staffers. But one member of his team soon veered into talking about his own personal problems. While Mr. Kirk pleaded with the man to stay on message, another participant argued it was important "to hear the whole story."

Later, with no team solutions to offer the other participants, Mr. Kirk winged his presentation, getting this time-honored advice from the psychologist: "She basically said, 'You gotta live with it,' " he recalls.

INTRODUCTION

An organization is a miniature society. It has clusters of groups and teams, which perform to achieve a common objective. One of the realities of organizational behaviour and its psychology is that we must work in and with group to accomplish our aspiration. No matter how much we value and protect our individuality; almost all our goals and targets can be achieved only when we work in a group. An organizations performance is to a great extent dependent on smooth functioning of groups in the organization. Hawthorne studies have shown the influence of groups on human behavior. Increase in output or performance by the workers in the Hawthorne study was due to the importance given to the group by the researchers. This emphasizes the importance of groups in organizational psychology. Goals to be achieved by the group bind the individuals together in a group. The behaviour of an individual in groups is something more than the sum total of each acting in his or her own way. The ideas generated jointly by a group will be richer and more creative than if the same was done by individual without any interaction among the group.

The Oxford English dictionary defines a group as a number of persons or things regarded as forming a unit on account of any mutual or common relation or classified together on account of common degree of similarities.

Defining Group

"A group is any number of people who have a common purpose or objective, interact with each other to accomplish their objective, are aware of one another and perceive themselves to be part of the group". (Huse and Bowditch (1977).

"A group is a set of two or more individuals who are jointly characterised by a network of relevant communication, a shared sense of collective identity and one or more shaped dispositions with associations." (David smith)

"A group is two or more persons who are interacting with one another in such a manner that each person influences and is influenced by each other" (Marvin shaw)

We can summarise from the above definitions that a group is the aggregation of a small number of persons who work for common goal, develop a shared attitude and are aware that they are part of the group.

Why people join groups?

People join groups due to varied reasons. Some of them are as follows:

1. **Safety and security reasons:** Employees join groups because it reduces the insecurity of being alone. For example, most of the times, a group of employees will meet management regarding pay hike rather than an individual employee. Employees develop more confidence when they are in groups. Besides, they can handle threats in a better way when they are in groups than when they are alone.

2. **Relatedness/belongingness needs:** Group provides an individual the required emotional support. Regular interaction with group members fulfills their need for affiliation. When employees do not get the feeling of belongingness, they are more likely to leave the job.

3. **Esteem needs:** The sense of recognition provided by the group is very important for an employee. This gives an increased feeling of self-worth.

4. **Sense of status:** Inclusion in certain groups give a sense of status to employees. For example, an employee who works in the head-quarters of a company may feel that he holds better status than a similar cadre employee in the subsidiary of the company.

5. **Sense of increased power/Synergy:** Fayol's principle of "Unity is strength" applies here. One plus one is more than two. What can't be achieved individually is frequently achieved by groups. One of the reasons for employees join trade union is for the increased power.

6. **For pooling of talents:** When the target to be achieved demands varied skills and knowledge, the management makes formal groups to accomplish the task.

7. **For becoming a leader:** People with an inborn leadership ability would want to form a group to lead them.

8. **Empowerment through sharing:** When people are in groups, there is an exchange of ideas and knowledge, skills, talents, values etc. This process enables the individual to acquire expertise, thus, members gain expert power.

Nature of group

Groups have the following features:

1. Interaction among members: Members of the group interacts with each other constantly.
2. Shared goals: Members of the group have a shared common goal.
3. Common identity: Members identify with each other as people of the same group
4. Interdependency: Members of the group are dependent on one another.
5. Two or more people are needed to form a group.

What is not a group?

Mere aggregate of people, people in a market, a crowd in a street corner watching some event etc. do not constitute to a group. The reason is, they do not interact, do not consider themselves to be a part of a group even if they know each other and do not share a common interest. They have their individual interest at heart in these cases.

TYPES OF GROUPS

Groups in organizations are categorized by sociologist and psychologists who study the social behaviour of people in organisation and divide them into different types of groups.

1. Formal groups :

These are the groups established by the organization to accomplish a specific task. They are deliberately created and the members are usually appointed by the organization, though in certain cases it does not hold good. The distinctive feature of formal group is the hierarchy of authority, with specified member rules and regulation. Rules, regulation, incentive and sanctions guide the behaviour of members of formal groups.

Cartwright and Zander (1974) identified 3 different types of formal groups viz:

a) **Command groups/Standing group:** It is a collection of employees who report to the same supervisor. It consists of supervisor who exercises formal authority over the subordinates. It consists of managers and their subordinates. Organizational charts show command groups. The performance of a command group has a direct impact on the organisation's performance. Leaders of the command group to a large extent determine the effectiveness of the group. Example of a command group will be a foreman and his team of workers in an organization.

b) **Committees:** Committees are created for accomplishing a specific assignment of the organisation. Committee members are assigned different tasks which have a common organizational objective. If the committee is dealing with a long term problem or task, the members may be changed or rotated. These kinds of committees are known as standing committees. Committees are usually created outside the command group structure to solve recurring problems. Tenure could be long [Ex:- Planning committee] or short [Ex:- University exam discipline committee]

c) **Task force:** is a temporary group which is created to solve the specific problems of employees of different departments. Employees work together to complete a task, but do not report to the same supervisor. They stay together till the task is completed. And once the task is completed the group is adjourned. Eg: A task force formed to solve the problem of many departments, consisting of representatives of each department. All command groups are task groups, but task groups cut across the organizational structure. The task may be a non-recurring problem

d) **Interacting Group:**- Work of one group member is contingent upon that of others, such as assembly line workers, who perform separate operations in a prescribed sequence

2. Informal groups :

Informal groups are formed within the structure of organization but they are formed by the members themselves and not by the organization. An informal group is formed when two or more individuals join together as a group in order to satisfy their social needs but not due to official job structure and organizational requirement. This group is formed out of interests, aptitudes, values, opinions, ideas and characteristics of the people.

Informal work groups can be broadly classified into 2 groups.

a) **Interest group:** When employees have a common interest, they form interest groups. It is made up of people who affiliate to achieve an objective of mutual interest that may have nothing to do with their formal task group identity. Sometimes, the interests of the employees will be overlooked by the management and interest groups helps employees to voice their opinions. E.g.: Employees who are interested in fitness will join together and convince the management to start a fitness center in the premise. Another example of interest group will be a group of university professors who organize a seminar on Mergers & Acquisitions.

b) **Friendship group:** Friendship groups are formed by employees who like to socialize with each other. This is developed based on common characteristics such as age, marital status, political views, college affiliations and sports. Such groups are important because they satisfy the affiliation needs of the members. And good relation with friendship group will bring tremendous impact on attaining organizational goals. Examples of friendship group will be a group of working women going out for lunch often to be with each other.

3. Primary groups

Members of this group will have intimate, face to face interaction and association on a regular basis. The members have a feeling of loyalty, camaraderie and share common values.

4. Reference groups

An individual identifies or wants to identify themselves to these groups. These are special type of informal groups that people use to evaluate themselves. It may not be an actual one that meets together, it can be a imaginary group. Ex: A reference group for a new university lecturer will be other scholars in the same discipline at other universities.

5. Cliques

Cliques consist of colleagues or those who commonly associate with each other regularly and more intensely than others and observe certain social norms or standards. The number of members tends to be smaller, rarely exceeding 5 – 6. The objective of forming a clique is to provide recognition to each other and exchange information of mutual interest. Cliques may have a positive or negative effect on the organizational climate. Positive cliques can set a positive precedence for overall staff team spirit.

Bad cliques can create a culture of fear and can cause excluded co-workers tremendous mental stress.

Vertical clique: People working in the same department, with members cutting across the hierarchy.

Horizontal clique: People of more or less same rank, working in the same area- the most common informal group.

Random/Mixed clique: The group draws members from different ranks, department or physical location. Eg: Same locality people, train passenger

The concept & nature of Teams:

A team is a formal work group. The team approach to managing organizations has a diverse and substantial impact on the organisation. All individuals who work in groups are not team members. A team is made by an organization for a specific purpose. Team members will have high level of interaction. This leads to the team members exchanging their skills and expertise. A team is a small number of people having shared goals and has an approach for which they hold themselves mutually accountable. Teams include people of mixed skills appropriate to the task to be done. Team members need technical, problem solving, decision making and interpersonal skills.

Definition of Team: A small number of people with complementary skills, who are committed to a common purpose, set of performance goals, and approach for which they hold themselves mutually accountable (Katzenbach & Smith)

E.g.: IT companies, which are based on clients projects, will have, at any given time, as many as 2000 teams and the strength of each team varies from 8 -10 depending on the size of the project.

Different types of teams

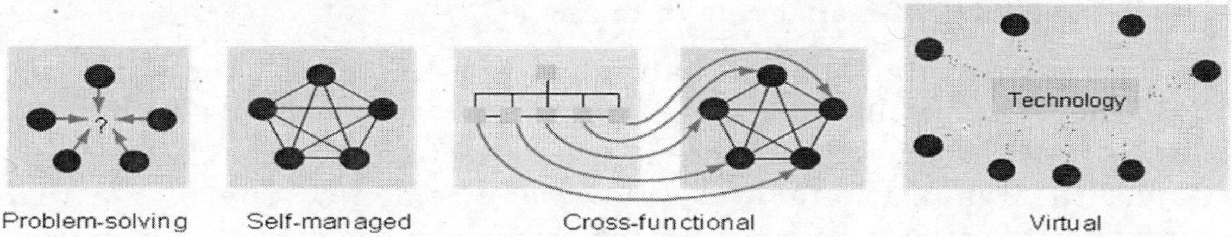

1. Problem solving/Process improvement teams

The individuals in the process improvement team perform each operation of the process or sub-process. Usually, the field of the team's activity is restricted to the work unit. During the course of the team's life, extra knowledge from other work areas may be combined on a constant or temporary-basis. It is disbanded when the objective has been obtained. When the addressed process constitutes many work units or the whole organization, a cross functional team may be more apt with work unit teams as sub teams.

2. Cross functional teams

A team about six to ten members represents a number of different functional areas, such as engineering, marketing, accounting, production, quality and human resources. It usually includes the customer and supplier. A design study team is the best example of cross functional team. These teams are usually temporary. The exception- a product support team, which would be everlasting and has an objective to work along a particular product line, service activity, or a particular customer. These teams break down functional area boundaries.

3. Natural work teams

These teams are now voluntary–they are made up of all the individuals of the work unit. They differ from quality control circles because a manager is a part of the team and the projects to be made better are selected by management. Certain individuals prefer not to work in teams for different reasons and managers should expect this and be ready to help employees become contented in the team environment or instead find work in another unit that does not require individuals to work in a team. Even though, "team work" is preferable; there may be problems such that its introduction should be arrested until there has been an ample turnover.

4. Self-directed/Self-management teams

They are a continuation of natural work teams minus the supervisor. Thus, they are the ultimate of the authorized organizations–they do the work as well as manage it. There is wide direction to organize their work subject to organizational work flow requirements. There is a team coordinator to act as a liaison with the senior management that may rotate among members. The team meets daily to plan their activities, and decisions are made usually by a consensus. Additional responsibilities may include; hiring, dismissal, performance evaluation, customer relations, supplier relations, recognition/reward and training. The team must have access to business information in order to plan, control and improve their processes. The members of self-managed teams are responsible for the goal accomplishment of the team. The leader of a team is identified by the members themselves. The employees are empowered to share various management and leadership functions in an organization. They plan, control and improve their work on their own. The team is empowered to discipline the underperforming team members. They set their own goals and inspect their own work. Schedules are created and review themselves. They prepare their own budget and coordinate their work with other departments of the organization. Inventory management is also done by them.

Difference between a group and a team:

Though many times we use the words team and groups interchangeably, they are different from each other in the following aspects.

GROUPS	CRITERIA	TEAMS
Formal establishment ←	Leadership	→ Shared roles
Individual ←	Accountability	→ Shared and individuals
Sum of individual outputs ←	Performance	→ Collective and synergize
Diverse ←	Skills	→ Complementary
Common goals ←	Orientation	→ Common Commitment

Groups can also be formed informally without any complementary skills whereas teams are always formed by the organization with people whose skills are complimentary. In groups, work performance depends on the work of the individual members, whereas the performance in the team depends on both individual contributions and collective effort of team members.

Groups and teams differ in the accountability of the job. In groups the supervisor holds individual members accountable for their work whereas in teams, members hold themselves accountable.

A group shares a common goal, but team members share a common commitment to purpose. The commitment to goal attainment is what differentiates teams from groups. Groups are responsive to demands regularly placed on them by the management, whereas teams are free to set their goals ,timing, and the approach they wish to adopt without interference from the management, once the vision and mission is been fixed. Group members possess diverse skills but the skills of team members are complimentary.

Formation of groups:

Groups in an organization do not have permanence. New hires, attrition, lateral entry, promotions etc will change the constitution of said groups. This lead to change in group tasks and goals. Hence there is a need to change the group constituents on a regular basis. Groups are formed and developed through various stages. Tuckman identified five stages of group formation.

Group formation stages:

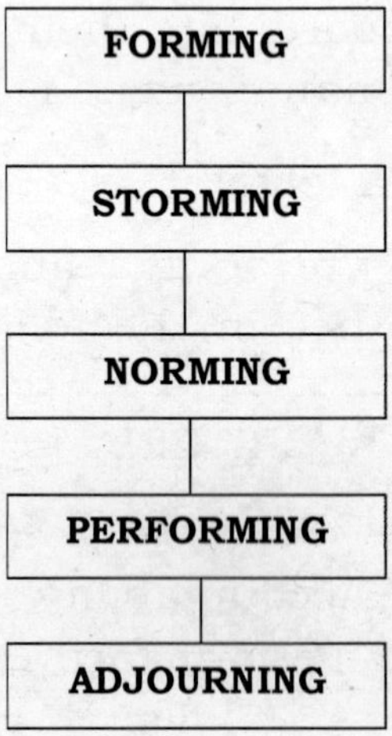

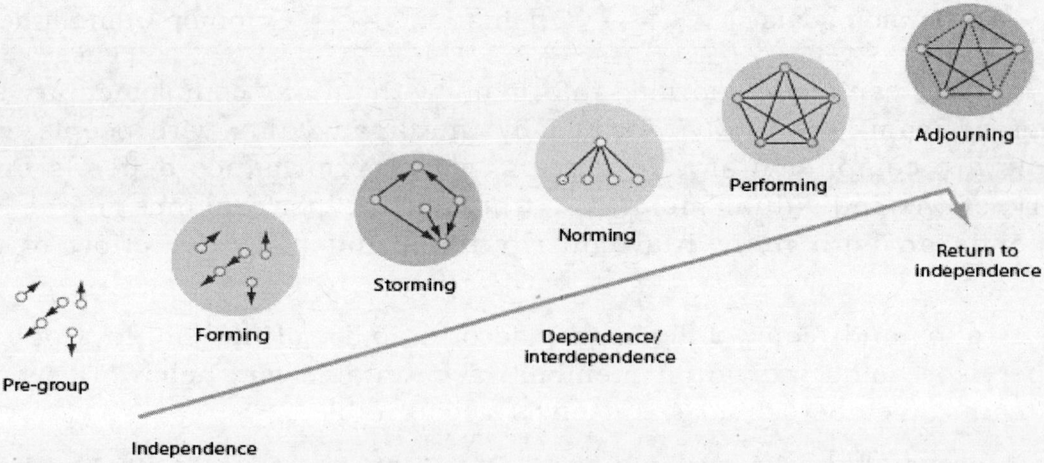

Individual issues	"How do I fit in?"	"What's my role here?"	"What do the others expect of me?"	"How do I best perform?"	"What's next?"
Group issues	"Why are we here?"	"Who is in charge and who does what?"	"Can we agree on roles and work as a team?"	"Can we do the job properly?"	"How do we disband?"

Stage 1 –Forming:

This is the first stage of group formation. Members try to know each other and form a common understanding between them. This stage is characterized by uncertainty and confusion. Members observe others, observe various events and issues and then decide what type of behaviour is acceptable. They use their energy in clarifying group goals. Thus, members "test the waters" during this stage which helps them to decide to be in the group or not. Forming stage is considered to be completed when individuals within the group feel that they are members of the group.

Stage 2- Storming

The storming stage is characterized bya considerable amount of conflict and confrontation among group members. Members often resist being ruled over by the group during this stage. There can be conflict over leadership. There may be conflicts about how much power is to be vested in the leader. Members are aware of the hierarchy and chain of command when the leader within the group is determined. This stage is supposed to be completed when the members are sure about their leader and the hierarchy.

Stage 3- Norming

The third stage in group development where the members settle, start cooperating and collaborating with each other and develop close relationship among themselves. Group cohesiveness increases and group members prefer to identify themselves with the group during the norming stage. Group members agree upon the standards to guide their behavior in the group. Members formulate common goal and expectations of the group.

Stage 4- Performing:

At this stage, group members are ready to take up group tasks. Group members work towards achieving group goals. In this stage, group members exert all their energies towards functioning and performing the tasks in order to attain set group goals. The real work of a group is finished at this stage.

Stage 5- Adjourning:

This is the last stage of group development. Temporary groups like committees, task force, commissions and teams reach this stage after completing their task as their task is non-continuous. After the completion of a task, the group is adjourned. But in ongoing work groups, there is no adjourn stage. They continue at the performing stage.

Advantages of using groups in decision making:

Groups come up with more alternatives. "Two heads are better than one". Besides when the group is involved in decision making, it fosters better acceptance of a decision. It can reduce bias while taking decision as well.

Disadvantages of groups in decision making:

A group decision could be dominated by one individual (or a minority). Making a group concurrence can be very time consuming. Sometimes members are pressurized for a consensus. It can lead to decreased or ambiguous responsibility among group members. It hampers the optimal use of resources. It can also lead to group think. Where group think: is a biased decision making resulting from group members striving for agreement.

Terminologies connected to group dynamics

1. Group Norms

"Group norms are prescriptions for acceptable behaviour determined by the group".

2. Group Roles

Role: A set of expected behaviour pattern attributed to someone occupying a given position in a social unit.

3. Group Cohesion

"The degree to which, group members are attracted to each other and remain within the group".

4. Group Think

Group think is generally seen in a negative light. It is an extreme form of consensus in which the group thinks as a unit rather than a collection of individuals. Free exchanges of ideas are inhibited. Group members are cowed down by dominating members imposing their ideas on others.

Group members try to promote a consensus at the possible expense of arriving at a more defective solution.

The group is so cohesive that its members lose sight of its ultimate goals for fear of disruption of the group itself.

6. Social Loafing

It is the tendency for individuals to spend less effort when working collectively than when working individually. The individual's expectation is that other group members will put the required effort for task completion and that they need not take the additional responsibility to ensure task completion. To reduce social loafing, teams should not be larger than necessary, and individuals should be held accountable for their actions .

To reduce social loafing , organizations can follow strategies like making the individual efforts clearly identifiable and accountable, emphasizing on the kind of important contributions of individual members, and keeping an appropriate group size.

POWER

"Power tends to corrupt; absolute power corrupts absolutely"

(Lord Acton)

The word power is derived from a French word "Pouvoir" which means "to be able". Power is the ability to influence people and events. Power is a general term. The term power can be applied to individuals, groups, teams, departments, organisations and countries. It is not an absolute or an unchanging term. It is dynamic and it changes as situations and individuals change. The influence a person casts on others could be covert (like attitudes, values, thinking etc.) and / or overt (like behavior and action of individuals).

Definition of power:

"Measure of a person's potential to get others to do what he or she wants them to do as well as avoid being forced to do what he or she does not want to do "(Kotter & Scheesinger 1979).

Influence means the actions that either directly or indirectly cause a change in the behavior and/or attitudes of another individual or group. Power is the capacity an individual has to influence the behavior of another individual so that he behaves in accordance to the wishes of the individual with power. *Dependency* is the key to power. Dependency is the relationship an individual A has with an individual B, when B possesses something the individual A desires. Dependency depends on importance, scarcity and non-sustainability of a resource. An individual can wield power over you only if he controls something you desire. The instant the desire ceases to exist, the wielded power fades.

Features of power:

1. Power arises from varied power bases
2. Power may exist, but may not be used.
3. Power is a function of dependency
4. Power does not have same effect on all individuals

Differentiating power from leadership:

Leaders use power as a means of achieving group/organizational goals. Power is different from leadership in many aspects. Power does not require goal compatibility whereas leadership requires the congruence of goals between leader and followers. Power needs mere dependence, not goal compatibility of individuals.

Differentiating power from Authority:

Many times the words power and authority are used interchangeably. But they are different in many sense. Power is one's ability to influence others whereas authority is the right to command. Power is exercised by an individual whereas authority comes from a position and hence is legitimate. Power moves downward while authority moves in all directions.

The importance of power in the organizational context:

1. Power helps in improving cooperation among employees to achieve organizational goal.
2. Power can be used in making and implementing decisions to facilitate new and more appropriate organizational goals.
3. Individuals with positional power decide the size of the organization, the adaptation of new technology etc.
4. Power has a say in the allocation of rewards as well.

Power bases:

Power bases are the sources from which one derives power. There are seven bases of power, as proposed by Hersey & Blanchard (1982). They are coercive, legitimate, expert, reward, referent, information and connection. All these power bases can be categorized into "Personal" and "Positional" power bases.

Coercive power:

This base of this power stems from fear. It is the power to give punishment or withhold it. An individual reacts to this power out of fear of a negative repercussion of noncompliance. Coercive power can come from infliction of physical pain or mental trauma, unpleasant treatment, promotion, demotion, suspension withholding praise etc. This is the power which is used most often and it is also often condemned.

Legitimate power:

It is the formal authority to control and use organizational resources for achieving organizational goals. It gives legal authority over organizational resources. It is the ultimate source of individual power in an organization. The pre requisite for legitimate power is the acceptance of authority by subordinates / members of the organization.

Expert power:

It is an informal power, which does not exist in al organizations. It is derived from the expertise, special skill and knowledge possessed by an individual. This is another very powerful source of power. Expert power is very important for a high task orientation leadership style. The technology boom has augmented the importance of expert power. Hence in all organizations, individuals with a specialized skill set always wield more power than the others.

Reward power:

Reward power is the opposite of coercive power. Compliance to this power produces positive effects or benefits. A person who distributes rewards that others consider valuable has power over the rest. Rewards could be either financial like the control over a pay package, raise in pay, bonuses etc. or nonfinancial like recognition, interesting work assignments, flexible time, autonomy etc. The issue with reward power is that it often involves a cost to the organization.

Referent power:

When an individual identifies with another individual who has desirable resources or suitable personality traits, the individual is said to have referent power. It develops from the admiration of an individual and wanting to be like him or her. Celebrity endorsements are classic examples of referent power. Referral power is generally acquired by charisma. Deep rooted referent power is often called as Charismatic power, where the emotions and feelings of the followers are influenced by the charismatic person. Market research surveys show that the Indian film actor Amitabh Bachan has the maximum referent power. This power base is highly useful in consumer behavior to influencing the buying behavior of individuals. On the flip side, charismatic power can't be delegated and the followers blindly follow the charismatic person without much thought given to the same decision or action.

Information power:

When individuals have access to and control over information which is not freely available, they are known to have information power. The greater the access and control over information, the greater is the power. Others develop dependency due to the information which is restricted with the people who wield the power. A person who is involved in grapevine communication tends to have more information than a manager and hence will wield more power. Grapevine communication, in other words known as rumor, is found to be almost 80 percent correct according to some research reports. Hence an individual who can provide more reliable information is understood to have a lot of information power. Organizations with an open culture will have lesser occurrence of information power.

Connection power / Networking power:

This power is dependent on who you know in the organization or outside the organization, both vertically and horizontally in the organizational structure. An individual is said to have connection power if he or she has connections with important and or influential people inside and outside the organization. It is a personal power base and not a positional power base. It goes with the saying "It is not important what you know but it is important whom you know". A high connection leader makes other people follow him because of the favor they gain or disfavor they avoid.

Out of the different bases of power, both expert and referent power are positively related to employee satisfaction with supervision, organizational commitment etc. Coercive power can have a negative effect on employee morale.

Activity: In your organization, what three things can you do to make people in your organization dependent on you? Write down your answers on a sheet of paper.

Power tactics often found in organizations

Individuals use different options to influence their bosses, co-workers and subordinates. Some of the power tactics used by individuals are as follows.

1. **Friendliness:** Being humble and friendly with people who have power and position. They often use flattery to get into the good books of powerful people. These individuals use the power of powerful people to do what they want in the organization by requesting them for certain allowances and/or favours.
2. **Assertiveness:** Being assertive includes setting a deadline for others to comply with a request, ordering others to do what they are expected to do, emphasizing on the importance of complying with the request, and repeated reminders
3. **Ingratiation:** It is considered as a"soft" political tactic. Here, an individual gets the other person do what he wants to do by putting that person in good mood. Praising the person prior to the request, exaggerating the importance of complying with the request, acting in a friendly and humble way etc are all ways of ingratiation.
4. **Rational persuasion:** It is the use of facts and information in a logical way so that the request for compliance looks logical and well prepared. The originator of the request is projected as a competent person.
5. **Sanctions- :** The use of sanctions means the use of organizational rewards and punishment for certain expected behavior of employees. Examples of sanction are subjective rating in performance appraisal, withholding promotions etc
6. **Bargaining:** Some benefits are given in exchange of complying with a request. This includes the give and take through a process of negotiation. The person seeking the favor may remind the other person of the benefits the former had done for him or her in the past to ensure that work is done.
7. **Coalition:** Persuading someone by seeking assistance of others. This involves getting help from other parties in the organisation, by building up alliances with subordinates and co-workers.
8. **Consultation:** Taking opinions of others while making a decision so that there is better compliance among group members.

9. **Inspirational appeal:** Generating enthusiasm among the colleagues by appealing to their values and beliefs.

10. **Pressure:** Putting pressure on individuals to get the work done. It amounts to seeking compliance by using demands, threats, or intimidation.

11. **Personal appeal :** Expecting/ demanding compliance based on friendship and loyalty

ORGANISATIONAL POLITICS

Organizational politics are the activities employees engage in to increase their power and use it to their advantage to achieve their goals. Employees engage in organizational politics to get things done that are specifically not assigned to them in their job descriptions. It is self-serving behavior which is not sanctioned by organizations.

Definition of organizational politics:

"Organisation politics is the management of influence to obtain ends not sanctioned by the organisation or to obtain ends through non sanctioned means." (Mayes and Allen (1977).

"Organizational politics involve those activities taken within organizations to acquire, develop and use power and other resources to obtain one's preferred outcomes in a situation in which there is uncertainty about choices ". (Pfeffer (1981)

Organizational politics has got close connections to power. When employees convert their power into action, it is termed as organizational politics. Individual engage in politics to increase their power. Organizational politics is more connected to resource allocation, decision making and conflict resolution. For the above said reasons when employees convert their power into action, organizational politics comes into existence. Individuals who have good political skills use their bases of power effectively.

Organizational politics can have negative as well as positive repercussions. The positive attributes of organizational politics are bringing parity between individual and organizational goal in pursuing organizational objectives, transparency in operations and adapting "win-win" situations. Sanctioned use of power for developing skills could be an example of the positive use of power. Most of the time, organizational politics are viewed from a negative perspective. It is characterized by "win – lose" situations, pursuit of personal goals and hidden agendas, ulterior motives etc. Withholding information could be an example of the negative use of power.

Why do people play politics in the organization?

1. Organizations consist of individuals who have differing values, goals and interest, which necessitates the existence of organizational politics.
2. Resource constraints can force employees to play politics to gain an upper hand in getting the required resources.
3. When organizations do not set clear performance objectives, chances of the occurrence of organizational politics are high.

Broad categorization of organizational politics

Organizational politics can be categorized into Legitimate & illegitimate organizational politics.

Legitimate political activities:

Legitimate politics are normal day to day behaviour. There will be too much compliance to rules and regulations on the part of the employee. Some of the examples of legitimate politics are forming coalitions with other like-minded people, bypassing the chain of command in the context of open door policy, complaining to your supervisor, developing outside contacts through professional activities etc

Illegitimate political activities:

When individuals pursue extreme political behaviors that violate certain norms it is termed as illegitimate politics. Activities like scapegoating, sabotaging your colleague, a group of employees calling in sick etc are examples of illegitimate politics.

Factors influencing its occurrence

From an individual's perspective

- **High self-monitors:** The presence of individuals who demonstrate different behavior at different occasions for individual benefit increases the chance of political behavior in the organisation
- **Internal locus of control:** If the majority of individuals belong to the internal locus of control group, i.e. they believe that they are the masters of their destiny, there will be a high occurrence of political behavior.

- **High need for power:** When an individual's cardinal traits are power oriented , they will politicize the work environment.
- **Large investment in the organization:** If there are individuals who have invested in the organization and have special interest, there will be political behavior demonstrated by them.
- **More perceived job alternatives :** When the employees find themselves to be having many job alternatives, chances of organization politics is high

From the organisation's perspective:

- **Pyramid shaped organization structure:** A pyramid shaped organization structure has power accumulated only at the top and the people at base of pyramid are virtually powerless. This can make lower level employees play politics.
- **High expectations of success:** When the top level management has set high targets of achievement, the organization may have a high level of political activity.
- **Existing pattern of resources is changing:** When there are strategic changes made in the company, which put constraints on resources, employees play politics to benefit from the constrained resources.
- **Opportunity for promotion:** When there are higher vacant posts, there is a very high chance of political behavior from employees' aspirants for the vacant post .
- **Subjective performance criteria:** When the performance criteria are subjective, employees will resort to playing politics by doing unethical things to get into the good books of the authority.
- **Low trust:** When the element of trust is low, the chances of occurrence of organizational politics are high.
- **Role ambiguity:** When there isn't a clear job description given to employees and job clarity is poor, high level of politics can occur in the organisation
- **Zero-sum reward allocation practices:** When the management adopts a zero sum reward policy i.e. when the total allocation of resources from management is fixed and some one's gain will be the other one's loss, employees resort to organizational politics .

- Political activity of top level management will automatically increase the occurrence of organization wide organizational politicking.

Types of political behavior in organizations

There are seven categories of political activities played by employees in organizations, according to Steven and Mary Ann Von. They are as follows:

1. **Attacking or blaming others:** A politically savvy individual will blame an individual or a group of individual who can pose threat to him in future. Spreading rumors about a rival to spoil his image is an example of this.
2. **Selective distribution of information:** Sharing information which is not freely available to only favorable people in the organization is another form of politics in organization.
3. **Controlling the information channels:** Controlling the lines of communication, especially the access to key people is an often used political strategy often used by secretaries of powerful people, who otherwise do not have any merit.
4. **Forming coalition:** Few employees who have common interests join hands together to receive favorable position in the organisation.
5. **Cultivating networks:** For gaining support and getting necessary information, employees form networks in the organisation
6. **Creating obligation:** Employees behave in such a way to create obligation from others so that they are obliged to support them in times of need.
7. **Managing impression:** Creating a favorable image in the organization by being nice to all other employees, helping them during the time of crisis etc. Generally done by high self-monitor.

"Politics is in the eye of the beholder"

"Political" Label		"Effective Management" Label
1. Blaming others	vs.	Fixing responsibility
2. "Kissing up"	vs.	Developing working relationships
3. Apple polishing	vs.	Demonstrating loyalty
4. Passing the buck	vs.	Delegating authority
5. Covering your rear	vs.	Documenting decisions
6. Creating conflict	vs.	Encouraging change and innovation
7. Forming coalitions	vs.	Facilitating teamwork
8. Whistle blowing	vs.	Improving efficiency
9. Scheming	vs.	Planning ahead
10. Overachieving	vs.	Competent and capable
11. Ambitious	vs.	Career-minded
12. Opportunistic	vs.	Astute
13. Cunning	vs.	Practical-minded
14. Arrogant	vs.	Confident
15. Perfectionist	vs.	Attentive to detail

Source : *Based on T.C.Krell,M.E.Mendenhall,andJ.Sendry , "Doing Research in the Conceptual Morass of Organisational Politics", paper presented at the Western Academy of Management Conference , Hollywood,CA,April 1987*

How do employees respond to organizational politics?

- Employees who are not willing to take part in organizational politics generally lose ground to political game players, will have reduced job satisfaction, increased stress and psychosomatic illness, and ultimately they quit their job.
- Employees who are moderately politically savvy will understand the undercurrents of the politics played in the organization by others and accommodate themselves.
- When individuals consider political behavior of others as a threat to their ego, they start responding with defensive behavior.

Defensive behavior

When employees perceive organizational politics as a threat rather than an opportunity, they respond with defensive behaviors like reactive and proactive behaviors to avoid action, blame or change. Defensive behavior is adopted to protect one's self-interest. The following are some examples of defensive behavior.

Avoiding Action:

1. *Over conforming:-* Strictly adhering to the rules of the organization in terms of job description etc.
2. *Buck passing:-*Transferring the accountability and responsibility for a task or decision to someone else.
3. *Playing dumb:-* Pretending to be ignorant or unable to do a task to avoid an unwanted task.
4. *Stretching:-* Unduly assigning too much time for the completion of a task so that the person appears to be occupied.

Avoiding Blame

1. *Buffing:-* Rigorously documenting all the work done by an individual to create an image of competence.
2. *Playing safe:-* Avoiding unfavorable situations like taking a neutral stand during the time of conflict, selectively taking up highly successive projects etc.
3. *Justifying:-* Giving a random explanation for a negative outcome.
4. *Scapegoating:-* Transferring the blame of a negative outcome onto someone to avoid blame.
5. *Misrepresenting:-* Selectively communicating a piece of information by manipulating and distorting the facts.

Avoiding Change

Prevention: Preventing the implementation of a change which is threatening.

Activity: Consider that you are the territory manager of an ayurvedic product in North India and your territory has registered 30 % decline in the sales of the product in the year 2013. Describe any 3 most suitable defensive behaviors you will use to reduce the consequences of decline in sale

Positive Effects of Organizational Politics

1. Employees find the strength to overcome personnel inadequacies
2. Politics helps the employees to cope with change.
3. During times of requirement, politics helps in substituting formal authority.

Flip side of Organizational Politics

1. It reduces the motivation level of employees.
2. Work output steadily deteriorates.
3. There is increased stress on the employee leading to employee turnover .
4. There is loss of productive time in politicking.

How to Play Positive Politics

1. Embed your personal goal in organizational goals. Camouflaging self-interest is effective and positive, if that serves a greater good.
2. Project the right image in the organization. Understanding the core values of the organization and cultivating an appropriate image which matches with the company image will go a long way in helping one set a stable stand in the company.
3. Gain access to organizational resources by way of improving your knowledge and skill
4. Improve visibility by taking up jobs critical to the organization.
5. Develop powerful allies.
6. Avoid members of the organization with a tainted image.
8. Make yourself indispensable to the organization.

Ethics in organizational politics

It is rather difficult to demarcate certain ethical political activities from unethical activities, as there are no clear norms that set both apart. Nevertheless, politics can be categorized under ethical activity if it answers in the affirmative for the following questions:

1. **Utilitarianism:** Is the political activity motivated by self-interest alone, which does not match with other employees' interest or the organization's interest? Example: A purchase manager giving the vendor ship of a raw material to a known person for personal gain, which may lead to procurement of inferior raw material, which affects the quality of produce. Since this violates the principle of utilitarianism, it is an unethical practice. As long as self-interests are consistent with organizational goals, the political activity to attain self-centric goals is ethical.

2. **Right:** Does the political activity respect the rights of other individuals in the organization? Example: Grabbing an opportunity which was previously assigned to a more meritorious colleague. As long as the rights of other party are not violated, the political activity can be called ethical.

3. **Justice:** Is the political activity fair and equitable? Example: A supervisor evaluating a favored employee on a higher rating and a disfavored employee on a lower rating without an objective criterion of evaluation will be unethical. If political activity conforms to standards of equity and justice, it's ethical to play politics.

Many companies have abused power and propagated politics in the organization with a Machiavellian justification that "The end justifies the means ". Though such strategies would have fetched an immediate reward, in the long run it will erode the good will of the company. Hence organizational politics should be used with caution.

CLOSING CASE

Damned If You Do, Damned If You Don't

Fran Gilson has spent 15 years with the Thompson Grocery Company rising through the ranks of this 50-store grocery store chain to become a regional manager, overseeing seven stores and earning approximately $95,000 a year. Fran also thinks she is ready to take on more responsibility, so she agreed to consider the position of vice president and regional manager for a national drugstore chain.

The only person at Thompson who knows Fran is looking at this other job is her good friend and colleague, Ken Hamilton, the director of finance. Fran tells Ken it is a dream job and expresses her positive excitement. She asked Ken last week if she could use his name as a reference. Ken agreed to give her a great recommendation. She made it very clear to the recruiter that Ken was the only person at Thompson who knew she was considering another job.

Jennifer Chung has been a financial analyst in Ken's department for five months. Fran met Jennifer through Ken. Fran's impression of Jennifer is quite positive. Jennifer came to Fran to talk. Fran sat her down and listened to her story. What Fran heard was hard to believe, but she had no reason to think Jennifer was lying. Jennifer said that Ken began making off-color comments and his behavior got progressively worse including leering and touching. Jennifer would ask him to stop and not do it again, but it fell on deaf ears. Yesterday, Ken reminded Jennifer that her six-month probationary review was coming up. "He told me that if I did not sleep with him that I could not expect a very favorable evaluation." Jennifer said that she had come to Fran because she did not know what to do or whom to turn to.

"I came to you, Fran, because you are a friend of Ken's and the highest ranking woman here. Will you help me?" Fran had never heard anything like this about Ken before. About all she knew regarding his personal life was that he was in his late 30s, single, and involved in a long-term relationship.

Question:

1. Analyze Fran's situation in an ethical sense. What is the ethically right thing for her to do? Is that also the politically right thing to do?

Test your knowledge

Multiple choice questions

1. A cohesive group will
   a) Always produce good results
   b) Will have multiple group leaders
   c) Are unlikely to be successful
   d) Will conform to the accepted level of output decided by the group
2. Groups formed as a consequence of organizational structure are
   a) Cliques
   b) Formal group
   c) Interest group
   d) Target group
3. In the Tuckman model of group formation, which stage develops guidelines and standards of acceptable behavior
   a) Storming
   b) Forming
   c) Norming
   d) Adjourning
4. Which one of the following is not implied in the definition of power?
   a) Influence
   b) Potential
   c) Dependency
   d) Discretion

5. Legitimate power is based on:
   a) Rewards.
   b) Fear.
   c) Position.
   d) Knowledge.

7. Celebrities are paid huge amount of money to endorse products in commercials because the advertisers believe the celebrities have ____ power.
   a) Coercive
   b) Referent
   c) Expert
   d) Reward

8. The most popular power tactic used by managers to influence subordinates is:
   a) Friendliness.
   b) Reason.
   c) Higher authority.
   d) Sanctions.

9. Reactive and protective behaviors to avoid action, blame, or change are termed:
   a) Political behaviors.
   b) Defensive behaviors.
   c) Coalitions.
   d) Impression management.

MODEL QUESTIONS

Section–A

(Each question carries 2 marks)

1. What is behaviour?
2. What are groups?
3. Define group
4. State the Nature of groups
5. What are the Functions of group?

6. Who are effective teams?
7. What is ethics?
8. What is defensive behavior?
9. What is politics?
10. What is organizational politics?

Section–B

(Each question carries 5 marks)

1. Explain the nature of behaviour
2. Write the function and formation of group behaviour
3. Write the importance of team in an organization
4. What are groups in organization? Give two examples
5. Why does organizational politics creep into organization?
6. What is the ethics? Why ethical behaviour is important in organizations
7. What is the basis of power? Explain with five examples
8. How can organizational politics be productive? Give examples
9. What are the benefits and costs of working with others?
10. Write a note on dependency and defensive behaviour

Section–C

(Each question carries 15 marks)

1. Write in detail the nature and contribution of group in achieving the goal of organisation?
2. What are formal and informal groups? Write in detail which could be the best in organisational culture
3. What are ethics? What gestures are called as ethical practices what kind of influence does it have on group and organisation
4. What are the basis of power. what are its implications in goal fulfilling process
5. Write harmful effects of organisational politics? How can this problem be averted?
6. Effective team and social influence do contribute for goodness of the organisation explain
7. Explain in detail the benefits of working in groups with appropriate examples

8. Why are groups made? What is the distinctive factor of multiple groups? What are the conducive factors to run group in-sprit?
9. Write in general on group behaviour, power and politics and its influence on organisational ethics.

REFERENCES

1. Nancy Langton & Stephen P. Robbins, Organisational behavior, Fourth Canadian edition, 2007, Pearson education Canada.
2. Organizational Behavior, Fred Luthans, 11th edition, Mc-Graw Hill International.

◈◈◈◈

Read More on the Web

Group dynamics refers to a system of behaviors and psychological processes occurring within a social group (intragroup dynamics), or between social groups (intergroup dynamics). Amongst the members of a group, there is a state of interdependence, through which the behaviors, attitudes, opinions, and experiences of each member are collectively influenced by the other group members. The formation of the group starts with some sort of bond or attraction between individuals. There are two approaches to group formation, namely the **social cohesion approach,** which states that group formation originates from interpersonal attraction, and the **social identity approach,** which states that a group forms when a collection of individuals perceive that they share the same social category, and that the formation of interpersonal relations is secondary.

A level of psychological distinctiveness is required for the formation of a group as well. Through interaction, individuals begin to develop group norms, roles, and attitudes which define the group, which are then internalized to influence personal behavior. An individual's identity (or self-concept) has two components: personal identity and social identity (or collective self). One's personal identity is defined by more individual qualities and attributes. In contrast, one's social identity is defined by his or her group membership, and the general characteristics (or prototypes) that define the group and differentiate it from others.

New members of a group must prove themselves to the full members, or "old-timers", to become accepted. Full members have undergone socialization and are already accepted within the group. They have more privilege than newcomers but more responsibility to help the group achieve its goals. Marginal members were once full members but lost membership because they failed to live up to the group's expectations. They can rejoin the group if they go through re-socialization. Depending on the self-esteem of an individual, members of the in-group may experience different private beliefs about the group's activities but will publicly express the opposite-that they actually share these beliefs. One member may not personally agree with something the group does, but to avoid the black sheep effect (where they are effectively cast our or disassociated with), they will publicly agree with the group and keep the private beliefs to themselves. If the person is privately self-aware, he or she is more likely to comply with the group even if they possibly have their own beliefs about the situation.

In turn, a group heavily influences the person's behaviour. Firstly, before joining a group: if a person is made to believe that the group to be joint is amazing, usually by an existing group member, and this image is constantly reinforced, he/she will believe the group is incredible, whether it is or isn't. After joining the group, and after gaining the acceptance of the same, he/she will slowly become critical of the group. Secondly, once the member is part of the group, his/perceptions of common situations, etc. are heavily influenced by the group. For example, he/she will like a new entry to the group; overriding his/her initial impression of the same, if the group as a whole likes that person. In larger groups, these dynamics can be very powerful- and can be both positive and negative.

This leads to something psychiatrists call **herd mentality,** or **mob mentality,** which describes how people are influenced by their peers to adopt certain behaviors, follow trends, and/or purchase items. This mentality refers to unique behavioral characteristics that emerge when people are in large groups. One reason for herd behavior is that people tend to do what others around them are doing. This usually is because those who join the group in certain behaviors figure that if several others are doing something, it must be worthwhile, or they would not be doing it. Two of the main factors are the greater anonymity that exists within a group and the distribution of responsibility for the group's actions. These factors sometimes make a person believe that they can act a certain way within a group and not have the same consequences that the same actions would have if he/she acted alone.

In every group, there is always an informal or formal hierarchy. Someone will always have a little more authority than everyone else. Certain people are hardwired to need authority and/or respect/appreciation. For this very reason, they look for ways to attain this; the methods employed for the same may or may not be ethical. Here, people use their power and play politics.

Power is a force that gives one communicator the ability to influence another communicator to take an action which would not otherwise be taken. But sometimes, there is an imbalance, where a less dominant person is overridden by a dominant person. This can be applied in organizational setups. Certain steps can be taken to correct this disparity, and quite often, it needs the participation of the group, and a neutral mediator.

- **Listen:** Listen to what the less dominant person has to say. Take damaging attention off him/her. Remove bias directed to him/her.
- **Ask questions:** so that the less dominant can express himself fully without apprehension.
- **Set an agenda:** where one can calmly discuss topics that are important to both types of person.
- **Set hypothetical situations:** sit with the less dominant person and create hypothetical 'what if" situations. This allows the person to be prepared for many possible outcomes beforehand.
- **Explore the need:** help the less dominant person voice his needs, structure them, discuss and establish possible ways of meeting the same. This empowers the person.
- **Terminate the mediation:** this method is usually used as a last resort. Not attaining an agreement is better than a bad agreement. Also, it reduces the chances of the mediator being seen as a co-conspirator by the organization.

Sources and References

http://en.wikipedia.org/wiki/Herd_mentality

http://en.wikipedia.org/wiki/Group_dynamics

http://www.wisegeek.com/what-is-mob-mentality.htm

http://www.mediate.com/articles/voylesr3.cfm (steps to counter power imbalances)

JAIN UNIVERSITY
Center for Management Studies

III SEM - BBM, Pre-final Exam - September - 2012

ORGANIZATIONAL PSYCHOLOGY

Time: 3 Hours **Max Marks: 80**

Note: i) The paper is divided into four sections A, B, C & D

ii) Follow the instructions given in each section carefully & answer the questions.

iii) Section D is Compulsory

SECTION – A

1. Answer any five questions. Each question carries two marks. **(5 x 2 = 10)**

a) Define Psychology.

b) What is Perceptual Constancy?

c) What is Rorschach Inkblot Test?

d) Define learning.

e) What do you mean by group cohesiveness?

f) Give the meaning of job enrichment.

g) Define Emotional Intelligence.

h) What is projection?

SECTION – B

Answer any two of the following. Each question carries five marks. **(2 x 5 = 10)**

2. Explain the different impression management strategies used by employees.

3. What are the three filing cabinets to store Long term memory?

4. What are the Characteristics of OB?

5. Explain the big five model.

SECTION – C

Answer any two of the following. Each question carries fifteen marks. (2 x 15 = 30)

6. What are the work related aspects of personality?

7. What are the Stages of Group Formation developed by Tuckman?

8. Explain the process of perception.

9. Explain the different factors that contribute to the formation of attitude.

SECTION – D

Answer all the three questions compulsory. Each question carries ten marks. (3 x 10 = 30)

10. Case Study

Perception in the Workplace: How it Does – and "Will" - Impact

Kevin lives in the US, and works within the real estate industry. Throughout his career he has become increasingly aware of the importance of intangible deliverables in a work context, as opposed, to simply performing the technical requirements of a role satisfactorily.

Issues such as being conscious that you are under a constant gaze, adopting different approaches when inter-relating with superior managers with different management styles and personality profiles and promulgating conspicuously what you are doing and the achievements one has realised, have all enable him to effectively raise his profile, operate effectively and enhance his profile at work.

The views expressed are personal, for illustrative purposes only and should not be related, or automatically applied to, other situations or scenarios.

Perception is one of the foundations of our society. It's what causes the stock market to reach fantastic heights or, as we have all seen recently, abysmal lows. Financially, professionally, even personally, this is a very important aspect in our lives. Nearly every waking moment, people simultaneously play two roles in the game of perception, those who are perceived and those who do the perceiving. Each role is crucial in future growth and success.

In my first job, I did not take perception as seriously as I should have. I figured success at work was simply a matter of me doing a better job than anyone else. For a while, I met these expectations, doing my job fast and efficiently, thinking that I had mastered the art of success on my first attempt. After a while, I stopped shaving and in some cases even missed a few showers, thinking that my physical appearance no longer mattered as long as I was performing efficiently. This lasted for a good amount of time and then came the performance review. It had stated I had done very well on the performance side; my work was of high quality and had no deficiencies. But the other section was full of negatives; employees confidently complained to their managers my grooming was not acceptable, I was not being respectful of others and I did not take the job I was working in seriously.

I was devastated by my overall "poor" performance review. It had never occurred to me that this would happen. I knew I worked hard and did a good job, everyone there admitted that my work was better than everyone else's. I struggled to understand why such excellent and efficient work would lead to such a "poor" review. Logically, it made no sense to me; I thought I should have at least gotten an "OK" review. While it was a painful way for me to learn this lesson, I later found it was due to in most part to perception.

I had done my work above and beyond what anyone else in my position did, but I had not shown much interest in communicating or in some cases, keeping clean and respectable. As a result, people perceived that I did not take the job seriously. While still upset at the results of my recent review, I decided to test a theory. I decided to see what would happen if I was really clean and very outgoing, but did not work as hard or barely at all. To my surprise, my following performance review was a marked improvement from the previous one. Even my efficiency was rated at a higher level. In reality, I knew my efficiency was actually lower than before (due to my "experiment"), so the reason for the higher rating was likely more due to a perception that my improvements in communication and cleanliness led to increased work output.

I wondered to a certain extend how much of a role perception had played into my performance. For a few weeks, I had actually done nothing at all except looked and acted good at work. The ruse worked, although temporarily. My manager approached me, and warned me that there were some complaints on things not getting done. Of course, I went back to working hard, but I was certain at this point perception played a major role. Had I have come in not having worked and not been social or even clean, I would have certainly been removed from my job.

Ultimately, I learned that perception is an important element of success in any job. In some cases, it can actually supplant real performance. While I do not think that this is the way it should be, this is the way it is. Being successful at any job is not merely whether or not you work hard, it is also reliant on how you look and how you interact with others. For people with Aspergers', this can be often hard to conceptualize. But people without Aspergers judge a person, fairly or not, in many cases on perception alone. Often, a mix of actual hard work and being perceived as a hard worker are the best mix. Too little of one thing can be just as bad as too much of another.

Questions:-

a) Bring out the changes that happened in Kevin's life. **(5 Marks)**

b) "Perception is an important element of success in any job." explain **(5 Marks)**

11. <u>ARTICLE</u>

Prejudice and Discrimination

Prejudice is a cultural attitude that rests on negative stereotypes about individuals or groups because of their cultural, religious, racial, or ethnic background. Discrimination is the active denial of desired goals from a category of persons. A category can be based on sex, ethnicity, nationality, religion, language, or class. More recently, disadvantaged groups now also include those based on gender, age, and physical disabilities.

Prejudice and discrimination are deeply imbedded at both the individual and societal levels. Attempts to eradicate prejudice and discrimination must thus deal with prevailing beliefs or ideologies, and social structure.

Prejudice and Discrimination in a Historical Context. As far as historical records show, no society or nation has been immune to prejudice and discrimination, either as victim or victimizer. Contemporary forms of prejudice and discrimination date back to when European colonizers penetrated and transformed previously isolated societies and peoples. The more extreme forms of discriminatory practices include genocide, slavery, legislated discrimination (such as *Apartheid*), discriminatory immigration laws, and disenfranchisement. Less extreme forms of prejudice and discrimination, but nevertheless pervasive and oppressive, include social exclusion at the institutional level (such as in schools and hospitals), and the more subtle forms practised by the media. Some groups appear to suffer from more persistent forms of discrimination, such as Jews (as in anti-Semitism) and the Roma (a.k.a. Gypsies), regardless of time and place.

As to the root cause of prejudice and discrimination there appears to be no clear acceptance of any theory of causation. Scholars do agree, however, that prejudice and discrimination are not universals as something humans are inherently born with. There is ample evidence that prejudice and discrimination are social constructions. If indeed prejudice and discrimination are inherent in the human condition, we would not be able to account for intermarriage and assimilation among highly differentiated human groups. There is, moreover, considerable evidence that prejudice is absent in young children (e.g. Allport, 1954).

Although there is no wide agreement as to the "cause" of prejudice and discrimination, there is a consensus that they constitute a learned behavior. The internalization of prejudice starts with parents and, later, teachers--the groups primary in the formation of attitudes within children. The media and social institutions solidify prejudicial attitudes, giving them social legitimacy. In a sense, it is incorrect to speak of "eradicating" prejudice, since prejudice is learned. (In a similar vein, one cannot eradicate evil except by ensuring the presence of goodness.) At best, one can reduce prejudice and discrimination. Society looks most often to education and legislation to alleviate prejudice and discrimination--for reasons still not clearly known, intergroup contact alone is not enough to reduce prejudice. On one hand, multicultural education, whether direct or indirect, constitute the mainstay of educational efforts to eliminate prejudice. On the other hand, the emphasis on civil rights, enlightened immigration policies, and mandates for quota hiring are the cornerstone of legal approaches to alleviating the effects of prejudice and discrimination. The most overlooked area in resolving the problems of prejudice and discrimination lies in the web of close relationships where genuine feelings of love can be fostered and strengthened. The private sphere may indeed be the last frontier where a solution to the problems of prejudice may have to be found.

Prejudice and discrimination produce immense effects in the psychological, social, political, and economic domains. Whether intended or not, the effects are compounded by the loss of self-worth, a sense of alienation from the wider society, political disempowerment, and economic inequalities. Klineberg (1968: 440) asserts that "Prejudice and ethnic hostilities constitute a major danger to peace both within a nation and among nations." As a consequence, the emergence of a new global moral order increasingly provides a leverage point to counter the effects of prejudice and discrimination. While many agree that the various international instruments to protect people against prejudice and discrimination are still not universally followed or even implemented, it is clear that a new international consciousness is indeed emerging and is, in fact, intensifying

Questions:-

a) What is prejudice? Explain its bad effects. **(5 Marks)**

b) Explain its causes of prejudice with the help of the above article. **(5 Marks)**

12. ARTICLE

What's stressful to one person may be all in a day's work for another. The difference appears to lie in our perceptions of various events. Mental health professionals believe personality plays a significant role in how we perceive stress.

People with "Type A" personalities, for example, are rushed, ambitious, time-conscious and driven. Studies suggest these traits, if not properly managed, can create stress-related illnesses. In contrast, the "Type B" personality is a much more relaxed, less time-conscious and driven person. Type B personalities are able to view things more adaptively. They are better able to put things into perspective, and think through how they are going to deal with situations. Consequently they tend to be less stress-prone.

The Development of Personality Type

But where do these differences in personality come from? A variety of social, biological, psychological and behavioral factors influence the development of our character. Scientists agree that a largely genetic personal chemistry, or in-born temperament, influences an infant to react to its environment in ways that can be assertive or shy. Such tendencies are further influenced by experiences. The combination of inheritance and experience form an individual's characteristic way of behaving, feeling and thinking — his personality.

Studies also show that men and women handle stress differently — a difference that some scientists attribute, in part, to estrogen. This hormonal difference may also account for the fact that women are three times more likely to develop depression in response to the stress in their lives than are men. Women, unlike men, also tend to have stronger social support networks to which they turn during times of stress. These social supports may help explain why women, in general, seem to be better able to cope with stress than men.

Recent research suggests that our response to stress could be influenced by our experiences in the womb. Scientists have been studying mechanisms by which maternal stress — and the resulting high levels of cortisol in her body during pregnancy — could affect the development of the baby. According to the research, if a mother has high cortisol levels, the fetus will have similarly high levels. As a result, this exposure could affect the level of receptors for stress-related substances in the brain, which may make them more susceptible to stressors later in life.

Even after birth, a mother's response to stress affects her baby. Research shows that if a mother is stressed or very depressed during the early weeks of her baby's life, she may not establish a good relationship with her child. Worse, there could be long-term consequences on the child's stress response, behavior and intelligence.

Chronic Stress Has Serious Health Implications

Even people with the most adaptable personalities can experience the effects of long-term stress if they lack a sense of control over aspects of their daily lives. Scientists studying stress in the workplace, for example, have found that those who perceive that they have the least control over their working environment suffer from the highest levels of stress-related illness. Experts recommend that managers work to ensure that their employees have some sense of empowerment in order to relieve an unnecessary source of chronic stress.

Caregivers of elderly or chronically ill family members are another group subject to chronic high levels of stress. For example, studies done on caregivers of Alzheimer patients show that chronically high cortisol levels significantly weakened their immune systems. Mental health professionals suggest that caregivers try to set very small goals in the care or recovery of their loved ones and take respite from their responsibilities to lessen their stress.

Questions:-

a) How do personality types impact people's responses to stress? **(5 Marks)**

b) Give your suggestions as a student of organisation psychology, to overcome such problems. **(5 Marks)**

****

THIRD SEMESTER BBM EXAMINATION OCTOBER- 2012

ORGANISATIONAL PSYCHOLOGY

Time: 3 Hours **Maximum Marks: 80**

SECTION - A

Answer any FIVE of the following questions. **5x2=10**

a. Define group dynamics.

b) What do you mean by Interactionalism approach of OB?

c) Bring out the difference between sensation and perception.

d) Give the meaning of id, ego, and super ego as per Sigmund Freud.

e) What is closure principle?

f) Explain the interference theory in the context of forgetting.

g) Briefly explain the Thematic Apperception Test.

h) What is a coercive power?

SECTION - B

Answer any TWO of the following questions. **2x5 = 10**

a) Bring out the challenges and opportunities for OB.

b) What are the external factors Influencing the Perception Process?

c) What are the Major contributing factors to Personality?

d) Explain the characteristics of an enriched job.

SECTION - C

Answer any TWO of the following questions. **2x15=30**

a) Explain the early and the contemporary theories of motivation

b) Explain the factors affecting the attitude formation.

c) What do you mean by emotional Intelligence?

Explain the five domes of emotional intelligence.

d) What are the different personality traits observed at organization?

SECTION - D

Answer all questions.

a) Case study

Maslow's theory at Kellogg's

Within Kellogg's every employee is motivated to work through each of these levels. As they do so, this provides positive effects for each employee and the organisation. For example:

Physiological needs - Kellogg's offers competitive salaries. This gives people the means to acquire the basic needs for living. The Kellogg's Cornflex flexible benefits programme allows employees to choose those benefits that suit them. This includes childcare vouchers, cash alternatives to company cars and discounted life assurance schemes. These savings and competitive salaries help workers' pay go further and so motivate them to be loyal to the company.

Safety needs - Kellogg's values the safety of all employees. The company is committed to providing a safe and healthy work environment to prevent accidents. Employees are however accountable - that means they have to take responsibility for observing the health and safety rules and practices. Kellogg's also offers employees a range of working patterns. Some may want to work part-time, others may want career breaks or undertake homeworking. This helps employees to choose the best option for a healthy work-life balance.

Social needs - These are associated with a feeling of belonging. Kellogg's operates weekly group 'huddles'. These provide informal opportunities for employees to receive and request information on any part of the business, including sales data and company products. This helps strengthen teams and enhances workers' sense of belonging. Having an open approach to communication keeps everybody focused on the company's aims helps individuals contribute to the company's K-Values. They include values such as being positive, seeing the best in people and recognising diversity. Kellogg's positively recognises and rewards staff achievements.

Self-actualisation - Kellogg's provides employees with the opportunity to take on challenging and stimulating responsibilities. For example, the business provides the opportunity for individuals to take ownership of projects. This enables them to develop and improve.

Laura Bryant joined Kellogg's straight after university in 2002. She joined the Field Sales team initially. This involved visiting five to ten supermarkets a day to develop relationships at a local level. After two years her hard work was rewarded and she was promoted to Customer Marketing Manager at Head office. This helped to raise her profile as she wanted to move into marketing. With support from her manger, laura made the transition from sales to marketing as assistant brand manager on rice krispies and frosties. In 2009 she was promoted again to manage the marketing plan for special K and she is now brand manager for kellogg's cornflakes. The company has helped motivate her to climb the hierarchy of needs and achieve her carrer ambitions.

Questions:

i. Bring out the relevance of Maslow's theory with reference to Kellogg;s 05

ii. Example the growth of Ms Laura Bryant and explain the key factor responsible for the same. 05

b. Article

How interest and attitude influence learning?

With greater interest, the processing of information at the time of learning becomes deeper. At the deepest level, the information is processed semantically, and is linked by a network of associations with various cues in the L TM. Therefore, they are learned and remembered better. A person interested to play cricket, read novels, or collect stamps would learn the act more quickly and maintain it for a longer period of time. The amount of effort spent on learning the skills that are interesting is much less, as the processing is automatic.

Individuals differ in their favorite ways of learning and remembering. Materials that are not interesting are not attended to at the time of learning. Materials that are unpleasant and painful are repressed back into deep chamber of unconscious, and therefore, are not available for conscious recall.

A learner has his unique learning style, which has been developed during the course of socialization. His approaches to the learning materials are based on his cultural background and unique pattern of abilities. Some have analytic, while others have relational approach to learning.

Those with a relational learning style learn materials best through exposure to a full unit or phenomenon. Parts of the unit are understood only by understanding their relationship to the whole. In contrast, people with an analytical learning style do best when they carry out an analysis of the principles and components underlying a phenomenon. After they master the fundamental principles and components, they are best able to understand the full content. The distinction between the two learning approaches is analogous to top-down and bottom- up processing.

Willlam James remarked that the greatest discovery of our generation is that human beings can alter their fate by changing their attitudes of mind. Attitude determines the subject's emotional and motivational dispositions towards the learning material. Most cognitive and complex forms of learning are greatly influenced by whether or not the subject has the right kind of attitude towards the learning situation.

Questions:

i. What is the importance of both interest and attention in learning? 05

ii. Explain the different styles of learning as mentioned in the above case. 05

C. Case study

Hindustan Lever Research Centre (HLRC) was set up in the year 1967 at Mumbai. At that time the primary challenge was to find suitable alternatives to the edible oils and fats that were being used as raw materials for soaps. Later, import substitution and export obligations directed the 'focus towards non-edible oil seeds, infant foods, perfumery chemicals, fine chemicals, polymers and nickel catalyst. This facilitated creation of new brands which helped build new businesses.

HUL believes in meritocracy and has a comprehensive performance management system, which ensures that people are rewarded according to their performance and abilities. Almost 47% of the entire managerial cadres are people who have joined us through lateral recruitment.

Over the years many break through innovations have taken place. Hindustan Lever Research gained eminence within Unilever Global R&D and became recognized as one of the six global R&D Centers of Unilever with the creation of Unilever Research India in Bangalore in 1997.

At Bangalore R&D center, a team of 10 scientists were appointed for a project on 'shampoo' line. Suranjan Sircar heading the team as Principal Research Scientist with the support of Vikas Pawar, _ Aparna Damle, Jaideep Chatterjee, Amitava Pramanik as Research Scientists. Suresh Jayaraman & Punam Bandyopadhyay were Research Associates.

Vikas Pawar came up with an idea of pet shampoos during brainstorming with the team. "Hey, why don't we target the pet care segment because in India, pet industry is being seriously looked at as a growing industry. I had been working on this concept for a few weeks & have done some initial research as well", said Vikas. "I think we should just focus on the dog segment & bring out a range of shampoos that are breed specific", contributed by Aparna Damle, who was a new unmarried scientist in the company. "Oh that's a really great idea, a breakthrough" said Jaideep & Amitava appreciating Aparna. The idea given by Aparna got support from both colleagues & head.

Vikas was although not comfortable with his credit being taken away. He also felt that creating brand specific shampoos would not be a profitable innovation thus, no point concentrating efforts on that. With this in mind he put his point forward but couldn't gather consensus.

After the discussion, Jaideep & Amitava being friends to Vikas, consoled him & showedconfidence in his plan & thoughts. "We understand what you are going through. The idea was yours & Aparna took all your credit. Don't worry we are with you & be careful from next time."

Nevertheless, in the meeting Aparna presented her proposal for the idea mentioningrequirements & chemical details. The meeting began with motivational speech & plan of action by the head of the team. A lot was discussed in detail & tasks were allotted alongwith deadlines. Immediately after the presentation Jaideep & Amitava approached Aparna & eulogized her research & proposal reiterating the importance of breed specific range of shampoos.

Vikas lay aside his ego & went ahead with full dedication & commitment, however during the tenure of the research he noticed poor attitude of team members. Punam was not regular with deadlines; she submitted her research on breeds four days after deadline. Suresh was asked to coordinate with members looking into chemical research but Vikas observed him most of the times in the recreation room, so he asked him "Hi, so what's the progress in chemical research so far?" Suresh replied that he had done whatever he was asked to do by senior scientist.

He reported this lack of commitment & proactive attitude to Suranjan Sircir & asked for an action against them. "Hmm ... I know what's happening in the team. I have worked for 20 years in this industry & from my experience I know what to do & when to do", here torted back. Finally the project got completed 4 months after deadline. Vikas went back to the lab; sitting & wondering at the flaws in the group.

Questions:

i. Analyze group behavior of the team. Study the informal & formal groups In this case. 05

ii. Point out flaws in the group & recommend solutions to overcome them. 05